The Economic Crisis:
Notes from the Underground

Thomas I. Palley
Independent Analyst
mail@thomaspalley.com

ISBN-10: 147500480X
ISBN-13: 978-1475004809
Library of Congress Control Number: 2012908925

May 2012

"In economics, a thought has not been thought until the right person has thought it."
James K. Galbraith

CONTENTS

PREFACE: HISTORY FROM BELOW

An old adage is "The winners get to write history" and that is certainly proving true in the current economic crisis. Open any major newspaper and the op-ed page contains articles by the same economists and policymakers as before the financial crash of 2008. Those who were the leading academic economists before the crisis remain the leading economists after the crisis, and the same holds for economic policymakers. Nowhere is this more clearly visible than Team Obama, which has relied on Larry Summers, Timothy Geithner, and Gene Sperling – all of whom had held top policy positions before the crisis.

One myth the winners are looking to promulgate is that the crisis was not predicted and not predictable. The claim that it was not predictable has a purpose as it excuses the economics profession from its catastrophic intellectual failure. That is why "black swan" explanations, which attribute the crisis to complexity and the convergence of extreme unlikely circumstances, are so popular. Likewise, the myth that the crisis was not predicted also has a purpose, as it implies no other theoretical perspective has a claim to doing better.

That said, to cover both sides of the table, a select few are credited with foreseeing the crisis. But here too, the intent is to smother the case for change by covering up the profession's intellectual failure rather than spotlighting it.

One favorite son is Raghuram Rajan, Professor of finance at the University of Chicago and former Chief Economist at the IMF. Rajan has been touted as foreseeing the financial crisis in his 2005 paper "Has Financial Development Made the World Riskier?" which was presented at the elite Jackson Hole conference of the Kansas City Federal Reserve Bank. Rajan deserves credit for his theoretical observations regarding how financial innovation can increase risk, but it is impossible to read his paper as predicting the financial crash. Moreover, it says nothing about the deeper crisis problems regarding chronic aggregate demand shortage rooted in deteriorated income distribution. Indeed, the paper's conclusion is actually sanguine: "I believe the changes, in general, expanded opportunities significantly and, even on net, have made the world tremendously better off (Rajan, 2005, p.360)." Once again, there is purpose in promoting Rajan as he is a top insider, which serves to insulate the establishment against charges of intellectual failure.

Another quasi-insider is Nouriel Roubini, former assistant secretary in the Treasury Department under Larry Summers in the late 1990s. Roubini [2005] did predict the financial crash and its aftermath for which he deserves credit – and he also deserves credit for his subsequent shift to a progressive Keynesian stance. However, it is also noteworthy that Roubini got the economics completely wrong. Thus, his explanation of a how a crash would develop ran as follows:

"The basic outlines of a hard landing are easy to envision: a sharp fall in the value of the U.S. dollar, a rapid increase in U.S. long-term interest rates and a sharp fall in the price of a range of risk assets including equities and housing."[1]

Viewed in this light, Roubini's astutely well-timed call of catastrophe represents market intuition rather sound theoretical analysis.

Contrary to the mainstream myth, the reality is several people operating from a critical outsider intellectual perspective did identify the roots of crisis. Economists Dean Baker [2002] and Robert Shiller [2005] both identified the house price bubble, though neither framed the bubble in terms of a fundamentally flawed economic paradigm. Wynne Godley and Gennaro Zezza [2006] clearly foresaw the serious macroeconomic danger inherent in rising U.S. household indebtedness and the U.S. trade deficit but did not predict the financial crash. Australian economist Steve Keen [1995, 2006] developed a theoretical framework that explains the crisis and started warning of its imminence in 2006.

I also anticipated an economic downturn of depression proportions – though I did not foresee the path involved financial crash. The last chapter of my 1998 book, *Plenty of Nothing*, is titled "Recipe for a depression". It warned that the economic system confronted a structural shortage of demand because of wage stagnation, worsened income inequality, and the exhaustion of credit-led growth. These themes of structural demand shortage and exhaustion of consumer credit were further developed in later papers [Palley, 2001, 2006a, 2006b].

When economic historians look at the current epoch I believe they will date the crisis as having begun with the stock market crash of 2001. The Bush administration and Federal Reserve managed to forestall developments via policies that promoted a house price bubble of epic proportions. However, the 2001-07 business cycle expansion was still the weakest on record [Bivens and Irons, 2008]. In effect, policy managed to delay and obscure developments, but at the cost of deepening the problem by adding a massive layer of debt.

Economists cannot predict daily movements of the stock market and we do not expect them to. However, we should expect them to identify imminent major developments. On this score the mainstream profession failed comprehensively. Moreover, it has continued to fail by under-estimating the severity and depth of the crisis. According to mainstream analysis the financial crash of 2008 caused a deep recession. The combination of restored financial stability, low interest rates, and massive fiscal stimulus should have been enough to right the economy. That was the thinking behind Federal Reserve Chairman Ben Bernanke's remarks about

---

[1] Roubini, N., and Setser, B. [2005], "Will the Bretton Woods 2 Regime Unravel Soon? The risk of a hard landing in 2005-2006," paper prepared for a conference organized by the Federal Reserve Bank of San Francisco, February, p. 5.

"green shoots" of recovery in March 2009. However, instead of a flourishing recovery, the economy has continued stuttering on the edge of recession and return to full employment is off the radar.

It is important to straighten the record, to provide a history from below, so to speak. That is the purpose of this book which collects short op-ed length articles starting in September 2005. Publishing them at this stage serves two purposes. First, and most important, they can help set the record right regarding the myth that none predicted the crisis. That is vital because exposing this myth is part of what is needed to make space for an alternative to failed neoliberal economic theory.

Second, the articles have stood the test of time and the issues raised have become even more salient. The economic articles provide condensed access to both theoretical and policy controversies that continue to be important and germane. The political articles frame the enormous political challenges we confront.

In the U.S., today's political choice between Democrats and Republicans is a choice between "bad" and "worse". A similar choice confronts voters in many countries. That political choice is linked to the dominance of mainstream economic theory which guides economic policy on both sides of the aisle. It is as if we are in a restaurant with two waiters (e.g. Democrats and Republicans), but only one chef (trained in mainstream economics). The challenge is to crack that monopoly and have progressives offer policies based on alternative economics. That is a double challenge. It means getting progressive politicians interested in economic theory and big ideas. And it means cracking the academic monopoly of mainstream economics.

Neither challenge is easy. The academy is a club and it resists change because club members benefit from their monopoly. Meanwhile, politicians consider themselves to be "practical" persons and have a disinterest in theory. They are also subject to the pull of money and money likes the existing mainstream economic paradigm. Finally, politicians are not economists and they look to the academy for advice. However, given the club monopoly they are all fed roughly the same policy diet. Together, this constitutes a powerful sociological system that is hard to crack.

That was the motive for my starting my blog, *Economics for Democratic and Open Societies*, in September 2005. The goal was to use the internet and emerging blogosphere to leapfrog the walls of the club. Those efforts from the underground now provide a chronicle of a crisis foretold and a chronicle of the catastrophic intellectual failure of mainstream economics.

Washington, D.C.
December 2011

REFERENCES

Baker, D. [2002], "The Run-up in Home Prices: Is it Real or is it Another Bubble?" Center for Economic Policy and Research, Washington, D.C., August.

Bivens, J. and J. Irons [2008], "A Feeble Recovery: The Fundamental Economic Weaknesses of the 2001 – 07 Expansion," EPI Briefing Paper No. 214, Economic Policy Institute, Washington D.C., December.

Godley, W., and G. Zezza [2006], "Debt and Lending: A Cri de Coeur," Policy Note 2006/4, The Levy Economics Institute of Bard College.

Keen, S. [1995], "Finance and Economic Breakdown: Modeling Minsky's Financial Instability Hypothesis," *Journal of Post Keynesian Economics*, 17 (4) (Summer), 607 – 35;

---- [2006], "The Recession We Can't Avoid," Steve Keen's Monthly Debt Report, November.

Palley, T. I. [1998], *Plenty of Nothing: The Downsizing of the American Dream and the Case for Structural Keynesianism*, Princeton: Princeton University Press.

----[2001 [2002]], "Economic Contradictions Coming Home to Roost? Does the U.S. Face a Long Term Aggregate Demand Generation Problem?" Working Paper 332, Levy Economics institute of Bard College, June 2001 and *Journal of Post Keynesian Economics*, 25 (2002), 9 - 32.

-----[2006a], "The Weak Recovery and Coming Deep Recession," *Mother Jones*, March 17.

---- [2006b [2007/8]], "The Fallacy of the Revised Bretton Woods Hypothesis: Why Today's System is Unsustainable and Suggestions for a Replacement," Public Policy Brief No. 85, The Levy Economics Institute of Bard College, 2006. Also published in *International Journal of Political Economy*, 36 (Winter), 36 – 52.

Rajan, R.G. [2005], "Has Financial Development Made the World Riskier?" Paper presented at the Jackson Hole Conference of the Kansas City Federal Reserve Bank.

Roubini, N., and B. Setser [2005], "Will the Bretton Woods 2 Regime Unravel Soon? The Risk of a Hard Landing in 2005-2006," paper prepared for a conference organized by the Federal Reserve Bank of San Francisco, February, p. 5.

Shiller, R.J. [2005], *Irrational Exuberance*, 2nd edition, Princeton University Press: Princeton, N.J.

ACKNOWLEDGEMENTS

I would like to thank profoundly Jamie Baker for her help over many years. Jamie has managed and maintained my website and she also prepared this manuscript for electronic publishing. Without Jamie's help these notes from the underground would never have seen daylight.

I THE CRISIS WAS PREDICTABLE

Letter to the Queen: The crisis was predicted

♦

The weak recovery and the coming deep recession

♦

Two views about a possible U.S. hard landing:
Foreign flight versus consumer burnout

♦

Asset bubble Keynesianism versus economic flexibility:
Challenging the Greenspan hypothesis

♦

Trade deficits matter

♦

Export-led growth: The elephant in the room

♦

The house price bubble: Won't get fooled again

LETTER TO THE QUEEN:
THE CRISIS WAS PREDICTED

July 29, 2009

Her Majesty The Queen
Buckingham Palace
London, SW1A 1AA

MADAM,

In response to your question why no one predicted the crisis you have recently received a letter from Professors Tim Besley and Peter Hennessy, sent on behalf of the British Academy. They claim economists' failure to foresee the crisis was the result of a "failure of the collective imagination." That claim is tendentious and will mislead you.

The failure was due to the sociology of the economics profession. This failure was a long time in the making and was the product of the profession becoming increasingly arrogant, narrow, and closed minded. One was compelled to adhere to the dominant ideological construction of economics or face exclusion. That was the mindset of the IMF and the World Bank with their "Washington Consensus", and it was the mindset of central bankers (including your own Bank of England) with their thinking about the sufficiency of inflation targeting and hostility to regulation.

The crisis was predictable and was predicted. See, for example:
1) "The Weak Recovery and the Coming Deep Recession," Mother Jones, March 2006.
2) "Debt and Lending: A Cri de Coeur," Levy Institute, April 2006.
3) "The Fallacy of the Revised Bretton Woods Hypothesis: Why Today's Financial System is Unsustainable," Levy Institute, June 2006.

Professors Besley and Hennessy's letter is another example of the economics profession's complete inability to come to grips with its sociological failure which produced massive intellectual failure with huge costs for society. This is a very serious social problem and we will all continue to pay the costs as long as it is unaddressed.

Respectfully yours,
Tom Palley

Posted on July 30, 2009 at thomaspalley.com. Also posted as "Let me explain, Ma'am...," The Guardian, Comment Is Free, July 31, 2009.

THE WEAK RECOVERY AND
THE COMING DEEP RECESSION

March 13, 2006

To quote Yogi Berra, "It's tough to make predictions, especially about the future." Many (including myself) expected that the bursting of the stock market and Internet bubbles in 2001 would cause a deep recession owing to large excesses of borrowing and spending by both the household and corporate sectors. Now we know that the recession of 2001 was fairly mild and of short duration, though the economic recovery has also been the weakest since World War II.

After having been wrong once, it's either brave or foolish to make a second prediction that the next recession will be deep and difficult to escape. But the facts point to it being just that—despite the optimism of the Federal Reserve. This is because the economic factors that helped escape the last recession have been largely exhausted and will not be available to fight the next recession.

The main reasons why the last recession was so relatively mild are the federal budget and interest rates. In fiscal year 2000 the federal government ran a budget surplus of $236 billion dollars, but within three years this had reversed to a deficit of $378 billion. The overall budgetary U-turn was therefore $614 billion dollars, equal to about six percent of economic output (gross domestic product). This turn provided an enormous injection of spending that helped prevent a deeper recession and jump start recovery.

The role of government spending in damping the recession and driving the recovery is evident in the employment statistics. From March 2001 (the beginning of the recession) to January 2006 government employment rose by 4.5 percent (one million jobs) to 21.9 million jobs. Over the same period, private-sector employment rose by just one percent. Government, which accounts for just 16 percent of total employment, therefore created half of all new jobs in the almost five years after the recession began. The private sector, which accounts for 84 percent of total employment, created the other half. Moreover, part of the increase in private-sector jobs involves government contract and defense-related work, so that the government's overall job contribution was even larger. In effect, increased government employment has masked persistent private-sector weakness.

This fiscal stimulus was accompanied by an extraordinary extended period of monetary ease that kept interest rates at historical lows. In 2000, the year before the recession, the Federal Reserve's target interest rate (the Federal funds rate) averaged 6.24 percent. When the recession began, the Fed cut this interest rate aggressively, lowering it to 1.67 percent in 2002 and 1.13 percent in 2003. Moreover, the Fed then held interest rates at historical lows three years after economic recovery had officially begun, so that the Federal funds rate was only

1.35 percent in 2004. Only since late 2004 has the Fed reversed itself and started systematically raising short-term interest rates.

There are three significant features about this monetary easing. First, it contributed importantly to warding off the recession and generating recovery. Second, the weakness of the private-sector recovery, despite the extraordinary scale of the fiscal and monetary stimulus, points to the underlying fragility of the private-sector economy. Third, the monetary easing has promoted massive consumer indebtedness and a housing price bubble, a combination that poses grave future threats.

The Fed's lowering of interest rates to forty-year record lows served to spur the recovery. It inspired a mortgage re-financing boom, providing immediate relief to households who were able to spend their mortgage interest savings. Lower interest rates also made houses more affordable, triggering a house price bubble that contributed significantly to escaping the recession.

Higher house prices increased homeowner equity, and many owners used this increased equity as collateral to borrow against. Their borrowing then financed consumption, which significantly explains the consumer-spending boom. Higher house prices have also allowed some existing homeowners to cash out, and some have spent part of their windfall. Meanwhile, homebuyers have financed house purchases with loans, which has increased the money supply. Lastly, rising house home prices have also created enormous profit margins for builders, providing an incentive to build new homes and spurring a construction industry boom.

The problem now is that these special conditions are largely spent. The projected federal budget deficit for fiscal year 2006 is $423 billion, approximately 3.3 percent of national output. With the budget already in deficit, this leaves less room for the type of U-turn that occurred in the last recession.

With regard to interest rates, the federal funds rate now stands at 4.5 percent—so there is room to lower it. However, lowering it is likely to have far smaller effects than last time. Why?

Homeowners have already significantly refinanced so that the stock of high interest rate mortgages available for refinancing has been depleted. Consumers are borrowed to the hilt, leaving less access for further borrowing. House prices are already at all-time highs by every measure—so lower interest rates are unlikely to spur another price boom, with all its expansionary effects. Instead, house prices could actually start falling as new supply continues to come on to the market, and this effect could be amplified by recession-induced job losses that trigger mortgage defaults by workers losing their jobs. Taken together, these factors point to future interest rate reductions likely being akin to pushing on a string.

Adverse domestic economic conditions will also be echoed globally. The 2001 recession was business investment-led, with little consequence for China and East Asia. This is because those economies export consumer goods and the American consumer kept spending. However, a consumption spending-led recession will quickly spill over into East Asia, triggering job losses and a decline in investment spending in those economies. Consequently, a U.S. recession will quickly ricochet around the globe.

This is not about predicting *when* the next recession will happen, but rather about its character. The "when game" is impossible. As Nobel Prize-winning economist Paul Samuelson once quipped, "The stock market has correctly predicted nine of the last five recessions." However, it is possible to anticipate future difficulties and proscribe possible remedies.

First, the Federal Reserve should be very careful about over-shooting with its rate hikes, and at this time it should take an inflation chill pill. Second, the current recovery has been extraordinarily weak, which should finally discredit the notion that tax cuts for the rich drive growth and job creation. Third, the speculative financial market paradigm—which has ruled the policy roost for twenty-five years—is out of gas. It is time for a new paradigm that links growth to rising wages rather than to asset price boom-bust cycles.

Originally posted as "The next recession" on March 13, 2006 on tompaine.com. Also posted as "The weak recovery and the coming deep recession" on thomaspalley.com on March 15, 2006 and Mother Jones on Friday, March 17, 2006.

TWO VIEWS ABOUT A POSSIBLE U.S. HARD LANDING: FOREIGN FLIGHT VERSUS CONSUMER BURNOUT

October 23, 2005

The current U.S. economic expansion is in its fifth year. At this stage, the possibility of its ending has raised two explanations that can be labeled the "foreign flight' and "consumer burnout" hypotheses. While both predict a recession, they rest on very different reasoning and have different implications for interest rates and exchange rate policy. The foreign flight hypothesis is also politically troubling since it can be easily tinged with xenophobia.

The foreign flight view argues that foreign lenders, who have financed the U.S. trade deficit, will eventually grow tired of doing so. Its logic is as follows. At some stage, foreign wealth holders will become saturated with U.S. financial liabilities, and they will cease buying additional debt. This will cause interest rates to spike and the dollar to plunge. The result will be financial market turmoil and recession.

The consumer burnout view also predicts a recession, but its logic rests on consumers exhausting their borrowing capacity. When this happens, consumer spending will slow, sending the economy into recession. Slowed spending may well link with an end of the housing price bubble since rising house prices have provided collateral that has backed consumer borrowing. From this perspective, rising house prices, household borrowing, and robust consumer spending are three sides of the same coin. Equity prices are also vulnerable owing to the prospect of diminished corporate profitability, and the dollar could fall if diminished U.S. prospects cause investors to tilt asset allocations overseas. However, interest rates are likely to fall rather than rise because government bonds will look relatively safe compared to equities.

One problem for policymakers is that the two views have many observational similarities, which tends to confuse the issue. Both predict recession, financial market turmoil, and a fall in the dollar. However, they differ regarding interest rates. The foreign flight hypothesis predicts an interest rate spike, whereas the consumer burnout hypothesis predicts that rates will fall. Interestingly, Wall Street bond traders appear to hold the latter view, as evidenced by falling long-term interest rates despite the Fed's raising of short-term rates.

There are also big differences regarding the exchange rate. The foreign flight hypothesis sees an exchange rate collapse as "triggering" the downturn, whereas the consumer burnout hypothesis has it "resulting" from the prospect of a downturn that causes investors to lose confidence in the U.S. economy.

The two views have important policy differences. In an economy, every lender needs a matching borrower, and every saver needs a matching spender. The foreign flight hypothesis sees lenders and savers as the ultimate constraint on economic activity. In particular, it identifies the supply of foreign credit and foreign investor portfolios as the constraint on the U.S. economy. The consumer burnout hypothesis focuses on spenders and borrowers, and identifies the level of domestic demand and consumer balance sheets as the ultimate constraint.

At the policy architecture level, the foreign flight view recommends increasing U.S. saving, whereas the consumer burnout hypothesis recommends safeguarding the integrity and sustainability of U.S. demand generation. The trade deficit matters for both. However, the foreign flight hypothesis recommends increasing U.S. saving, whereas the consumer burnout hypothesis emphasizes switching expenditure from imports to domestic goods. Indeed, household saving need not increase. What is needed is that the composition of consumption change, thereby generating jobs and income that sustain consumer borrowing.

More specifically, the foreign flight hypothesis could suggest that the Fed raise rates to defend the dollar should it weaken. The consumer burnout hypothesis unambiguously recommends that the Fed lower interest rates and let the dollar slide in managed fashion as a way of maintaining domestic demand. However, this will be problematic for the rest of the world, which currently relies on U.S. demand.

Finally, the foreign flight view has troubling political overtones because it is easily tinged with xenophobia. Bondholders, domestic and foreign, are pretty much alike. Indeed, a run on the dollar is more likely to be triggered by better-informed domestic "Wall Street" investors. That is the history of capital flight episodes. The trade deficit is a major problem because of its adverse impact on the structure of U.S. income and demand generation. We should talk of it in those terms, and resist talking about it in terms of foreign bogeys.

Posted on October 23, 2005 at thomaspalley.com.

ASSET BUBBLE KEYNESIANISM VERSUS ECONOMIC FLEXIBILITY: CHALLENGING THE GREENSPAN HYPOTHESIS

November 12, 2005

If you have a pulpit and say something over and over again, that something may eventually come to be believed. No one has a bigger pulpit than Alan Greenspan, Chairman of the Federal Reserve, who for the last decade has been saying that the secret of America's prosperity is its economic flexibility. But there is another explanation, which is asset bubble Keynesianism. It too can make for a jolly old time – at least for a while.

We are now approaching the post-Greenspan era when consumers may finally have "maxed-out," and the new era promises to test the two hypotheses. If Mr. Greenspan is right, we have nothing to fear. The good times will keep rolling. If he is wrong, the American economy could face a day of reckoning, at which time it will be important to re-examine the economic policies and rhetoric of the last two decades.

The Chairman's thinking was recently on display (October 12, 2005) in a preliminary farewell speech titled "Economic Flexibility," made to the National Italian American Foundation. So too was his propensity to re-write economic history. The years 1945 – 1975 witnessed the fastest annual economic growth rate in American history, and the country grew together with all sharing in prosperity. Since then, growth has slowed and we have grown apart, with those at the bottom getting a smaller share of the economic cake. However, these facts did not deter the Chairman from declaring the period 1945 – 75 to be one of growing failure, and the ensuing period to be one of great success. A case of "If history does not support theory, too bad for history."

The Greenspan view is eloquently simple. The key to resilient prosperity is economic flexibility, which "is most readily achieved by fostering an environment of maximum competition. A key element in creating this environment is flexible labor markets." Such flexibility makes "the economy more resilient to shocks and more stable overall" and is key to growth in standards of living.

Even granting Chairman Greenspan his (contentious) claims about U.S. prosperity, there is another explanation of why growth has been more stable and why America avoided a deep recession after the 1990s stock market bust. That explanation is America has been borrowing its way out of successive crises, and has enjoyed a bout of "asset bubble Keynesianism." Spending rather than flexibility has stabilized the system. However, borrowing can store up trouble if not used wisely, and America's borrowing has been allowed to leak away through the trade deficit. Now, households are burdened with debt, and by frivolously using up our credit, the American economy is poorly positioned to escape future economic shocks.

It is easy to mistake the borrowing binge for economic flexibility, since increased access to credit has been the result of financial innovation and deregulation. The 1980s introduced the junk bond market. The 1990s introduced the home equity loan, and today we have the interest-only home loan. We have also shifted from defined benefit to defined contribution (401k) pension plans. Paradoxically, these make us worse off in retirement, but we feel better and spend more pre-retirement. When the stock market goes up, people feel wealthier when their 401k statements come in, and they can also borrow against 401k wealth. None of this happened under earlier pension arrangements.

There is one area where financial deregulation and innovation have truly helped. That is the shift from state banking to national banking, which means individual banks now lend across wide regions. This has diversified risk, helping avoid cascading bank failures when loans have gone bad. Another innovation that has helped spread risk is securitization, which is a form of second-hand loan market. This has enabled banks to bundle loans and sell them to insurance companies and pension funds. However, risk can be spread but not gotten rid of, so the system is still exposed to a really big bust.

Not only has Chairman Greenspan misinterpreted the economic effects of financial innovation and deregulation, he also deeply misunderstands competition. The Chairman laments that "Many working people, regrettably, equate labor market flexibility with job insecurity", and he proposes maximum competition. But if competition is to deliver shared prosperity, it must be nested in a set of rules that ensures appropriate income distribution and prevents undesirable forms of competition. All of this must be done while preserving the incentive to produce. Mr. Greenspan's view, which has prevailed in the design of globalization, recognizes none of this and takes us back in the direction of 19th century style competition.

If the asset bubble Keynesianism hypothesis proves correct, policy will need to revisit the questions of financial regulation and unbridled competition. There are better forms of Keynesianism that ensure a robust level of spending based on fair and stable structures of income generation. That should be the goal of economic policy.

Posted on November 12, 2005 at thomaspalley.com.

TRADE DEFICITS MATTER

September 22, 2006

Over the last several years the U.S. trade deficit has persistently set new records, hitting $717 billion in 2005, equal to almost 6 percent of GDP. China, in particular has contributed to the deficit, and now accounts for just shy of one-third of the total. By any historical standard, the economic warning lights are flashing red.

Interestingly, both the *laissez-faire* right and Keynesian left sometimes give comfort to the *status quo* with claims that trade deficits do not matter. From the right comes the argument that trade deficits don't matter because they simply reflect the actions of consenting adults doing what they choose through markets. Indeed, deficits are good, being the way that consenting adults obtain their utility maximizing lifetime consumption outcomes.

From the left comes the argument that the massive U.S. trade deficit with China benefits both countries. U.S. consumers get lots of cheap goods in return for which they give over paper I.O.U.s that are costless to print. Meanwhile, China creates millions of jobs and builds modern factories that are transforming it into an industrial superpower, and it also accumulates billions of dollars in financial claims against the United States. From this perspective, trade deficits don't matter because there are no limits or consequences to either government or private borrowing, and because manufacturing does not matter either.

According to the logic of left and right, the U.S. would benefit even further if China devalued its exchange rate and ran a larger trade surplus. If the Chinese want to give away their production at artificially low prices, more fool them and we should willingly accept the gift. When something sounds too good to be true, that's usually because it is not true. Both left and right are wrong. Large persistent trade deficits do matter.

Before turning to why trade deficits matter, it is necessary to dispel a straw man argument. Trade deficit deniers often begin by rhetorically speculating what if the deficit were to disappear overnight, and they rightly observe that U.S. inflation would immediately rise owing to lack of industrial capacity. This would force the Federal Reserve to raise interest rates, and might also compel higher taxes and government spending cuts.

However, this is a straw man. No one is arguing for going "cold turkey" on trade. Instead, there is need to begin a process of adjustment whereby the U.S. trade deficit is gradually reduced over the next few years. This adjustment will be difficult, but the longer it is delayed the more difficult and dangerous it will be. If you are unfit and wish to get fit, it is unwise to go out and immediately run a marathon. Likewise, continuing to smoke and generally over-indulge makes getting fit more difficult and dangerous. These analogies hold for the U.S. economy and its trade deficit.

Why then do persistent large trade deficits matter? The first reason concerns jobs. The current U.S. economic recovery has been the weakest since World War II, and this is significantly due to the trade deficit. In past recoveries, consumer spending created hundreds of thousands of domestic manufacturing jobs. This time round it has leached out of the economy in the form of spending on imports and created jobs in China and elsewhere.

For trade deficit deniers from the right the failure to create jobs is because Americans don't want to work. If they did they would lower their wage demands and job creation would follow. This glibness ignores the fact that lowering wages would quickly bankrupt most households who would be unable to pay their mortgages. That in turn would cause the financial system to collapse, giving rise to another Great Depression.

For deficit deniers on the left, the job shortage can be remedied by larger budget deficits and more private borrowing. The reasoning is budget deficits have no consequences and there is no limit to the amount of money banks can create or consumers can borrow. That reasoning is false. There are significant adverse consequences to both excessive budget deficits and excessive private sector indebtedness, and the U.S.'s extraordinary trade deficits have resulted in both being higher than would have otherwise been needed to restore U.S. full employment.

Regarding budget deficits, these can pose problems for the future because interest must be paid, which means reduced revenues available for other purposes. With regard to foreign-held U.S government debt, when foreigners spend the interest that will be good for U.S. jobs and incomes. However paying interest will consume available tax revenues so that maintaining government services could require higher taxes that may be politically difficult to accomplish. Moreover, unlike domestic bondholders, interest payments to foreign holders are not taxed, which amplifies their future budget impact.

Regarding private sector debts, accumulated debt burdens promise to be a drag on future U.S. demand growth and economic activity. Individual households have credit limits. Accumulated debts are deflationary because interest must be paid and because they constrain future borrowing. The problem is that U.S. household debts have grown far faster than income, in part due to the trade deficit that has resulted in job creation offshore rather than onshore.

Not only has the trade deficit burdened the demand-side of the U.S. economy, it has also burdened the supply-side. First, the undervalued exchange rate has resulted in many U.S. manufacturing companies closing factories because they cannot compete. Some companies have simply gone out of business, while others

12

have re-located or sub-contracted production to East Asia. Second, many companies have re-directed investment to China rather than building new modern capacity in the United States. This has weakened the U.S. industrial base, and also made the task of trade deficit adjustment more difficult.

To trade deficit deniers on both right and left these effects apparently do not matter because manufacturing jobs can be replaced without consequence by service sector jobs. Boeing is one of the crown jewels of America's industrial base. According to such reasoning, Boeing could close shop, move to China, and then export aircraft to the United States. Boeing workers could be re-employed as service sector street sweepers with the same pay and America would be better off because it would have cleaner streets.

This is false. Manufacturing is key to prosperity, being a major center of productivity growth and innovation. When manufacturing moves offshore, associated research and development activities often go too. Additionally, international trade remains concentrated in goods, which means that over the long haul countries need goods to sell to finance imports. Behind the arguments of the trade deficit deniers is a tacit assumption that should the U.S. ever exhaust its international credit, it can quickly and simply reconstruct its industrial base. Unfortunately, that is not how real world manufacturing operates. Individual manufacturing firms are clusters of knowledge, skills, and capital, themselves clustered in industries. Once firms and industries are destroyed it is costly and difficult to reassemble them.

Lastly, both left and right also ignore the fact that persistent trade deficits raise financial stability and strategic concerns, which are particularly acute regarding China given uncertainty about whether it will become a geo-political friend or rival. The concern is that countries could start selling their holdings of U.S. financial assets, triggering financial disruption and higher interest rates. However, this concern should not be overstated, and xenophobic appeals of right-wing nationalists and left-wing populists should be resisted. The history of capital flight episodes shows that it is domestic investors who have tended to trigger panics, as they are better informed and therefore head for the exits first. That suggests Wall Street rather than foreigners will trigger any run on the dollar.

Posted on September 22, 2006 at thomaspalley.com. An earlier version of this article titled "Deficits do matter" appeared in The Guardian, Comment is Free on April 27, 2006.

EXPORT-LED GROWTH:
THE ELEPHANT IN THE ROOM

January 13, 2006

Psychologists refer to the "elephant in the room" phenomenon as a condition where people talk about everything except the most important issue. I recently (January 10, 2006) attended a conference at Washington's prestigious Institute for International Economics on the likelihood of a financial crisis in developing countries. All morning the elephant sat quietly in the room sipping coffee.

The expert panelists puzzled over why global financial markets are so calm despite rising U.S. interest rates and the record trade deficit. Interest rate spreads between the U.S. and emerging market (EM) countries are at record lows, and foreign direct investment is flowing abundantly into these countries. This rosy picture was explained by reference to permanent policy changes. EM countries have improved their macroeconomic policies; run trade surpluses; restrained spending in the boom; and improved public finances by extending debt maturities, lowering their foreign currency debt, and refinancing at lower interest rates.

However, there is another deeper cause of this rosy condition. That cause is export-led growth, which is the elephant's name. What's the deal with export-led growth? EM countries export manufactured consumption goods to the U.S., in return getting financial claims against the U.S. These exports generate large trade surpluses that fund improved public finances. Additionally, EM countries get large flows of foreign investment since multinational corporations are happy to build export production platforms that take advantage of cheap labor and undervalued exchange rates.

The other side of the transaction has the U.S. getting cheap consumer goods – lots of them. It also runs a trade deficit that American banks finance by issuing dollar deposits to EM countries. To the extent that countries use these deposits to buy U.S. debt, this lowers interest rates, which is good for the U.S. housing market. If they buy U.S. assets, this bids up asset prices and makes U.S. households wealthier. The downer is that the U.S. sacrifices its manufacturing base since existing production and much new investment are off-shored via multinational foreign direct investment.

This configuration explains the health of emerging market economies. As long as the U.S. keeps importing, they can keep exporting and the merry-go round keeps turning. The sixty-four million dollar question is what could stop it? And if it stops, what follows?

One possible stopper is if foreign countries cease holding their earnings in dollars. This would cause the dollar to fall, raising import prices and lowering U.S. consumer import purchases. But foreign governments have no interest in this, as it would kill their "golden goose". Moreover, alternative yen and euro investments pay lower interest rates than dollar investments.

A second possible stopper is if the Federal Reserve raises interest rates high enough to tank the housing market, driving down house prices. This would make households poorer, likely tip the U.S. into a recession, and reduce consumption spending. That would reduce imports, which would quickly be felt in emerging markets. This scenario is a real possibility, but policy can avoid it.

A third possible stopper is if Americans cease their consumption binge because they feel over-extended. Alternatively, local American banks may tighten lending because they doubt households' credit-worthiness and think house prices are inflated so that housing collateral is unsound. In this case, the flow of credit financing consumption would dry up at its base, and imports would quickly fall. This is another credible scenario, and it is one that is harder for policy to impact. The Fed controls the price of credit, but a local borrower and lender must seal the deal to activate that credit. Even China's willingness to lend to local American banks cannot force that transaction.

Once consumption spending falls the U.S. economy will slow, possibly even falling into recession. Imports will fall, ricocheting back to emerging market countries whose exports will tumble. On the financial side, EM countries' trade surpluses will fall. On the industrial side, there will be excess capacity and lost jobs. Excess capacity will discourage foreign direct investment, while rising unemployment risks a return of political instability. The depth and duration of such a downturn is the next sixty-four million dollar question. That will depend on the extent of excess capacity and the scale of U.S. household over-indebtedness. It will also depend on whether emerging economies can replace exports with domestic sales, but don't count on that as their record is poor.

That brings us back to the opening conundrum. Why no mention of export-led growth? One reason is that trade is a touchy subject in Washington, and trade has enough problems without being tied to global financial instability. Export-led growth also shows that trade is not a level playing field, confirming critics' claims about countries manipulating exchange rates and pursuing mercantilist policies that subsidize their manufacturers. Finally, the export-led growth story implies the U.S. is relying on import-led growth that sacrifices the manufacturing base, which is a doubtful long run national growth strategy. So why do people ignore the elephant? To quote Bill Clinton, "Denial, it's not just a river in Egypt."

Posted on January 13, 2006 at thomaspalley.com.

THE HOUSE PRICE BUBBLE:
WON'T GET FOOLED AGAIN

April 8, 2006

One of my all-time favorite rock albums is The Who's "Who's Next" and one of my favorite tracks on that album is "Won't Get Fooled Again." Right now there is much talk of a housing bubble, making for the possibility that a lot of people are getting fooled.

There are two ways to assess whether there is a housing bubble. The first can be termed the "historical approach," and it involves looking at the historical relationship between house prices, levels of income, interest rates, and demographic factors. According to that approach house prices look significantly out of whack.

The second can be termed the "comparable cost approach," and it involves comparing the relative cost of renting versus buying. A recent study by Professors Gary and Margaret Smith of Pomona College in Southern California uses this approach and concludes that house prices are generally not over-valued. Their findings have quickly been advertised by the mainstream media (New York Times, Saturday April 1, 2006), but the comparable cost approach has serious limitations. In the spirit of openness, here are some cautions about their conclusion.

People buy houses to enjoy the accommodation services that houses provide. An alternative way to get those services is to rent an equivalent house. If over the lifetime of occupancy, a house can be rented for less than it can be purchased this would suggest house prices are over-valued. Such a comparison involves a complicated calculation involving assumptions about future rents, future home ownership costs, and future house price appreciation that determines what an owner gets when they sell. Using this method, and assuming future annual rent increases and house price appreciation of three percent, the Smiths found that house prices were fair to under-valued, except in a few areas.

The main problem with the Smith's study is that it assumes away the bubble. Their baseline calculation assumes a three percent annual increase in house prices, which automatically means no bubble. If prices keep rising, there cannot by definition have been a bubble.

That leads to the core problem with the comparable cost approach, which is that it provides no insights into future prices of houses or rents. Instead, it compares existing house prices with existing rents and factors in an assumed future path for prices and rents. That makes it a good tool for framing the "rent or buy" decision, but not for predicting future prices. It is possible that rents today are too high and could fall and drag down house prices. Alternatively, house prices

16

could fall and drag down rents. There is some evidence that both may happen, but this vital evidence is ignored.

House builders are reporting record profits, which means that cost of building homes is significantly below the price of homes. Consequently, builders have an incentive to keep building homes and adding to the supply of homes until prices return closer to building costs. Given today's prices and costs, new house construction promises to keep the lid on home prices and possibly lower them.

The same holds for the rental market. Real estate investment trusts have also reported record profits. This suggests that rental properties are profitable, providing an incentive to build more rental units, which will keep the lid on rents. This incentive is strengthened by the fact that rental supply has been reduced by conversion of rental units into condominiums.

Either of these effects – flat home prices or flat rents – dramatically changes the conclusion that houses are fairly valued under the comparable cost approach. Note, that neither prices nor rents need to fall to generate the conclusion that people in many locales are over-paying. All that is needed is for prices or rents to flat-line, in which event buying a house is a poor investment at today's prices.

A second core problem with the comparable cost approach is that it completely ignores risk. For renters, the main risk is faster than expected future rental price increases. For buyers, the main risk is capital loss, and this risk is closely linked to how long one holds the house. If you hold a house for thirty years, it is unlikely you will incur a capital loss because the long-run trend of house price appreciation will dominate temporary price fluctuations. However, if you hold it for less than ten years, the likelihood of loss is much larger - particularly after a period of rapid home price increases.

Given the leveraged nature of home buying, small decreases in home prices can inflict large losses on owners. Consider a $500,000 home with an initial ten percent down payment. If the house price falls ten percent, the owner loses one hundred percent of their equity. If the price falls twenty percent, they end up with negative equity of $50,000 that would probably bankrupt most households. This can have lifelong consequences by denying future access to credit, which can also prevent future home purchases.

These considerations are especially important to young buyers who often buy condominiums. The holding period for young buyers is shorter, exposing them to greatly enhanced risk of loss. Moreover, home prices do not even have to fall to impose large losses. Remember, the cost of selling a home is six percent. For the above $500,000 example, the exit cost is $30,000 and that wipes out more than half of the initial equity investment. The important point is that houses are illiquid and risky investment. Such investments usually trade at a discount to flexible liquid investments (i.e. renting), and homes (especially condominiums) should therefore sell at a slight discount to renting.

If there is a bubble, it is likely heavily concentrated in the condominium market. However, the effects will ramify throughout the residential real estate market. Many condo owners could find their equity wiped out, and condos are often the first step on the housing market ladder. Consequently, condo market weakness will ripple into broader housing market weakness. Over the long run prices will recover, but as the great British economist John Maynard Keynes remarked, "In the long run we're all dead."

Posted on April 8, 2006 at thomaspalley.com.

II AMERICA'S EXHAUSTED PARADIGM

The debt delusion

♦

America's exhausted growth paradigm

♦

A second Great Depression is still possible

THE DEBT DELUSION

February 8, 2008

A second big American interest-rate cut in a fortnight, alongside an economic stimulus plan that united Republicans and Democrats, demonstrates that U.S. policymakers are keen to head off a recession that looks like the likely consequence of rising mortgage defaults and falling home prices. But there is a deeper problem that has been overlooked: the U.S. economy relies upon asset price inflation and rising indebtedness to fuel growth.

Therein lies a profound contradiction. On one hand, policy must fuel asset bubbles to keep the economy growing. On the other hand, such bubbles inevitably create financial crises when they eventually implode.

This is a contradiction with global implications. Many countries have relied for growth on U.S. consumer spending and investments in outsourcing to supply those consumers. If America's bubble economy is now tapped out, global growth will slow sharply. It is not clear that other countries have the will or capacity to develop alternative engines of growth.

America's economic contradictions are part of a new business cycle that has emerged since 1980. The business cycles of Presidents Ronald Reagan, George H.W. Bush, Bill Clinton, and George W. Bush share strong similarities and are different from pre-1980 cycles. The similarities are large trade deficits, manufacturing job loss, asset price inflation, rising debt-to-income ratios, and detachment of wages from productivity growth.

The new cycle rests on financial booms and cheap imports. Financial booms provide collateral that supports debt-financed spending. Borrowing is also supported by an easing of credit standards and new financial products that increase leverage and widen the range of assets that can be borrowed against. Cheap imports ameliorate the effects of wage stagnation.

This structure contrasts with the pre-1980 business cycle, which rested on wage growth tied to productivity growth and full employment. Wage growth, rather than borrowing and financial booms, fuelled demand growth. That encouraged investment spending, which in turn drove productivity gains and output growth.

The differences between the new and old cycle are starkly revealed in attitudes toward the trade deficit. Previously, trade deficits were viewed as a serious problem, being a leakage of demand that undermined employment and output. Since 1980, trade deficits have been dismissed as the outcome of free-market choices. Moreover, the Federal Reserve has viewed trade deficits as a helpful brake on inflation, while politicians now view them as a way to buy off consumers afflicted by wage stagnation.

The new business cycle also embeds a monetary policy that replaces concern with real wages with a focus on asset prices. Whereas pre-1980 monetary policy tacitly aimed at putting a floor under labor markets to preserve employment and wages, it now tacitly puts a floor under asset prices. This is not a matter of the Fed bailing out investors. Rather, the economy has become so vulnerable to declines in asset prices that the Fed is obliged to intervene to prevent them from inflicting broad damage.

All these features have been present in the current economic expansion. Wages have stagnated despite strong productivity growth, while the trade deficit has set new records. Manufacturing has lost 1.8 million jobs. Prior to 1980, manufacturing employment increased during every expansion and always exceeded the previous peak level. Between 1980 and 2000, manufacturing employment continued to grow in expansions, but each time it failed to recover the previous peak. This time, manufacturing employment has actually fallen during the expansion, something unprecedented in American history.

The essential role of asset inflation has been especially visible as a result of the housing bubble, which also highlights the role of monetary policy. Despite the massive tax cuts of 2001 and the increase in military and security spending, the U.S. experienced a prolonged jobless recovery. That compelled the Fed to keep interest rates at historic lows for an extended period, and rates were raised only gradually because of fears about the recovery's fragility.

Low interest rates eventually jump-started the expansion through a house price bubble that supported a debt-financed consumer-spending binge and triggered a construction boom. Meanwhile, prolonged low interest rates contributed to a "chase for yield" in the financial sector that resulted in disregard of credit risk.

In this way, the Fed contributed to creating the sub-prime crisis. However, in the Fed's defense, low interest rates were needed to maintain the expansion. In effect, the new cycle locks the Fed into an unstable stance whereby it must prevent asset price declines to avert recession, yet must also promote asset bubbles to sustain expansions.

So, even if the Fed and U.S. Treasury now manage to stave off recession, what will fuel future growth? With debt burdens elevated and housing prices significantly above levels warranted by their historical relation to income, the business cycle of the last two decades appears exhausted.

It is not enough to deal only with the crisis of the day. Policy must also chart a stable long-term course, which implies the need to reconsider the paradigm of the past 25 years. That means ending trade deficits that drain spending and jobs, and restoring the link between wages and productivity. That way, wage income, not debt and asset price inflation, can again provide the engine of demand growth.

Distributed by Project Syndicate on February 8, 2008 at project-syndicate.org. Also posted on February 26, 2008 at thomaspalley.com.

AMERICA'S EXHAUSTED GROWTH PARADIGM

April 11, 2008

The American economy is most likely in recession, and high debt and housing-sector problems spur fears that this downturn could be far more severe than the recessions of 1991 and 2001. The Federal Reserve and Treasury have taken unprecedented actions to stimulate the economy through interest-rate cuts, infusions of liquidity, and tax cuts, all of which are entirely justified but constitute short-term economic firefighting.

While America certainly needs to deal with the latest trough in the business cycle, we also need to recognize that the growth paradigm that has driven our economy for the past generation is exhausted. That also has implications for the global economy, which has relied on America as the buyer of last resort. Should the American economy slow, it is not clear other countries have either the capacity or the will to develop alternative engines of economic growth.

The recent economic expansion began in November 2001 with an extended period of jobless recovery, and for most of the expansion, employment growth remained below par. That compelled the Federal Reserve to lower interest rates despite a so-called recovery, to keep rates low for an extended period, and to raise them only gradually thereafter. The Fed's actions prevented a relapse into recession, but only by triggering a bubble in housing prices. They also fostered a chase for yield among investors that led to a disregard of risk, and that has come home to roost in the form of house-price deflation and massive losses in credit markets.

Why was the expansion so weak despite the massive tax cuts of 2001 and large increases in military and security spending? The answer is the overvalued dollar and a trade deficit that drained spending, jobs, and investment from the economy. As a result, much of manufacturing failed to participate in the expansion. Indeed, manufacturing actually lost 1.8 million jobs between the end of 2001 and the end of 2007. That is unprecedented, as never before has manufacturing lost jobs during an expansion.

The U.S. policy of a strong dollar bears substantial blame for the trade deficit. The policy was initiated by the Clinton administration on the advice of Treasury Secretary Robert E. Rubin, and the Bush administration continued it. The effect has been to make imports cheaper and exports more expensive, thereby increasing imports, decreasing exports, and encouraging off-shoring of production. That, in turn, caused job cuts in manufacturing, reductions in production capacity, and reduced investment in domestic manufacturing.

Trade policy has also played a significant role by encouraging American corporations to move production offshore and shift to global sourcing.

Compounding those trends were the export-led growth policies of China and other East Asian countries. Those policies promoted Asian exports and foreign direct investment in those economies, while hampering American exports.

The trade deficit and disregard for manufacturing are part of a broader policy paradigm in place since 1980 that created a new kind of business cycle. The business cycles during the administrations of Ronald Reagan, George H.W. Bush, Bill Clinton, and George W. Bush have strong similarities and are very different from those before 1980. The similarities are the detachment of wages from productivity, large trade deficits, inflation, losses in manufacturing jobs, and rising household debt.

The post-1980 business cycle has relied on financial booms and cheap imports. Financial booms have provided collateral to support increased borrowing that has financed spending on consumption. Increased borrowing has also been supported by easing of credit standards, and by financial innovations that have widened access to credit. Meanwhile, cheap imports have ameliorated the effects of wage stagnation.

That pattern contrasts with the earlier business cycles that rested not on borrowing but on wage growth tied to productivity growth and full employment. Spending, combined with full employment encouraged investment, which increased productivity and fueled higher wages.

The shift from the old to the new business cycle was the result of profound political change associated with Reagan's election in 1980. It inaugurated a period in which business has been ascendant and labor battered. The shift was intellectually rationalized by economists such as Milton Friedman. The old business cycle rested on the combination of New Deal institutional innovations that strengthened labor, combined with demand-management measures pioneered in Keynesian economics. The new business cycle rests on policies that have sought to erode and repeal New Deal institutions, and demand management has been redirected to lowering inflation rather than securing full employment. Indeed, the language of full employment has been discarded.

The differences between the post-1980 and pre-1980 business cycles are starkly illustrated by policy. Previously the trade deficit was viewed as a serious problem because it was a leakage of spending from the economy that undermined employment and production. Since 1980 the trade deficit has been viewed as a helpful form of inflation control, and it has also helped hide the effects of wage stagnation.

The new business cycle has also changed monetary policy. Previously it was geared to supporting labor markets, maintaining full employment and wages, and encouraging the spending that drove investment and productivity growth. Now monetary policy supports asset prices in order to encourage borrowing, and rising wages are viewed as an inflationary threat.

The problem is that the post-1980 paradigm is tapped out. After a quarter-century borrowing binge, many households have hit their debt limits. Likewise, prices of assets (especially houses) are at elevated levels and at risk of falling, in some cases precipitously. In other words, this business cycle needs inflation in asset prices plus borrowing to drive spending.

More fundamentally, it is unclear how growth can be restored. Consumers won't be able to borrow their way out of this recession as they have the past couple. Lower interest rates are likely to be far less effective than before, with their effect similar to pushing on a slack string. Previously households had unused access to credit, which provided a launching pad for recovery. Now many are in debt to the hilt, and banks are far less willing to lend to risky borrowers anyway.

Mortgage refinancing is also likely to have weaker effects. First, the pool of high-interest-rate mortgages has largely been refinanced in prior recessions, leaving fewer mortgages worth refinancing. Second, falling house prices will make banks less willing to refinance existing mortgages, which may exceed house values.

The bottom line is that the post-1980 business cycle, which has relied on a combination of asset price inflation and persistent increases in borrowing, appears exhausted. Not only does the economy stand to lose the economic octane that those processes provided, it could fall into a downward spiral if asset prices decline and households shun further debt. Under these conditions, the Federal Reserve is likely to be able to do little to jump-start growth.

We need a new economic paradigm that restores the link between wages and productivity growth, and again makes wage income the principal engine of demand. Remedying the generation-long rupture of the wage-productivity link will require the restoration of policies aimed at full employment. Full employment will give workers bargaining power. That will encourage wage increases, which will fuel spending, productivity, and investment. Achieving full employment will require coordination of monetary, fiscal, and exchange-rate policies toward that end.

Also necessary is a change in the balance of power in labor markets. That will entail reforms and vigorous enforcement of labor law to end employer intimidation preventing workers from joining unions and bargaining for fair contracts. The minimum wage should be tied to average wages so that it rises as the economy grows. And unemployment insurance must be broadened and extended.

America must also start to close the trade deficit, which has hemorrhaged spending and undermined manufacturing. A new exchange-rate policy should prevent overvaluation of the dollar relative to the currencies of major trading partners. Only a clear and lasting commitment to such a policy will convince businesses to invest again in American manufacturing.

Lastly, developing economies must be weaned from their policies of export-led growth, and must focus on the development of domestic markets. In the realm of trade policy, that means putting an end to unfair international competition based on undervalued exchange rates, export subsidies, and unfair trade restrictions. That will require a new international economic architecture that promotes fair and balanced trade— a task that will require enlightened American leadership.

Published in The Chronicle of Higher Education, Section: The Chronicle Review, Volume 54, Issue 31, Page B10, April 11, 2008 and on forums.chronicle.com.

A SECOND GREAT DEPRESSION IS STILL POSSIBLE

October 11, 2009

Over the past year the global economy has experienced a massive contraction, the deepest since the Great Depression of the 1930s. But this spring, economists started talking of "green shoots" of recovery and that optimistic assessment quickly spread to Wall Street. More recently, on the anniversary of the Lehman Brothers crash, Federal Reserve Chairman Ben Bernanke officially blessed this consensus by declaring the recession is "very likely over".

The future is fundamentally uncertain, which always makes prediction a rash enterprise. That said there is a good chance the new consensus is wrong. Instead, there are solid grounds for believing the U.S. economy will experience a second dip followed by extended stagnation that will qualify as the second Great Depression. Some indications to this effect are already rolling in with unexpectedly large U.S. job losses in September and the crash in U.S. automobile sales following the end of the "Cash-for-Clunkers" program.

That rosy scenario thinking has returned to Wall Street should be no surprise. Wall Street profits from rising asset prices on which it charges a management fee, from deal making on which it earns advisory fees, and from encouraging retail investors to buy stock which boosts transaction fees. Such earnings are far larger when stock markets are rising, which explains Wall Street's genetic propensity to pump the economy.

As for mainstream economists, their theoretical models were blind-sided by the crisis and only predict recovery because of the assumptions in the models. According to mainstream theory, it is assumed that full employment is a gravity point to which the economy is pulled back.

Empirical econometric models are equally questionable. They too predict gradual recovery but that is driven by patterns of reversion to trends found in past data. The problem, as investment professionals say, is "past performance is no guide to future performance". The economic crisis represents the implosion of the economic paradigm that has ruled U.S. and global growth for the past thirty years. That paradigm was based on consumption fuelled by indebtedness and asset price inflation, and it is done.

There is a simple logic to why the economy will experience a second dip. That logic rests on the economics of deleveraging which inevitably produces a two-step correction. The first step has been worked through, and it triggered a financial crisis that caused the worst recession since the Great Depression. The second step has only just begun.

Deleveraging can be understood through a metaphor in which a car symbolizes the economy. Borrowing is like stepping on the gas and accelerates economic activity. When borrowing stops, the foot comes off the pedal and the car slows down. However, the car's trunk is now weighed down by accumulated debt so economic activity slows below its initial level.

With deleveraging, households increase saving and re-pay debt. This is the second step and it is like stepping on the brake, which causes the economy to slow further akin to a double dip. Rapid deleveraging, as happening now, is equivalent to hitting the brakes hard. The only positive is it reduces debt, which is like removing weight from the trunk. That helps stabilize activity at a new lower level, but it does not speed up the car as economists claim.

Unfortunately, the car metaphor only partially captures current conditions as it assumes the braking process is smooth. Yet, there has already been a financial crisis and the real economy is now infected by a multiplier process causing lower spending, massive job loss, and business failures. That plus deleveraging creates the possibility of a downward spiral which would constitute a depression.

Such a spiral is captured by the metaphor of the Titanic, which was thought to be unsinkable owing to its sequentially structured bulkheads. However, those bulkheads had no ceilings, and when the Titanic hit an iceberg that gashed its side, the front bulkheads filled with water and pulled down the bow. Water then rippled into the aft bulkheads, causing the ship to sink.

The U.S. economy has hit a debt iceberg. The resulting gash threatens to flood the economy's stabilizing mechanisms, which the economist Hyman Minsky termed "thwarting institutions".

Unemployment insurance is not up to the scale of the problem and is expiring for many workers. That promises to further reduce spending and aggravate the foreclosure problem.

States are bound by balanced budget requirements and they are cutting spending and jobs. Consequently, the public sector is joining the private sector in contraction.

The destruction of household wealth means many households have near-zero or even negative net worth. That increases pressure to save and blocks access to borrowing that might jump-start a recovery. Moreover, both the household and business sector face extensive bankruptcies that amplify the downward multiplier shock and also limit future economic activity by destroying credit histories and access to credit.

Lastly, the U.S. continues to bleed through the triple hemorrhage of the trade deficit that drains spending via imports, off-shoring of jobs, and off-shoring of new investment. This hemorrhage was evident in the cash for clunkers program in which eight of the top ten vehicles sold were foreign brands. Consequently, even enormous fiscal stimulus will be of diminished effect.

The financial crisis created an adverse feedback loop in financial markets. Unparalleled deleveraging and the multiplier process have created an adverse feedback loop in the real economy. That is a loop which is far harder to reverse, which is why a second Great Depression remains a real possibility.

Posted on October 11, 2009 in the FT Economists' Forum. Also posted on October 12, 2009 at thomaspalley.com.

III FAILURE OF MONETARY POLICY: BEFORE THE CRISIS

The questionable legacy of Alan Greenspan

♦

Ben Bernanke and the winner's curse:
The torment of the Fed's Chairman-designate

♦

The Fed and America's distorted expansion

♦

Demythologizing central bankers and the Great Moderation

♦

Re-thinking that 1970's inflation show

♦

Market bondage

♦

One hand clapping for Ben Bernanke

THE QUESTIONABLE LEGACY OF ALAN GREENSPAN

October 16, 2005

Alan Greenspan will retire as Chairman of the Federal Reserve in January 2006, and his retirement promises a flood of swooning retrospectives. Writing anything else at this moment risks the charge of churlishly raining on the parade. However, there are good grounds for a more critical reading of Greenspan's eighteen-year tenure at the Fed.

As Fed Chairman, Greenspan has been one of the world's most powerful policymakers for almost two decades. During that time he has been a leading booster of globalization and financial deregulation, developments that have contributed to a new U.S. boom-bust cycle founded on financial exuberance and cheap imports. Financial exuberance has driven up asset prices and supported consumer borrowing and spending. Cheap imports have contained inflation and partially compensated households for wage stagnation and heightened economic insecurity. The new cycle is a Faustian bargain, the price of which will be paid when the bust phase begins.

The Greenspan Fed's support for this new boom-bust cycle is evident in its disregard of the over-valued dollar and persistent growing trade deficits, which have damaged U.S. manufacturing. To Greenspan, the over-valued dollar has been a boon that has helped contain inflation by cheapening imports. Side-by-side, the trade deficit has been viewed as the product of "consenting adults" taking advantage of beneficial trading opportunities afforded by globalization. Meanwhile, manufacturing has been tacitly analogized to agriculture, and its decline rationalized as part of an inevitable transformation into a post-industrial society.

Lastly, the Greenspan Fed has shown a deep aversion to financial market regulation. Thus, it refused to use existing regulatory instruments (margin requirements) to curb the stock market bubble of the 1990s. And more importantly, it has refused to contemplate new regulations that could have helped curb the subsequent housing price bubble.

The chickens are now coming home to roost. Though the housing price bubble helped escape the recession of 2001, it has left households saddled with debt. However, the economic expansion has still proven fragile owing to the massive leakage of spending out of the economy via the trade deficit. This leakage is a problem, but it is difficult to address owing to de-industrialization and the new economic environment associated with globalization and financial deregulation.

In the pre-globalization era large trade deficits could be corrected by dollar depreciation (as happened in 1985). To prevent inflation from increased domestic consumption and reduced imports, interest rates could be increased. Taxes could also be raised and government spending cut.

However, such corrections are now far more difficult. First, globalization has allowed the trade deficit to reach record levels, making the scale of adjustment unprecedented and the inflation danger greater. Second, de-industrialization means that America may lack the manufacturing capacity to replace imports, which means the only way to close the trade deficit may be through recession and unemployment that lowers incomes and import purchases. Third, higher interest rates could burst the housing bubble, triggering recession.

Unwinding structural imbalances is always difficult, but the current difficulty is compounded by scale and circumstance. Debt-financed consumption has borrowed demand from the future. That means even without economic shocks, the economy is already headed for a period of weaker demand. If house prices fall, wiping out consumer wealth, that weakness could be severe and the Fed may have difficulty containing it. Lowering interest rates, to stimulate the economy, may be little more than "pushing on a string." With expectations of falling house prices, buyers are likely defer purchases no matter what the interest rate, as happened in Japan after its property bubble burst in 1990.

The Greenspan Fed has cavalierly allowed imbalances to develop, brushing aside dangers with blithe references to the flexibility of the U.S. economy. The next Fed Chairman must take exchange rates and trade deficits seriously. Globalization means that exchange rates matter more, not less. The system of financial regulation must also be rebuilt. Financial innovation makes asset price bubbles more powerful, and the Fed must be able to contain them without recourse to the blunderbuss of interest rates that wreaks havoc on innocent sectors.

Posted on October 16, 2005 at thomaspalley.com. Also posted on Mother Jones on November 2, 2005.

BEN BERNANKE AND THE WINNER'S CURSE: THE TORMENT OF THE FED'S CHAIRMAN-DESIGNATE

November 4, 2005

In economics there is a phenomenon known as the "winner's curse" whereby the winner of an auction over-pays. The most that she should have paid is the second-highest bid, which is the highest value attached by all other bidders. This curse provides a useful analogy for thinking about the recent selection of Federal Reserve Chairman Alan Greenspan's replacement. There is a good chance that the winner, Ben Bernanke, may end up with a bout of the winner's curse.

Within Washington there is a new trend to appoint academic research economists to leading economic policy positions. Several recent Federal Reserve governors and district bank chairpersons are former academics or researchers, as is Chairman-designate Bernanke. This trend is disturbing. Academic economists believe in economic models. Though the economy is subject to shocks that make outcomes unpredictable, the economy's structure is supposedly known through their models. This view contrasts sharply with that of Chairman Greenspan who held strong ideological convictions about markets and government, but believed the economy's structure was unknowable. This belief kept Greenspan open despite the strength of his convictions, and it made him an uncanny central banker. The new danger is that academic policymakers will be less open and more inclined to ignore new facts in favor of their theories.

That said, Chairman-designate Bernanke is probably one of the most open-minded academics. He began his career studying the devastating effects of the Great Depression's deflation on the U.S. banking system, which explains his concern about deflation in the last recession and why he advocated such deep interest rate cuts. Unfortunately, financial markets have less sympathy with this view. Consequently, they may initially punish him as being potentially "soft" on inflation. One curiosum about his pedigree is that in many regards his intellectual profile better fits a new Democrat. That raises a puzzle regarding the basis of the romance between Bernanke and the Bush administration.

As Federal Reserve Chairman, Bernanke faces several major challenges. The first is that he is taking office at an extremely difficult economic moment. On one hand, the economy exhibits significant financial fragility that calls for interest rate caution: on the other, it is suffering a bout of oil price inflation. Though higher interest rates are not appropriate for dealing with such inflation, financial markets deem that they are and are pushing for higher rates. This comes just as the "Greenspan premium," earned through a decade of costly anti-inflation policy, is being replaced by the "Bernanke discount." The net result is that Chairman Bernanke will have less room for maneuver and will be under greater pressure to raise rates to prove his anti-inflation credentials. That could spell trouble for the U.S. economy.

A second challenge is that there is a very good chance of a very hard landing within the next two years. Economic policy is like a game of hot potato, and the person who gets blamed is the person holding the potato when the music stops. Chairman Greenspan baked this potato, but it is likely Chairman Bernanke who will end up holding it. If the housing bubble bursts and recession ensues, lower interest rates will likely have a similar effect to "pushing on a string." This is because lower rates will not benefit households that re-financed previously when rates were down, while others will find it difficult to refinance because home values will have fallen.

A final challenge facing the new Chairman is how to deal with asset price bubbles without recourse to the blunderbuss of higher interest rates, which harms innocent economic sectors. Here, Bernanke will have to reverse his earlier views. This has already started regarding his views on inflation-targeting, which now looks ill-advised in light of today's complex inflation and Europe's poor economic performance under inflation-targeting. Bernanke has written that asset prices should not be considered independently of their impact on overall inflation. If it transpires that there has been a housing bubble that wreaks widespread havoc when it bursts, he will have to change his views. In principle, that is quite easy. The difficult part is choosing to do so.

Posted on Mother Jones, November 4, 2005. Also posted as "Winner's curse: The torment of Chairman-designate Bernanke" on thomaspalley.com on November 4, 2005.

THE FED AND AMERICA'S DISTORTED EXPANSION

September 11, 2007

The U.S. economy has been in expansion mode since November 2001. Though of reasonable duration, the expansion has been persistently fragile and unbalanced. That is now coming home to roost in the form of the recent sub-prime mortgage crisis and the on-going deflation of the house price bubble.

As part of the fallout, the Federal Reserve is being criticized for keeping interest rates too low for too long, thereby promoting credit and housing market excess. However, the reality is low rates were needed to sustain the expansion. Instead, the root problem is a distorted expansion caused by record trade deficits and manufacturing's failure to fully participate in the expansion.

If the Fed deserves criticism it is for endorsing the policy paradigm that has made for this pattern. That paradigm rests on disregard of manufacturing and neglect of the adverse real consequences of trade deficits.

By almost every measure the current expansion has been fragile and shallow compared to previous business cycles. Beginning with an extended period of jobless recovery, private sector job growth has been below par through most of the expansion. Though the headline unemployment rate has fallen significantly, the percentage of the working age population that is employed remains far below its previous peak. Meanwhile, inflation-adjusted wages have barely changed despite rising productivity.

This gloomy picture justified the Fed keeping interest rates low. However, it begs the question of why the economic weakness despite historically low interest rates, massive tax cuts in 2001 and huge increases in military and security spending triggered by 9/11 and the Iraq war?

The answer is the over-valued dollar and the trade deficit, which more than doubled between 2001 and 2006 to $838 billion, equaling 6.5 percent of GDP. Increased imports have shifted spending away from domestic manufacturers, which explains manufacturing's weak participation in the expansion. Some firms have closed permanently, while others have grown less than they would have otherwise. Additionally, many have reduced investment owing to weak demand or have moved their investment to China and elsewhere. These effects have then multiplied through the economy, with lost manufacturing jobs and reduced investment causing lost incomes that have further weakened job creation.

The evidence is clear. Manufacturing has lost 1.8 million jobs during the expansion, which is unprecedented. Before 1980 manufacturing employment hit new peaks every expansion. Since 1980 it has trended down, but it at least recovered somewhat during expansions. This business cycle it has fallen during

41

the expansion. The business investment numbers tell a similar dismal story, with spending being much weaker than in previous cycles.

These conditions compelled the Fed to keep interest rates low to maintain the expansion. That policy worked, but by stimulating loose credit and a house price bubble that triggered a construction boom. Thus, residential investment never fell during the recession and has been stronger than normal during the expansion. Construction, which accounted for 5 percent of total employment, has provided over twelve percent of job growth. Meanwhile, higher house prices have fuelled a borrowing boom that has enabled consumption spending to grow despite stagnant wages. This explains both increased imports and job growth in the service sector.

The overall picture is one of a distorted expansion in which manufacturing continued shriveling while imports and services expanded. This pattern was carried by an unsustainable house price bubble and rising consumer debt burdens, and that contradiction has surfaced with the implosion of the sub-prime mortgage market and deflation of the house price bubble.

The Fed is now trying to assuage markets to keep credit flowing. It has recently lowered interest rates and will lower them further if the economy slows further. On one level that is the right response and it may even work again – though it does increasingly seem like sticking fingers in the dyke to prevent the flood. However, the deeper problem is the policy paradigm behind the distorted expansion, which is where the Fed is at fault and where it deserves criticism.

The ideological and partisan Alan Greenspan wholeheartedly endorsed corporate globalization and promoted the White House and Treasury's unbalanced expansion policies. The Fed's professional economics staff also seems to have dismissed domestic manufacturing's significance and endorsed corporate globalization in the name of free trade. Consequently, the Fed has tacitly supported the underlying policy paradigm that has given rise to America's distorted expansion. Despite talk about reducing global financial imbalances, the Bernanke Fed still seems locked in to this paradigm and that is where constructive criticism should now be directed.

Posted on September 11, 2007 at thomaspalley.com. Published in Dollars and Sense, Issue 273, November/December 2007. Also posted on September 13, 2007 as "The Fed and the U.S.'s distorted expansion" on Asia Times Online.

DEMYTHOLOGIZING CENTRAL BANKERS AND THE GREAT MODERATION

April 2, 2008

It is often said that the winners get to write history, which matters because the way we tell history frames our understandings. What is true for general history also holds for economic history, and the way we tell economic history affects our expectations and aspirations for the economy.

The last twenty-five years have witnessed a boom in the reputation of central bankers. This boom is based on an account of recent economic history that reflects the views of the winners. Now, with the U.S. economy entering troubled waters that reputation may get dented. More importantly, there is an opportunity to tell an alternative account of recent history.

The raised standing of central bankers rests on a phenomenon that economists have termed the "Great Moderation." This phenomenon refers to the smoothing of the business cycle over the last two decades, during which expansions have become longer, recessions shorter, and inflation has fallen.

Many economists attribute this smoothing to improved monetary policy by central banks, and hence the boom in central banker reputations. This explanation is popular with economists since it implicitly applauds the economics profession by attributing improved policy to advances in economics and increased influence of economists within central banks. For instance, the Fed's Chairman is a former academic economist, as are many of the Fed's board of governors and many Presidents of the regional Federal Reserve banks.

That said, there are other less celebratory accounts of the Great Moderation that view it as a transitional phenomenon, and one that has also come at a high cost. One reason for the changed business cycle is retreat from policy commitment to full employment. The great Polish economist Michal Kalecki observed that full employment would likely cause inflation because job security would prompt workers to demand higher wages. That is what happened in the 1960s and 1970s. However, rather than solving this political problem, economic policy retreated from full employment and assisted in the evisceration of unions. That lowered inflation, but it came at the high cost of two decades of wage stagnation and a rupturing of the link between wage and productivity growth.

Disinflation also lowered interest rates, particularly during downturns. This contributed to successive waves of mortgage refinancing and also reduced cash outflows on new mortgages. That improved household finances and supported consumer spending, thereby keeping recessions short and shallow.

43

With regard to lengthened economic expansions, the great moderation has been driven by asset price inflation and financial innovation, which have financed consumer spending. Higher asset prices have provided collateral to borrow against, while financial innovation has increased the volume and ease of access to credit. Together, that created a dynamic in which rising asset prices have supported increased debt-financed spending, thereby making for longer expansions. This dynamic is exemplified by the housing bubble of the last eight years.

The important implication is that the Great Moderation is the result of a retreat from full employment combined with the transitional factors of disinflation, asset price inflation, and increased consumer borrowing. Those factors now appear exhausted. Further disinflation will produce disruptive deflation. Asset prices (particularly real estate) seem above levels warranted by fundamentals, making for the danger of asset price deflation. And many consumers have exhausted their access to credit and now pose significant default risks.

Given this, the Great Moderation could easily come to a grinding halt. Though high inflation is unlikely to return, recessions are likely to deepen and linger. If that happens the reputations of central bankers will sully, and the real foundation and hidden costs of the Great Moderation may surface. That could prompt a re-writing of history that restores demands for a return to true full employment with diminished income inequality. How we tell history really does matter.

Posted on April 2, 2008 in The Guardian, Comment is Free and at thomaspalley.com. Also posted as "Demythologizing Central Bankers" on Asia Times Online on April 8, 2008.

RE-THINKING THAT 1970'S INFLATION SHOW

June 16, 2008

The Federal Reserve has recently received much criticism from economic conservatives who claim it has ignored inflation, thereby risking a rerun of the 1970's inflation show. In response, renowned Princeton economist Paul Krugman has come to the Fed's defense arguing today's inflation is fundamentally different from that of the 1970s.

Krugman is right, but his arguments do more than defend the Fed. They also unintentionally demolish the foundations on which central banks have based monetary policy the past twenty-five years. In effect, re-thinking the inflation of the 1970s also compels re-thinking economic policy.

The essence of Krugman's argument is that we are not watching a rerun of the '70's show because this time round there is no mechanism for creating a price - wage spiral. That is because unions are now dead so that workers are unable to ask for wage increases that match prices. As an example, Krugman contrasts the United Mine Workers contract of 1981 which bargained a three year eleven percent annual average wage increase with current conditions. Where now are the unions demanding 11-percent-a-year increases? Indeed, where are the unions, period?

Today's reality is indeed characterized by absence of a price - wage spiral mechanism, and it is the reason why the Fed's easy monetary policy is unlikely to cause general inflation. However, that raises a critical additional point.

Recognizing that the inflation of the 1970's was the result of a price - wage spiral triggered by conflict with unions over income distribution, compels rejection of the theory of the natural rate of unemployment. This theory has dominated economists' thinking about inflation for over a generation and has twisted public thinking.

The late Milton Friedman was the originator of the theory of the natural rate of unemployment, yet according to Friedman unions have absolutely nothing to do with inflation. Instead, inflation is everywhere and always an exclusively monetary phenomenon. For Friedman, the only role of unions is to increase unemployment, which fundamentally contradicts the union wage – price spiral story of inflation

That means if the union price - wage spiral story of inflation is correct (which it is), Friedman's natural rate theory is wrong and policymakers should abandon it. Instead, the focus of policy can formally return to probing the boundaries of full employment.

Moreover, since inflation involves conflict over income distribution, there remains an unsolved policy challenge of how to fairly distribute income at full employment without triggering inflation.

Seen in this light, it becomes clear that Friedman's natural rate theory has been used to justify running policy in a business friendly way. Thus, in the 1980's high interest rates were used to tamp down inflation, thereby causing unemployment and weakening unions by weakening manufacturing. In effect, fighting a price - wage spiral with high interest rates is a form of class based policy that breaks the spiral by undercutting the bargaining power of workers.

A final implication concerns the economics profession and its teaching of economics. In the 1980s Friedman's natural rate of unemployment theory became the mainstay of economics textbooks. However, if the union wage – price spiral story of inflation is correct, it is time to re-write those textbooks. Today's students deserve a theory that explains both the inflation of the 1970s and why the Fed is right in downplaying current inflation fears.

Natural rate theory asserts the economy self-organizes with full employment, and that inflation is the result of monetary policy trying to push the economy beyond the natural unemployment rate. The theory is fundamentally ideological and it flooded into the academy as part of the conservative capture of economics in the 1970s. It has always struggled to fit the facts, and now may finally be the time to discard it.

Posted on June 16, 2008 at thomaspalley.com and The Guardian, Comment Is Free on June 18, 2008. Also posted as "Time is up for Friedman" on Asia Times Online on June 19, 2008.

MARKET BONDAGE

August 15, 2007

With Wall Street beset by a crisis of confidence and the mortgage-backed securities market seizing up, there is urgent need for an immediate emergency Federal Reserve interest rate cut. This sudden need has also revealed how today's financial system places monetary policy in bondage to markets. That system has evolved over the past twenty-five years with the Fed's approval, and the current crisis starkly reveals need for reform.

An emergency rate cut is needed to prevent the sub-prime mortgage meltdown from spiraling into a full-blown recession. By immediately lowering the base cost of credit, a rate cut can make existing mortgage securities more attractive to investors and also encourage continued flows of mortgage finance for the housing market.

Such continued financing is critical. In its absence mortgage availability will shrink and mortgage rates rise, thereby deepening the housing market slump. That is likely to trigger additional mortgage defaults and reductions in construction activity, thereby perhaps even causing a recession. In this event, the spiral of credit deterioration stands to deepen, jumping from the sub-prime mortgage market to the entire housing sector and the economy more broadly.

In response to this threat the Fed has already moved to inject significant temporary additional liquidity into money markets, effectively lending billions of dollars to banks to prevent their having to make further asset sales under current distressed conditions. Central banks in Europe, Japan, and elsewhere have done the same. However, because the costs of recession promise to be so large, the Fed must also move to cut rates.

As recently as ten days ago Fed policy was focused on containing inflation. Now, within the blink of an eye, the evaporation of confidence among Wall Street lenders has created conditions warranting an emergency rate cut to save the economy. This power of financial markets is rooted in a new business cycle that emerged in the 1980s and which has made the economy increasingly dependent on debt to fuel expansions. The creation of debt in turn relies on highly leveraged financial intermediaries that package and re-package loans while promising liquidity they are unable to deliver. As a result, the system has become fragile.

Increased financial fragility is one feature of the new system. A second and worse feature is that increased debt is part of a complex for shifting value from the real sector to the financial sector - a phenomenon known as "financialization". This increases profits in the financial sector at the expense of the real economy. Meanwhile, the new structure also implicitly compels monetary policy to rescue the financial sector if it gets into trouble. This amounts to a policy stick-up whereby the Fed is forced to provide the get-away car for fear that not doing so will result in even greater economic damage.

Today's system places monetary policy in a double bind. In good times the Fed is forced to raise interest rates to maintain lender beliefs that inflation will remain low. Those beliefs ensure investors are willing to make the loans needed to fuel the system. However, the result is higher interest rates and curtailed expansions that hold down wages and employment, thereby limiting the share of productivity growth going to working families.

In bad times, such as we are now experiencing, the Fed is obliged to come to the rescue of lenders for fear that if they stop lending the economy will tank. Moreover, this fear deepens the greater the level and burden of debts. Worse yet, such intervention creates a problem known as "moral hazard" that can aggravate the need for rescues. Having the Fed intervene to prevent financial meltdowns tacitly puts a floor under financial markets. That floor acts as a form of insurance for investors and speculators, who knowing that they are protected against large losses, channel more funds into even higher risk investments and loans.

The Fed has actively promoted the new system through deregulation. Its claim has been the risks of the financial system imploding are less because risk is spread. That claim is now being shown to be false.

For two decades working families have felt the effects of the policy head-lock imposed by financial market demands for ultra-low inflation. Now, financial markets are exercising their other demand for interest rate cuts to preserve asset values in order to prevent recession.

The threat posed by the current crisis is such that the Fed should meet this demand. That means immediately cutting rates and continuing to judiciously provide emergency liquidity. However, once the storm passes Congress and the Fed must address the systemic problems and policy distortions that have been exposed by the current crisis.

Posted in The Guardian, Comment is Free on August 15, 2007 and at thomaspalley.com on August 16, 2007.

ONE HAND CLAPPING FOR BEN BERNANKE

August 26, 2009

President Barack Obama's nomination of Ben Bernanke to a second term as Chairman of the United States Federal Reserve represents a sensible and pragmatic decision, but it is nothing to celebrate. Instead, it should be an occasion for reflection on the role of ideological groupthink among economists, including Bernanke, in contributing to the global economic and financial crisis.

The decision to nominate Bernanke is sensible on two counts. First, the U.S. and global economies remain mired in recession. Though the crisis may be over in the sense that outright collapse has been avoided, the economy remains vulnerable. As such, it makes sense not to risk a shock to confidence that could trigger a renewed downturn.

Second, Bernanke is the best among his peers. He did eventually come to understand the nature and severity of the crisis, and then took decisive steps that contributed to halting the economic free-fall. That record, combined with doubts that any of his peers would have done better, means replacing him with another mainstream candidate makes little sense.

These two factors justify Bernanke's reappointment, but the faintness of praise is indicative of the deeper problems that his leadership has exposed. Those problems concern the state of economics and economic policy advice.

One such problem is Wall Street's implicit veto over the Fed. After all, a major reason for reappointing Bernanke is to avoid rocking financial markets. This also explains why Bernanke's only rivals are from his peer group – the only people whom financial markets would be willing to accept.

In the 1990's, placating financial markets was also invoked to justify the reappointment of Bernanke's predecessor, Alan Greenspan, and it is now perennially invoked to block change at the Fed and other central banks. In effect, financial markets have established an implicit veto over much of economic policy and the people who can hold top policymaking positions, and it is time to think how we can escape that hold.

A second problem concerns the state of economics. Though Bernanke may be the best in his peer group, the fact is that the economic crisis decisively proved him and his peers to have been wrong. As a group, they joined in the adulation of Greenspan, whom one leading economist proclaimed "the greatest central banker who ever lived." Almost without exception, mainstream economists failed to foresee the crisis, and even the few who did, got the logic and unfolding of events wrong.

49

For his part, Bernanke led the intellectual charge toward inflation targeting by central banks, arguing that setting a target for annual inflation was a full and sufficient framework for monetary policy. Such thinking contributed to neglect of asset and credit markets, promoted intellectual disregard for regulation, and fostered laissez-faire excess, because macroeconomic belief in the sufficiency of inflation targeting paired logically with microeconomic belief that credit markets would take care of themselves. In Greenspan's words, the "self-interest of lending institutions" would protect shareholders and the economy from lending excess.

This thinking explains why the Fed under Bernanke's leadership was so slow to respond to the crisis, which began in August 2007 yet did not elicit a coherent and comprehensive response until November 2008. The Fed certainly would have reacted sooner had it not been attached to a model of banking more appropriate to the 1950's. Oblivious to the role of the shadow banking system, the Fed did not understand how its implosion would undermine the traditional banking system. The Fed simply failed to comprehend the significance of traditional banks' large holdings of mark-to-market assets and their own engagement in shadow banking via off-balance-sheet "structured investment vehicles."

Any dispassionate assessment of the Fed's thinking before and well into the crisis shows that it failed to understand the economics of its own bailiwick, banking and financial markets. Moreover, the Fed promoted broader economic views about deregulation and the self-stabilizing nature of markets that the crisis has discredited.

Though circumstances dictate that Bernanke is the best candidate and should be reappointed, the real challenge is to ensure a thorough intellectual housecleaning at the Fed in order to open space for alternative economic views. The great danger is that reappointing Bernanke will be interpreted as a green flag for a flawed *status quo*.

That is where public debate and Bernanke's Senate confirmation hearings enter the picture. Those hearings should be an occasion for critical examination of what went wrong, and why. If that happens, Bernanke's reappointment can serve as a trigger for constructive change rather than an endorsement of a discredited paradigm.

Distributed by Project Syndicate on August 26, 2009.

IV FAILURE OF MONETARY POLICY: DURING THE CRISIS

Meltdown moment: What must be done

◆

Preventing a financial crash

◆

The liquidation trap

◆

Why Federal Reserve policy is failing

MELTDOWN MOMENT: WHAT MUST BE DONE

March 10, 2008

Last week's default of Thornburg Mortgage had an ominous sound, like the cracking of sheet ice. Wall Street now sits atop a potential collapse of confidence in asset valuations, threatening a panic that will wipe away both sound and unsound financial institutions. The week's events also reveal how the Federal Reserve's bail-out policy has failed to address the underlying problem of credit market seizure. Here's what's going on, and what must be done to prevent a meltdown.

By way of background, Thornburg Mortgage is a leading lender specializing in Alt-A mortgages for purchases of higher priced homes that exceed Fannie Mae's and Freddie Mac's conforming loan limit of $417,000. By all accounts its mortgage backed securities constitute good credit structures with the underlying mortgages still intact. The problem at Thornburg is not classic insolvency, but rather the evaporation of willingness to hold even mortgage backed securities backed by sound assets. This has caused security prices to tumble, lowering the value of Thornburg's collateral and thereby triggering margin calls from banks that it has been unable to meet.

Similar stories are being played out in many parts of the market. Thornburg and other financial intermediaries are now threatened with bankruptcy that poses two grave public threats. First, if these firms liquidate their mortgage portfolios that will further depress asset prices, thereby potentially triggering margin calls at other firms that could generate dangerous ripple effects. Second, putting additional mortgage lenders out of business will make it even more difficult to buy and sell homes, which promises to further depress house prices. These are exactly the effects policy should be avoiding.

The irony behind this debacle is that part of the problem is due to margin calls from banks. However, banks are currently being bailed-out by the Federal Reserve, which has provided them with tens of billions of dollars of subsidized credit through its term auction facility. In effect, the institutions the Fed is bailing-out are the same ones putting downward pressure on financial markets. Indeed, the banks are being given subsidized credit for problems similar to those experienced by Thornburg. Thus, there was an earlier loss of confidence in banks' assets that threatened their ability to renew roll-over funding for their activities. This risked causing banks to default, triggering margin calls and fire-sales of their assets that would have caused major asset price deflation and the destruction of credit provision.

The Thornburg story illustrates two things. First, the Fed's policy privileges banks, bailing them out while letting perish other financial institutions that are no more guilty. Second, the Fed's current policy has not solved the problem of financial instability. Though the banks have been ring-fenced, they are now causing problems elsewhere through loan margin calls. Moreover, these calls could collectively come back to haunt banks by driving down the price of assets that they also own. Consequently, even the banks remain at risk despite the Fed's term auction facility.

In today's crisis environment the problem in financial markets is not the level of interest rates, or even the size of the Fed's term auction facility. The problem is getting liquidity to those links in the financial chain that are most stressed. Reliance on the normal channels of distribution does not work when confidence has evaporated and markets have seized-up.

There is a very simple and fair solution to this problem. That solution is for the Federal Reserve to open its term auction facility to all publicly traded financial intermediaries rather than just deposit taking institutions. That means giving access to insurance companies, mortgage investment trusts, mutual funds, and hedge funds. These firms would be subject to the same borrowing terms as banks, and would have to post collateral of identical quality.

Such a change would level the playing field in financial markets and remove the unfair subsidy to banks. Most importantly, it would tackle the problem of credit market seizure that is afflicting all financial institutions. In a world where distinctions between financial intermediaries have become increasingly blurred, broadening access to the term auction facility is the logical and correct policy.

The Federal Reserve's current policy is failing because it is structured for the world of the past in which depository institutions dominated lending. Thus, current policy restricts access to emergency liquidity to deposit taking institutions, ignoring how lending has become detached from deposit taking. The challenge of the day is preventing a meltdown that destroys sound lenders and sound assets. That calls for widening access to temporary emergency liquidity. Afterward, there will be time to visit the question of regulatory reform and more permanent policy change.

Posted on March 10, 2008 at thomaspalley.com.

PREVENTING A FINANCIAL CRASH

March 17, 2008

With the collapse of Bear Stearns, financial markets are moving closer to a crash that risks grave harm to the economy and the lives of working people. The Federal Reserve's recently created Term Auction Facility (TAF) and Term Securities Lending Facility (TSLF) move policy in the right direction. However, more needs to be done if a crash is to be prevented.

One way of thinking about Fed policy is in terms of the institutions the Fed deals with, the assets the Fed deals in, and the collateral the Fed accepts. The TAF and TSLF both expand the Fed's transactions menu, but the Fed has resisted expanding the set of institutions it deals with. Thus, initially only depository institutions were given access to the TAF, and only primary government securities dealers have access to the TSLF.

That is not adequate. Had Bear Stearns had access to the TAF its collapse might have been avoided. Now, the Fed has decided to give liquidity access to securities dealers like Bear Stearns, which is welcome but still belated.

The Fed's failure to expand the set of institutions it deals with reflects failure to adapt to the new world of financial intermediation. Previously, lending was dominated by banks, which meant the Fed could address liquidity shortages threatening the supply of credit by providing liquidity directly to banks. Today, lending is increasingly separated from banks. First, banks sell many of the loans they originate so that the ultimate lender is not a bank. Second, many originating lenders are non-bank firms. That means the credit supply is vulnerable to disruptions among these other lenders.

The current problem is that asset prices are falling owing to lack of confidence, triggering margin calls on these non-bank lenders. That has compelled them to sell assets, further driving down prices and triggering further calls. Some lenders have been unable to meet these calls, threatening bankruptcy even though their underlying loans are still performing. That threatens a cascade of asset price collapse.

The Fed's new facilities are a good move that broadens capacity to protect against liquidity disruptions. However, the Fed should further widen the set of institutions it deals with. Limiting dealings to depository institutions and primary government securities dealers protects banks and Wall Street's major brokerage houses, but leaves too much of the system unprotected and creates inefficiencies.

Firms outside the Fed's ring of protection must set up complex transactions with firms inside the ring to access emergency liquidity. That is good for insiders' fee income, but it raises the cost of distributing liquidity and creates unnecessary transactions that can be disrupted. Meanwhile, restricting access to the Fed's liquidity auction facility fails to discover the true price of liquidity that would be paid if all had auction access, which is tantamount to not getting liquidity to those who need it most. That is inefficient, and it also provides a subsidy to institutions inside the ring of protection.

In addition to expanding the institutions the Fed deals with, the Fed should consider further judicious expansion of the categories of securities it accepts as collateral under its auction (TAF) and securities lending (TSLF) facilities. Any additional collateral categories should be assessed at deeply discounted values as they will be more risky. That will protect taxpayers from bearing losses if the collateral under-performs.

Even equities could potentially be accepted, but this would involve crossing a bright line as they are a different form of legal obligation. By accepting equity collateral, the Fed could acquire an ownership stake in firms, which would move it beyond its current role of setting interest rates and providing liquidity to the financial system.

Among economic commentators there has been much misleading chatter about limits imposed by the size of the Fed's balance sheet. The reality is the Fed has no practical limit to its balance sheet as it can always directly purchase financial assets. There is no need for that now, but in the meantime the Fed might further increase the size of its auction facility and should definitely widen the set of auction participants.

Critics will inevitably claim such changes are inflationary. That has been the history of every innovation in central banking. However, the reality is innovations are only inflationary if used in an inflationary way. With regard to the current crisis, that means the Fed will have to withdraw liquidity convincingly once the crisis has abated.

Finally, stopping a financial crash does not get the U.S. economy out of the woods. There remains the underlying residential mortgage debt crisis, and many risky mortgages will go bad as will the mortgage backed securities in which they are embedded. There is also the problem of recession, which calls for reviving aggregate demand and getting the economy growing again. Both the mortgage debt crisis and the recession need their own tailored policy responses. However, if the Fed fails to prevent a crash, the mortgage crisis will be deeper and a recession far more severe.

Posted on March 17, 2008 at thomaspalley.com.

THE LIQUIDATION TRAP

September 17, 2008

The U.S. financial system is caught in a destructive liquidation trap that has falling asset prices cause financial distress, in turn compelling further asset sales and price declines. If unaddressed, it risks sending the economy into deep recession – or even depression.

Current conditions are the result of bursting of the house price bubble and the end of two decades of financial exuberance. That exuberance was fostered by a cocktail of forces.

First, economic policy replaced wages and productive investment as the engines of growth with debt and asset inflation. Second, greed and free market ideology combined to promote excessive risk-taking and restrain regulators. This was encouraged by audacious claims that mathematical economic models mapped reality and priced uncertainty, making old-fashioned precautions redundant.

Recognition of the scale of financial folly has created a rush for liquidity. This is causing huge losses, triggering margin calls and downgrades that cause more selling, damage confidence, and further squeeze credit. That is the paradox of deleveraging. One firm can, but the system as a whole cannot.

Having failed to prevent the bubble, regulatory policy is now amplifying its deflation. One reason is mark-to-market accounting rules that force companies to take losses as prices fall. A second reason is rigid capital standards.

Application of mark-to-market rules in an environment of asset price volatility can create a vicious cycle of accounting losses that drive further price declines and losses. Meanwhile, capital standards require firms to raise more capital when they suffer losses. That compels them to raise money in the midst of a liquidity squeeze, resulting in fresh equity sales that cause further asset price declines.

Bad debts will have to be written down, but it is better to write them down in orderly fashion rather than through panicked deleveraging that pulls down good assets too.

This suggests regulators should explore ways to relax capital standards and mark-to-market rules. One possibility is permitting temporary discretionary relaxations akin to stock market circuit breakers.

Later, regulators must tackle the underlying problem of price bubbles. Currently, central banks are only able to control bubbles by torpedoing the economy with higher interest rates. New flexible measures of control are needed.

One proposal is asset based reserve requirements, which systematically applies adjustable margin requirements to the assets of financial firms.

The Fed must also lower interest rates, and not just for standard reasons of stimulating spending. Lower short term rates are needed to make longer term assets (including houses) relatively more attractive, thereby shifting demand to them and putting a bottom to asset price destruction.

Fears about a price – wage inflation spiral remain misplaced. Instead, the threat is deep recession triggered by the liquidation trap. If inflation is a wild card, now is the time to use the credibility the Fed has earned. Emergency rate reductions can be reversed when the situation stabilizes.

The great irony is central banks can produce liquidity costlessly. Usually the problem is restraining over-production: today, it is over-coming political concerns about "bail-outs". Those concerns are legitimate, but they also risk inappropriately restricting liquidity provision and unintentionally imposing huge costs of deep recession.

At the moment the Fed is protecting banks and the treasury dealer network but leaving the rest of the system in the cold. That is perverse given how the Fed went along with expansion of the non-bank financial system. Instead, the Fed should consider an auction facility that makes longer duration loans available to qualified insurance and finance companies too.

The facility's guiding principle should be an expanded version of the Bagehot rule. Accordingly, the Fed would auction funds at punitive rates, with loans being fully collateralized. The goal should be to facilitate repair of distressed financial companies with minimum market disruption and at no taxpayer expense. By creating an up-front facility, the Fed can get ahead of the curve and reduce need for crisis interventions that are always more costly and disruptive.

Among financial conservatives there is a view that financial markets deserve punishment for their "sins" and only that will cleanse them. This view is often presented in terms of need to restore market discipline and stay moral hazard.

The view from the left is strangely similar, arguing Wall Street "fat cats" need to be punished. Asset prices should fall, banks must eat their losses, and all but the most essential financial firms should be allowed to fail.

Both views have a moralistic dimension, and both risk unnecessary economic suffering. The mistakes of the past cannot be undone. All that can be done is to minimize their costs and then truly reform the system so that they are not repeated.

Posted on September 17, 2008 at thomaspalley.com. Also posted on Asia Times Online on September 19, 2008.

WHY FEDERAL RESERVE POLICY IS FAILING

October 2, 2008

The Federal Reserve and U.S. Treasury continue to fail in their attempts to stabilize the U.S. financial system. That is due to failure to grasp the nature of the problem, which concerns the parallel banking system. Rescue policy remains stuck in the past, focused on the traditional banking system while ignoring the parallel unregulated system that was permitted to develop over the past twenty-five years.

This parallel banking system financed vast amounts of real estate lending and consumer borrowing. The system (which included the likes of Thornburg Mortgage, Bear Stearns and Lehman Brothers) made loans but had no deposit base. Instead, it relied on roll-over funding obtained through money markets. Additionally, it operated with little capital and extremely high leverage ratios, which was critical to its tremendous profitability. Finally, loans were often securitized and traded among financial firms.

This business model has now proven extremely fragile. First, the model created a fundamental maturity mismatch, whereby loans were of a long term nature but funding was short-term. That left firms vulnerable to disruptions of money market funding, as has now occurred.

Second, securitization converted loans into financial instruments that could be priced according to market conditions. That was fine when prices were rising, but when they started falling firms had to take large mark-to-market losses. Given their low capital ratios, those losses quickly wiped out firms' capital bases, thereby freezing roll-over funding.

In effect, the parallel banking business model completely lacked shock absorbers, and it has now imploded in a vicious cycle. Lack of roll-over financing has compelled asset sales, which has driven down prices. That has further eroded capital, triggering margin calls that have caused more asset sales and even lower prices, making financing impossible for even the best firms.

Though the parallel banking system engaged in riskier lending than the traditional banking system, those differences were a matter of degree. Traditional banks like Washington Mutual, Wachovia, and Citigroup have also all lost huge sums. However, the traditional banking system is more protected for two reasons.

First, traditional banks are significantly funded by customer deposits. Ironically, such deposits can be withdrawn on demand and are in principle even more insecure than short term roll-over funding. However, they stay in place because of federally provided deposit insurance.

Second, traditional banks are significantly shielded from mark-to-market accounting because they hold on to many of their loans. These loans are therefore priced by auditors on a mark-to-realization basis. However, if they were securitized their market value would be significantly lower owing to current disruptive market conditions.

The bottom line is that the banking system is in better shape not because of its virtues, but because of policy. Deposit funding is safe because of deposit insurance. Banks are spared mark-to market losses because of different accounting rules. And the Federal Reserve is providing banks with massive liquidity infusions through its discount window and its various emergency auction facilities.

Policy has therefore ring-fenced traditional banks. But in the meantime it has left the parallel system in the cold, leaving a gaping hole in the policy dyke.

This policy stance reflects the Fed's continuing attachment to an antiquated view of the system whereby it takes responsibility for traditional banks and nothing else. Such a policy makes no sense and will fail. The Fed encouraged development of the parallel system, and that system undertakes many of the same activities as traditional banks. Meanwhile, failure of the parallel banking system will continue putting downward pressure on asset prices and lender confidence.

The Treasury's proposed seven hundred billion dollar asset purchase program will help put a needed floor under asset prices. However, it does nothing to tackle the parallel banking system's roll-over funding crisis that is crimping lending and pushing firms into bankruptcy. That is causing distress to spread far beyond the mortgage market, undermining the ability of any asset purchase program to put a floor under asset prices.

The urgent implication is the Fed (and other central banks) must extend its safety network to include the parallel banking system. Just as the traditional banking system needs liquidity assistance, so too does the parallel system. That assistance can be provided through such vehicles as the discount window and Federal Reserve auction facilities, and it should be allocated to qualified firms able to post appropriate collateral.

A credit based system is a chain, and a chain is only as strong as its weakest link. The Federal Reserve's antiquated view has it protecting links connected to the traditional banking system while neglecting everything else. That is a recipe for failure.

Posted on the FT Economists' Forum on October 2, 2008 and at thomaspalley.com on October 6, 2008.

V THE ECONOMICS OF GLOBALIZATION

A Galbraithian lens on globalization

♦

Barge economics: The new economics of trade

♦

Super-sized: What happens when two billion workers join the global labor market?

♦

Manufacturing meets Wal-Mart: The economics of global out-sourcing

♦

Globalization and IT: Setting the record straight

♦

Why the world pays dollar tribute

♦

Decoupling vs. the concertina effect

♦

Globalization lock-in: What should be done?

♦

Can globalization fail? Lessons from history

A GALBRAITHIAN LENS ON GLOBALIZATION

May 2, 2006

John Kenneth Galbraith died on April 29, 2006 at the age of 97, having led a life filled with honor and accomplishment. Unfortunately, his ideas are largely ignored by today's economics profession. His recent death marks an occasion for spotlighting the continuing relevance of those ideas and the ideological narrowness of a profession that makes no space for them.

The period 1890 – 1940 includes the Progressive (1900 – 1916) and New Deal (1932 – 1940) eras. During this fifty-year period America came to grips with the problems that arose with its transformation into a mechanized, industrialized, urbanized society. Whereas the Progressive era highlighted the human excesses of raw capitalism and took the first tentative steps toward taming them, the New Deal era confronted the instability of capitalism and enacted reforms that saved the system from itself.

Today's era of globalization is showing signs of problems similar to those seen earlier. In labor markets there has been a decline in workers' bargaining power, while the global economic system has shown proclivities toward financial instability and deflation. These parallels suggest that there are lessons to be learned from reflecting upon the reforms of the Progressive and New Deal eras. Such reflection inevitably leads to John Kenneth Galbraith's analysis of that period, published in 1952 under the title of *American Capitalism: The Concept of Countervailing Power*.

The core problems of the Progressive and New Deal eras were the callousness of the economic system and its inability to maintain sufficient purchasing power for full employment. Behind this lay the problems of monopoly and deflation. By charging high prices, monopoly erodes purchasing power. So too does deflation because it increases the value of debts. The New Deal tackled these problems through a combination of regulation and the creation of modern fiscal policy.

Regulation served the twin purposes of controlling monopoly and putting a floor under prices. Not only did it extend to key industrial sectors, it also included labor markets through legislation establishing the minimum wage, the forty-hour week, and the right to join unions. This established a wage floor that, in one swoop, tackled both the Progressive era problem of callousness and the Depression era problem of inadequate purchasing power. Side-by-side, modern fiscal policy was built upon an expanded government sector whose purchasing power was more stable, and which could also be mobilized in downturns to offset declines in private sector spending.

These policy interventions reinforced stabilizing features within the system. This is where Galbraith's concept of countervailing power enters. The problem of monopoly arose with the emergence of large powerful corporations. However, the system partially addressed this problem itself through the development of large corporations on both sides of the market. Consequently, big buyers confronted big sellers, thereby generating countervailing power between buyers and sellers that helped keep prices down and stable.

In labor markets, it was the development of trade unions that created countervailing power. This ensured that workers were also represented by big sellers that could go head-to-head with big buyers. In this regard, New Deal labor legislation was critical since it promoted unions. Prior to the legislation, employer opposition had stalled union coverage at about fifteen percent of employment. Afterward, it rose to almost thirty-five percent.

A Galbraithian lens suggests that the countervailing power equilibrium that prevailed after World War II has been dislodged. In labor markets, the process started with the inability of unions to organize the expanding service sector. At the same time that the service economy was growing away from unions, manufacturing started going mobile through the development of multinational production methods.

Additionally, a retail revolution was taking place through big box discount stores exemplified by Wal-Mart. These discounters have adopted a global sourcing model that scours the world for the lowest price – the so-called "China price" – and then requires American manufacturers and workers to meet it or lose the business. This model now extends to every retail segment, and it creates a race to the bottom by putting the entire consumer goods manufacturing sector in global competition. To stay competitive, American manufacturers must either slash pay at home or move production offshore. Moreover, this global sourcing model is now being applied in capital goods manufacturing, with assemblers like Ford, General Motors and Boeing adopting it.

A Galbraithian analysis points to the need to rebuild countervailing power. That requires organizing workers in the service sector and in firms such as Wal-Mart. American businesses also have an interest in the re-building of countervailing power as global sourcing has undermined the position of sellers. Enabling domestic suppliers to compete in a globalized economy calls for new institutional arrangements limiting unfair international competition based on labor exploitation, environmental neglect, and under-valued exchange rates. The bottom line is that Galbraith's economic analysis remains as trenchant and relevant as it was fifty years ago, and the logic of countervailing power provides vital insights into today's problematic of globalization.

Posted on May 2, 2006 at thomaspalley.com.

BARGE ECONOMICS:
THE NEW ECONOMICS OF TRADE

October 1, 2007

The classical theory of comparative advantage has driven U.S. trade policy for the past fifty years. That policy, in combination with technical innovations that have lowered costs of transportation and communication, has opened the global economy. Yet paradoxically, this opening has rendered classical trade theory obsolete. That in turn has left the U.S. economically vulnerable because its trade policy remains stuck in the past and based on ideas that no longer hold.

The logic behind classical free trade is that all can benefit when countries specialize in producing those things in which they have comparative advantage. The necessary requirement is that the means of production (capital and technology) are internationally immobile and stuck in each country. That is what globalization has undone.

Several years ago Jack Welch, former CEO of General Electric, captured the new reality when he talked of ideally having "every plant you own on a barge". The economic logic was that factories should float between countries to take advantage of lowest costs, be they due to under-valued exchange rates, low taxes, subsidies, or a surfeit of cheap labor. Globalization has made Welch's barge a reality. However, in doing so it has made capital mobility rather than country comparative advantage the engine of trade. And with that change, "free trade" increasingly trades jobs and promotes downward wage equalization.

The U.S. and European response to Welch's barge has been competitiveness policy that advocates measures such as increased education spending to improve skills; lower corporate tax rates; and investment and R&D incentives. The thinking is increased competitiveness can make Europe and the U.S. more attractive to businesses.

Unfortunately, competitiveness policy is not up to the task of anchoring the barge, and it can even be counter-productive. The core problem is corporations are globally mobile. Thus, government can subsidize R&D spending, but the resulting innovations may simply end up in new offshore factories. Moreover, competitiveness policy easily degenerates into a race to the bottom. For instance, if the U.S. cuts corporation taxes, other countries may match to stay competitive. The result is no gain for the U.S., while profit taxes are lowered and tax burdens shifted on to wages, which widens income inequality.

Worse yet, capital mobility prompts countries to adopt unfair policies to increase their relative business attractiveness. These policies include disregard of environmental damage; suppression of labor to keep wages low; direct subsidies;

and under-valued exchange rates. All are visible in China, which is the poster-child for such abuses.

A critical consequence of Welch's barge is the creation of a "corporation versus country" divide. Previously, when corporations were nationally based, profit maximization by business contributed to national economic success by ensuring efficient resource use. Today, corporations still maximize profits, but they do so from the standpoint of their global operations. Consequently, what is good for corporations may not be good for country.

When companies raise profits by rearranging production according to global cost patterns, those shifts can lower country income. For instance, when Boeing transfers production to China, the U.S. loses high value adding jobs and national income can fall. Moreover, though Boeing makes larger short-run profits on its Chinese production, even it may lose in the long run if it inadvertently creates a rival Chinese aircraft producer.

From an American worker perspective, the global economy has always had abundant supplies of cheap labor. In the past American workers were still able to compete and benefit from trade. The critical difference today is American corporations are taking their capital and technology offshore and equipping low-wage foreign workers. Those investments undermine American workers because that foreign production is intended for the U.S. market.

The emergence of barge-like corporations has reduced the scope for effective competitiveness policy, increased the temptations for unfair policy, and created a wedge between corporate and national interests. This poses two critical policy challenges. First, there is need for rules against unfair competition, which is where exchange rate rules and labor and environment standards enter.

Second, there is need to close the wedge between corporation and country. In the U.S. that calls for such measures as ending preferential tax treatment of profits earned offshore; making it illegal for corporations to reincorporate outside the U.S. to escape U.S. tax laws; and new tax arrangements that encourage jobs and value creation within the U.S.

Addressing globalization's challenges poses enormous analytical difficulties. Unfair competition must be prevented and companies re-anchored. But this must be done without losing the benefits of real trade based on comparative advantage or ending investment that fosters development. These economic challenges are compounded by political difficulties. In Washington, elite policy thinking is funded and lobbied for by corporations. Consequently, corporations control trade policy at a time when corporate interests differ from the national interest. That is also increasingly true in Brussels. Fifty years ago what was good for GM may really have been good for the U.S. With Jack Welch's barge, that may no longer hold.

Posted October 1, 2007 as "Jack Welch's Barge: The New Economics of Trade" at thomaspalley.com and in Asia Times Online on October 3, 2007. Also posted as "The new economics of trade: Factories on barges and the race to the bottom" on Alternet.org on October 1, 2007.

SUPER-SIZED: WHAT HAPPENS WHEN TWO BILLION WORKERS JOIN THE GLOBAL LABOR MARKET?

September 25, 2005

There is a famous theorem in international economics – the Stolper-Samuelson theorem – that says when a rich capital-abundant country (such as the U.S.) trades with a poor labor-abundant country (such as China), wages in the rich country fall and profits go up. The theorem's economic logic is simple. Free trade is tantamount to a massive increase in the rich country's labor supply since the products made by poor country workers can now be imported. Additionally, demand for workers in the rich country falls as rich country firms abandon labor-intensive production to the poor country. The net result is an effective increase in labor supply and a decrease in labor demand in the rich country, and wages fall.

The relevance of the Stolper-Samuelson theorem is clear. For the last two decades, U.S. policy makers, from both major political parties, have worked assiduously to create a global market place in which goods and capital are free to move. Over the same period, two and one half billion people in China, India, Eastern Europe and the former Soviet Union have discarded economic isolationism and joined the global economy. Now, these two tectonic shifts are coming together in the form of a "super-sized" Stolper-Samuelson effect, and they stand to have depressing consequences for American workers.

Much attention has been devoted to the adverse impacts of the U.S. trade deficit, particularly with China. And the U.S. government has been rightly criticized for failing to apply adequate pressure to get China to remedy its unfair and illegal trading practices. However, no one in Washington is talking about the deeper question of what happens to wages when two billion people from low wage countries join the global labor market.

Such an event is unprecedented in history. In the past, countries joined the international economy through a slow evolutionary process. Initially, they would export a few goods in which they specialized and had natural competitive advantage. Thereafter, countries would gradually deepen their involvement in international trade. The process was one of gradual integration, and production was largely immobile across countries.

Globalization has changed this by accelerating the process of international integration. It has also made capital, technology, and methods of production mobile, marking a watershed with the past. The new order is exemplified by China's recent experiences. In less than two decades, China has become a global manufacturing powerhouse through massive foreign direct investment and technology transfer. The impact of this transformation on the U.S. economy is seen in the trade deficit, the loss of manufacturing jobs, and downward pressure on wages.

Whereas classical free trade connected goods markets across countries, globalization creates a global labor market and moves jobs. Previously trade arbitraged goods prices, now it also arbitrages wages through job shifting. With the emergence of China, India and Eastern Europe, the dam of Socialism that held back two billion workers has been removed. If two swimming pools are joined, the water level will eventually equalize. That is what is happening with globalization. Manufacturing has already been placed in competition across countries, with dire consequences for manufacturing workers. The internet promises to do the same for previously un-tradable services, and higher-paid knowledge workers will start feeling similar effects.

Not since the industrial revolution has there been a transformation of this magnitude, and that revolution took one hundred and fifty years to complete. By comparison the new revolution is a mere twenty-five years old. These developments have a significance that goes far beyond the currency manipulation and WTO rules violations that have been the focus of trade deficit policy discussions. There is no reason to think the end is in sight, and American workers can look forward to the international economy exerting downward pressure on wages and work conditions for the next several decades.

As is so often the case, workers have understood the new reality long before economists and policymakers. Workers realize that trade is no longer a matter of exchanging exotic commodities for manufactured products, and that the new system involves trading their jobs and arbitraging wages. Especially bitter, is the fact that the process of globalization is being driven by large American multinational corporations that American workers helped build. U.S. policymakers have also abandoned American workers by promoting free trade agreements that have *de facto* created a global labor market that threatens workers' livelihoods and economic security.

Globalization demands that we begin anew the task of establishing fair and just rules that make the economy work for all. This challenge is the same as that faced by American workers at the beginning of the twentieth century. Unions, minimum wages, and fair labor practices were essential to meeting that challenge, and they are essential again. But such tools are no longer sufficient when applied nationally. They must be applied globally. That means China, India and other industrializing developing countries must agree to, and enforce, core labor standards and worker rights. Trade cannot be free without worker freedom and the right to share in the wealth created.

Successive administrations have pushed free trade without worker protections and they have given the green light to a global system without core labor standards. Through poor diplomacy and lax enforcement we have given away access to U.S. markets and valuable negotiating leverage without getting commitments on labor standards in recent free trade agreements. The consequences of these trade policies and the reality of the new global system must be exposed so that our approach can be changed. This is a task that will not be easy given Washington's captive economic policy elite and big business' interest in concealing the new reality.

Posted on September 25, 2005 at thomaspalley.com. Also posted as "The great labor threat" on TomPaine.com on September 29, 2005.

MANUFACTURING MEETS WAL-MART:
THE ECONOMICS OF GLOBAL OUT-SOURCING

October 1, 2005

General Motors and Ford have both recently announced plans to restructure their parts supply arrangements, the result of which will be the loss of thousands of middle-class manufacturing jobs. These plans involve slimming down the number of suppliers, as well as forcing domestic suppliers to match the lowest global price (the "China price") if they wish to retain business.

Every day factories close across the United States, but only occasionally do we get a clear look into the brutal logic of corporate globalization. Geologists learn the most from extreme events such as earthquakes. Likewise, events such as the Ford and GM announcements give us a window into the economics of global out-sourcing. And what we see is that U.S. manufacturing is now converging rapidly on the Wal-Mart model, a model that drives the "race to the bottom."

Understanding the Wal-Mart model requires understanding the "big box" discount store revolution in American retailing. These discounters are epitomized by Wal-Mart, which is the most efficient at squeezing workers globally (as well as the most efficient at squeezing American workers). Their business model rests on scouring the globe for the lowest price, putting firms and workers in global competition with each other.

This process started forty years ago, when the newly established discount retailers (Wal-Mart was founded in 1962) started putting California suppliers in competition with New York suppliers. Since all operated in the United States under U.S rules and labor laws, the process was not unfair. However, even then there were flaws because U.S. law permitted different labor laws across the states, thereby creating incentives and pressures for manufacturing to move south to non-union, so-called "right-to-work" states.

Since then Wal-Mart has gone global with its buying strategy, and it now puts Chinese suppliers in competition with suppliers from Mexico, Indonesia, Sri Lanka, as well as the United States. This global buying strategy would have posed little threat thirty years ago. But that was an era of classical free trade, and the rules of classical free trade no longer apply. Globalization has changed everything by making technology and methods of production mobile, and by lowering business coordination costs. These techniques were developed in America, and American multi-national companies took them global. The Wal-Mart global buying strategy plugs into this new economic order and moves it into hyper-drive. In effect, the big box discount retailers have changed the nature of global competition, and have become an even more important mechanism of global labor arbitrage than foot-loose production by multi-national corporations.

The Wal-Mart global buying strategy is now being adopted by the automobile industry and manufacturing. Having pioneered multi-national production, the producers are starting to supply themselves using the Wal-Mart business model. It is in this sense that manufacturing has met Wal-Mart. The Big 3 auto producers – GM, Ford and Chrysler - used to be vertically integrated companies that significantly supplied their own parts. The first stage of the game involved Ford and GM spinning-off Visteon and Delphi, who were then put in competition with other U.S. auto parts suppliers. Now, the game is going global, and U.S. suppliers (including Visteon and Delphi) are being made to match the "China price." This is the logic embodied in the Ford and GM announcements.

Moreover, the process is also happening in the aerospace industry, though there it has been slower to get going owing to greater national security and quality control constraints. However, Boeing's new 787 will be built using the Wal-Mart model, and the implication is that Boeing supplier workers have a rendezvous with Wal-Mart in their future.

If "Manufacturing meets Wal-Mart" is Act I, there may yet be a second act that can be labeled "Manufacturing meets The Gap" The Wal-Mart strategy has auto manufacturers outsourcing parts supply but retaining most of their assembly operations in the United States. However, it is easy to imagine a future in which assembly is also shipped offshore, and GM and Ford just slap a badge on cars and then sell them through their domestic distribution networks. This is The Gap model of globalization. The Gap does not own factories, but instead sub-contracts production, brands the product, and then charges for the brand in its stores. This has already happened for appliances and tools: think of Black & Decker. The auto producers can also clearly go this way. However, for reasons of quality control, in the immediate future they will either own the factories (as in Mexico) or enter into joint-ventures (as in Japan). Making cars remains more difficult than branding T-shirts and compels greater involvement for the time being.

The Wal-Mart – Gap business model reveals the inexorable and cruel competitive logic of globalization. No company can avoid it since any company that does not go that route will be competed into extinction by others that do. This reveals that the problem of globalization cannot be addressed at the individual company level. The problem is systemic, and must therefore be addressed systemically. That means addressing the problem of unfair labor competition, the problem of unfair competition based on a devalued exchange rate, and the problem of countries which export without reciprocal intent to import.

However, while it is true that the market's economic logic compels individual companies to pursue this path, it is not the case that companies are innocent. American manufacturing, as represented by the National Association of Manufacturers, has collectively worked hard to create the current system. Manufacturers supported NAFTA, PNTR with China, and most recently CAFTA, and they opposed the inclusion of labor standards in all of these agreements. The commercial logic of the system they helped create is now coming home to roost, and they bear some responsibility for the system's creation.

Posted on October 1, 2005 at thomaspalley.com.

GLOBALIZATION AND IT:
SETTING THE RECORD STRAIGHT

October 12, 2006

Over the last three years there has been an explosion of public concern about the wage and employment impacts of global outsourcing. As a result, worries about globalization have begun to move up the income ladder, infecting white-collar middle-class workers. For instance, a poll conducted in May 2004 for the Associated Press reported that sixty-nine percent of Americans believe outsourcing hurts the economy. Recognizing the potential threat this shift of public opinion poses to corporate globalization, business groups have been busy playing a game of catch-up seeking to allay these new more broadly shared public fears.

Recently, the world renowned Washington D.C. based Institute for International Economics (IIE) released a study praising the benefits of off-shoring the information technology (IT) industry, titled "Accelerating the Globalization of America: The Role for Information Technology." The study argues that IT is good for the economy, and globalization is good for IT. *Ergo*, globalization is good for the economy. The only problem is that the argument does not stack up.

The IT industry provides an opportunity for observing the effects of global outsourcing on a cutting-edge "new economy" sector. A close inspection of the facts confirms the fears of the public, not the claims of corporations. The IT industry is not the apparel or shoemaking industry, which means the adverse effects of global out-sourcing cannot be casually dismissed as just the inevitable shedding of outmoded industry.

The study's thesis is that IT investment yields a high rate of return for the economy. Moreover, IT investment is very price sensitive, so that lower IT prices yield a proportionately larger increase in IT investment spending. Finally, globalization has driven down the price of IT products. Putting the three pieces together, globalization has been good for the economy by driving down IT prices, increasing IT spending, and thereby spurring growth.

Sounds very reasonable. Unfortunately, there is little evidence that globalization has caused lower IT prices, and without that the argument crumbles. IT hardware prices are driven by two factors – long-term trends and the business cycle. The long-term price trend captures the impact of technological innovation, and the trend of prices has been down for a long time. That trend is sometimes referred to as Moore's law - after Gordon E. Moore a co-founder of Intel – and it states that the unit cost of computing power halves every eighteen months. Moore's law was coined in 1965, long before the current period of globalization began, and there is no evidence that globalization has accelerated the trend of computing power price decline.

With regard to the business cycle, there is clear evidence that the price of computing power (DRAM or dynamic random access memory) is related to the utilization of DRAM production capacity. Prices fall when there is excess capacity and they rise when capacity is tight. That is standard supply and demand analysis, which rests on economic principles that applied long before globalization. The only contribution of globalization is that much DRAM production capacity is now offshore because U.S. corporations have been building new capacity offshore rather than at home.

All of this casts huge doubt over the claim that globalization has benefited the economy by benefiting IT. However, whereas the benefits are in doubt, the costs are not. One clear cost is that the U.S. IT hardware industry has been significantly hollowed out. The U.S. used to run an IT goods trade surplus. Now, it runs a huge IT trade deficit, with many U.S. companies importing products made offshore by their subsidiaries or under license by foreign producers. In 2005 the U.S. trade deficit in information and communications products was $83.2 billion. The deficit with China alone was $50.8 billion, reflecting the huge off-shoring of IT production that has taken place.

With regard to jobs, there has also been a clear contraction in the level of U.S. IT employment. In 1999 there were 4.9 million technology-related jobs, but this had fallen to 4.6 million in May 2005 – a loss of 300,000 jobs. The bulk of these job losses were for workers earning less than $30,000 per year, but there was also significant job loss of 140,000 among computer programmers who made an average of $67,400 per year.

With regard to wages, the average real wage for lower paid technology related jobs was essentially stagnant between 1999 and May 2005. For mid-level computer support specialists whose annual pay averaged $43,380 in 2005, real wages actually fell 1.3 percent annually over this six-year period. However, the real pay of higher skill tech workers rose 1.6 percent per year. The bottom line is that global outsourcing of the U.S. IT industry has not been good for workers in the bottom half of the wage distribution. The IT sector therefore appears to be following a similar path to manufacturing, confirming the fears of working families about outsourcing.

An underlying claim is that outsourcing of IT hardware production has been a boon to the U.S. economy because it leads to lower IT prices from which the U.S. economy benefits. According to this logic, the U.S could benefit from outsourcing of its IT R&D capacity and from outsourcing its software industry. Indeed, these developments are to be encouraged, and under current globalization policy they are. Yet, this entire way of thinking has recently been challenged by Nobel laureate in economics, Paul Samuelson. Samuelson has shown that when the U.S. off-shores those industries in which it has historically held a comparative advantage (such as IT), the U.S.'s future gains from trade and standard of living can fall.

Changes in the structure of the U.S. IT industry are being driven by corporations, which are intent on maximizing their own profits. In a nationally based economy, such as was the case in the 1950s and 1960s, profit maximization by companies tends to maximize national income. In a global economy, that is not the case. Instead, profit maximization promotes the maximization of global income rather than national income. Companies are happy to outsource because they earn the profits on outsourced production, but that does not maximize national income. This fundamental insight is not yet appreciated within Washington policy circles.

There is no disagreement that IT is good for the economy. There is also agreement that globalization relies significantly on IT. However, there are two dangers. The first is that opposition to the current form of globalization gets misinterpreted as opposition to technology – a misinterpretation that advocates of corporate globalization encourage with charges that opponents are "Luddites". The second danger is that globalization gets credited with the benefits of IT because of its heavy reliance on IT - that's tantamount to a case of bait and switch.

The debate over globalization is not about the benefits of IT, and opposition to globalization does not mean opposition to technology. Instead, the debate is about the character of globalization – the absence of labor standards, the absence of rules for exchange rates, the implications of outsourcing for workers, and changed power relations that enable corporations to set economic policy and collar productivity gains for their top management and owners. The lesson from Moore's law is that the benefits of IT would have flowed regardless of expanded globalization, and for working families they might have been even larger under an alternative globalization.

A final generic lesson for policymakers concerns numbers and public debate. The enormous resources of the business community means that it can commission studies, launch them with fanfare, and then broadcast their findings. In this way controversial calculations can quickly become received fact. That is a problem for which there is no easy solution. However, it does suggest that policymakers and journalists be skeptical of studies about trade and globalization promising four course free lunches.

Posted on October 12, 2006 at thomaspalley.com.

WHY THE WORLD PAYS DOLLAR TRIBUTE

June 30, 2006

The U.S. dollar is much in the news these days and there is a sense that the world economy may have become excessively reliant on the dollar. This reliance smacks of dysfunctional co-dependence whereby the U.S. and the rest of the world both rely on the dollar's strength, but neither is well served by it.

The U.S. dollar is the world's premiere currency, with approximately two-thirds of world official foreign exchange holdings being dollars. Moreover, many countries appear willing to run sustained trade surpluses with the U.S., supplying everything from t-shirts to Porsches in return for additional dollar holdings. This willingness to exchange valuable resources for paper IOUs represents a form of dollar tribute.

Many foreign policymakers complain about the U.S.'s special advantage, which allows it to run enormous trade deficits without apparent market sanction. Whereas balance of payments considerations constrain other countries to run tight economic policies, no equivalent constraint appears to hold for the United States. This advantage is rooted in the dollar's special role as the world's reserve currency.

For the U.S. one major benefit of the dollar's reserve currency role is that it increases the demand for U.S. financial assets. This drives up prices of stocks and bonds and lowering interest rates, thereby increasing household wealth and lowering the cost of borrowing money. Additionally, the U.S. government gets seignorage (a free loan) from the hundreds of millions in dollar bills held offshore. Printing a one hundred dollar bill is almost costless to the U.S. government, but foreigners must give over one hundred dollars of resources to get the bill. That's a tidy profit for U.S. taxpayers.

Increased foreign demand for U.S. assets also appreciates the dollar, which is a mixed blessing. On one hand, consumers benefit from lower import prices. On the other, it makes U.S manufacturing less internationally competitive because an over-valued dollar makes U.S. exports more expensive and imports cheaper. Reserve currency status therefore promotes trade deficits and de-industrialization.

The conventional explanation of the dollar's reserve currency status is a "medium of exchange" story. The U.S. has historically been the largest and richest currency area, with the largest share of world output and trade. This has provided incentives for other countries to hold and use dollars. Additionally, the fact that many governments over-issue their own money and create high inflation, encourages foreign citizens to protect themselves by holding dollars instead of domestic currency.

81

A second theory of reserve currencies, associated with the political left, is based on U.S. military power and the Pax Americana. The argument is that U.S. military power provides the security that protects the global market system, and New York is the new Rome. Countries, such as Saudi Arabia, hold reserves in dollars because New York is a political safe haven, and because that is how they help cover the costs of enforcing the Pax Americana.

These two theories are mutually reinforcing. Thus, to the extent that the dollar is widely used and is also a safe haven, investors will tend to rush into dollars in times of uncertainty. Consequently, central banks in other countries need to accumulate large dollar reserve holdings to protect against financial disruptions that result from sudden exits by investors, as happened in East Asia in 1997.

There is a third unrecognized theory that can be labeled the "buyer of last resort" theory of reserve currencies. Put bluntly, the tribute other countries pay the U.S. through their trade surpluses is the result of their failure to generate adequate consumption spending in their own markets, be it due to poor income distribution or bad domestic economic policies. This forces them to rely on the American consumer.

The logic of this third theory is easily illustrated. Over the last decade, while Europe and Japan stagnated, the U.S. grew on the back of robust consumer spending. This spending has sucked in imports, helping growth in Europe, East Asia, and Latin America, and making the U.S. the major engine of global growth.

East Asian countries (especially China) have been particularly willing to run trade surpluses with the U.S. because this has fuelled export-led growth. These countries rely on exports to keep their factories operating. Export success then attracts foreign direct investment that advances development. Under-valued exchange rates are vital for this strategy as it keeps exports competitive. Countries have therefore channeled their trade surpluses into dollars, keeping the dollar over-valued and enabling them to sell in the U.S. market. This explains both the continuing strong demand for dollars despite the U.S. trade deficit, and the dollar's dominance in official foreign exchange holdings.

Ironically, America's dispensation from trade deficit discipline stems from other countries' failure to develop an equivalent of the American consumer. Countries want to industrialize with full employment, but they lack adequate internal demand. Consequently, they must rely on the U.S. market. It is also why Germany supplies BMWs and Mercedes-Benzes in return for paper dollar IOUs.

Conventional theory says the dollar will only lose its dominance when countries become saturated with dollar holdings. At that stage they will cease buying and may even sell dollars, causing a fall of the dollar. The problem with this story is that countries have no incentive to sell dollars, as this would kill the golden goose of export-led growth.

The buyer of last resort story suggests a different take. One reason the dollar could topple is if countries finally manage to develop their own consumption markets. Euroland is most capable of doing this, but for the moment it is gripped by policymaking that is obsessed with inflation and afraid of growth. China needs to improve its income distribution in a way that links income distribution to productivity. Unions are the natural way to do this, but they are blocked by China's totalitarian political system that fears unions.

An alternative source of collapse is if American consumers reduce spending because they feel over-extended, the Fed raises interest rates too high, or American banks tighten lending standards. In this event, the U.S. economy would stall and the dollar could fall owing to diminished U.S. economic prospects.

All three theories have merit, but in today's economic environment the buyer of last resort theory is especially relevant. As long as other countries fail to generate sufficient demand in their own markets, they will be compelled to rely on the U.S. market and pay dollar tribute.

However, none are well served by this co-dependence. Other countries are resentful of the U.S.'s special situation that exempts it from trade deficit discipline. Side-by-side, U.S. long-term economic prospects are undermined by the erosion of the manufacturing sector, while U.S. workers face wage and job pressures from imports that are advantaged by the dollar's over-valuation. Moreover, all are vulnerable to a sudden stop of the system resulting from financial over-extension of the U.S. consumer.

This suggests that the rest of the world needs to develop an alternative to the U.S. consumer. That will require raising wages in developing economies, and encouraging consumption in Europe and Japan. Such measures would stabilize the global economy by providing a second engine of growth, and it would also correct the large global financial imbalances that have developed as a result of over-reliance on the U.S. consumer.

Posted on June 30, 2006 at thomaspalley.com. This article was originally published by YaleGlobal Online as "Why Dollar Hegemony is Unhealthy" on June 20, 2006.

DECOUPLING VS. THE CONCERTINA EFFECT

September 7, 2008

Over the last year, as the U.S. economy has slipped toward (and likely into) recession, there has been much talk of decoupling. According to this idea the global economy has decoupled from the U.S. economy and can continue growing even if the U.S. goes into recession.

That idea is now proving fragile. Instead of decoupling, the global economy is showing signs of a concertina effect. Thus, as the U.S. economy grinds to a halt, much of the rest of the world seems to be also slowing and bumping in behind.

Ever since the East Asian financial crisis of 1997 the U.S. has served as the locomotive of the global economy. This locomotive role has had U.S. consumers engage in a ten year consumption binge financed by debt and rising house prices. That binge pushed the household saving rate to record lows, and it also resulted in record U.S. trade deficits.

Trade data show the U.S. has run large trade deficits with every major industrial region of the global economy – Europe, Japan, China, East Asia, Canada and Mexico. That pumped spending into these regions, fuelling their growth.

This economic arrangement has created a dependence on the U.S. market, and that dependence has been further deepened by policies of export-led growth. Unable or unwilling to grow their own domestic markets, countries have relied on policies that explicitly promote exports.

In many developing countries these policies have had the added benefit of attracting foreign direct investment (FDI). Thus, exports have kept factories busy, while the prospect of future exports has tempted companies to relocate production facilities to developing economies.

In effect, developing countries have gotten a twofer – export led growth plus FDI. Meanwhile, the U.S. economy has benefitted from cheap imports, but its manufacturing sector has been eroded and consumers have loaded up on debt in an unsustainable fashion.

The bursting of the U.S. house price bubble has shifted this process into reverse, slowing U.S. import growth and replacing financial exuberance with financial fear. But rather than global decoupling, there are signs of a shared global slowdown.

The NAFTA economies of Canada and Mexico are clearly vulnerable because of their large trade dependence on the U.S. and their tight integration into the U.S. supply chain. In Europe, Ireland, Spain and Italy are either in recession or on the cusp of recession. Growth has also slowed sharply in the U.K. and France, and Japan has also lowered its growth outlook.

Germany, which is Europe's largest economy, was supposed to replace the U.S. locomotive. However, it is one of the world's most export dependent economies. German growth has kept going longer than other European economies because of low consumer debt and export growth to OPEC economies, but Germany is now also slowing. Moreover, its policies of wage restraint and hyper-export competitiveness pose a menace rather than a help to the overall European economy.

The hope that China could pull East Asia through a U.S. slowdown was always a fiction. A quick inspection of China's trade shows that its trade deficits with other East Asian economies are derived from its trade surpluses with the U.S. China assembles imported parts from the rest of East Asia and sells the assembled product in U.S. markets. That means when the U.S. slows, the slowdown ripples back via China into the broader East Asian economy.

The commodity exporting economies of Australia, Latin America, and Africa have all done well from the commodity price boom. However, if the industrial economies of North America, Europe and East Asia slow, that can be expected to negatively impact commodity prices and exports.

Closer co-movements of national economies are a logical consequence of corporate and financial globalization since it makes economies more inter-dependent. Those co-movements can become a concertina when they are driven by a common factor such as export-led growth that relies on debt-financed U.S. consumers serving as buyer of last resort.

The key to avoiding a concerted global downturn is for developed economies to sustain confidence in financial markets, resist misdiagnosed calls for a war on inflation, and initiate policies that strengthen demand. Meanwhile, developing countries must continue spending even as their exports to the U.S. slow. These countries now have the foreign exchange reserves to ride out a weakened trade outlook. The open question is whether they have the sources of internal demand.

Developing that internal demand is a core problem. However, it remains off the development policy agenda because the current paradigm is obsessed with the supply-side and neglects income distribution and development of the demand-side. As long as that is so, the global economy will remain beset by an unstable and inadequate configuration of demand.

Posted on September 8, 2008 at thomaspalley.com. Originally posted as "The economic concertina" on September 7, 2008 in The Guardian, Comment Is Free.

GLOBALIZATION LOCK-IN:
WHAT SHOULD BE DONE?

May 14, 2007

"Lock-in" is a concept developed by economic historians to describe how economies get tied in to using inefficient technologies. It also applies to institutions as economies and societies can get locked into sub-optimal institutional arrangements. This has relevance for globalization where the arrangements governing trade and the global economy may be sub-optimal, posing problems of how to change them. The economics of lock-in helps understand the problem and suggests how to solve it.

Lock-in arises because a technology that is adopted first may gain a competitive advantage that encourages others to adopt it, even though other technologies are superior and would be chosen if all were at the same starting point. An example of lock-in is narrow gauge railroad that is less efficient than broad gauge on which railcars are more stable and can carry greater loads. Once a stretch of narrow gauge has been laid, there is an incentive for additions to be narrow gauge to fit the existing track. Moreover, the incentive increases as the size of the rail network grows.

Lock-in has enormous relevance for globalization, which has seen the creation of new institutions and patterns of economic activity. Trade agreements have created new rules, fostering new patterns of global production and setting the basis for future trade and investment negotiations. Another example of lock-in is removal of international capital controls that has changed financial flows and would be difficult and costly to restore.

Globalization lock-in matters because today's global economy has been designed with little attention to labor and social issues. This is because the system was largely stitched together in the last quarter of the 20th century, a period of labor weakness and *laissez-faire* revival. Consequently, arrangements were forged without attention to labor, social, or environmental concerns.

Corporate proponents of the system are trying to deepen the extent of lock-in through "competitive liberalization". This involves negotiating bilateral trade agreements that tie ever more countries into arrangements without standards, and these agreements become the launching point for future regional and multilateral agreements. In this fashion, the bar is cemented ever lower.

The economics of lock-in suggest an escape from this problem. Recalling the example of narrow gauge railroads, the market can produce a gradual escape by cherry-picking the most profitable parts of the existing network, causing it to gradually implode. Thus, parallel wide gauge track may be built on the most profitable segments of the existing narrow gauge network, draining the latter's profitability while promoting the gradual build-up of a wide gauge network.

This provides a metaphor for globalization. The global economy has built a narrow gauge railroad and now needs to find a way to build a broad gauge replacement. That points to several directions relevant for both the U.S. and Europe. First, countries should stop building more narrow gauge track, which means no more trade agreements without high quality labor and environmental standards. Additionally, agreements must have exchange rate provisions guarding against currency manipulation and unfair competition based on undervalued exchange rates.

Second, the U.S. and Europe should start cherry-picking the existing "narrow gauge" trade system and promote "broad gauge" trade agreements. For instance, they could negotiate a U.S. - Europe Trans-Atlantic free trade agreement (TAFTA) that includes proper labor and environmental standards and exchange rate provisions. Similar agreements could be negotiated with Canada, Japan and South Korea. All of these countries would have little difficulty complying with standards, and together they comprise over eighty percent of the global economy. Such a trading bloc would quickly become a "broad gauge" magnet for other countries.

Third, country shareholdings in the IMF and World Bank may in future be adjusted to reflect the greater contribution of developing countries to the global economy. If this happens, it should be part of a *quid pro quo* whereby the IMF and World Bank commit to promote labor and environmental standards.

The bottom line is that it is still possible to escape globalization lock-in. The key is replacing corporate sponsored downward competitive liberalization with progressive upward competitive harmonization. The newfound willingness of the U.S. to include standards in its Peru and Panama FTAs is a step in the right direction. However, these agreements severely limit workers' rights to sue for enforcement and they also lack provisions against exchange rate manipulation. That leaves plenty of room for improvement in future agreements.

Posted on May 14, 2007 at www.thomaspalley.com. Also posted as "Globalization lock-in" in Policy Innovations on May 16, 2007.

CAN GLOBALIZATION FAIL?
LESSONS FROM HISTORY

April 13, 2006

Around the world there are growing rumbles about globalization, and these rumbles are not confined to activist anti-globalization movements. In East Asia, the financial crisis of 1997 left a jaundiced sense of globalization, though robust economic recovery has tempered that. Globalization's standing has also been badly damaged in Latin America by the meltdown of the Argentine economy in 2000 and successive financial crises in Brazil in 1999 and 2001. In Europe, new fear about globalization is surfacing in a range of countries. In Poland it has taken the form of concern about foreign capital taking over the Polish banking system, and foreign takeover fears also permeate France and Italy. In France and Germany, working people link globalization with pressures to dismantle the social democratic state.

Among Americans, outsourcing of service sector jobs has become a top concern, possibly the top concern. Opposition to free trade has crept up the income and social-strata ladder to include educated white-collar workers. This new opposition comes on top of existing resentments among blue-collar workers at the loss of well-paying manufacturing jobs.

These developments have raised concerns about the durability of globalization among its supporters. In April 2005, Martin Wolf of "The Financial Times" gave a lecture titled "Will Globalization Survive?" at Washington's prestigious pro-globalization Institute for International Economics. More recently, Harvard professor Jeffry Frieden published a new book, "Global Capitalism: Its Fall and Rise in the 20th Century," that was featured at a recent International Monetary Fund book forum. Frieden is a supporter of globalization, yet the final section of his book is titled 'Global Capitalism Troubled," and he ruminates on the possibility that, like the globalization of the 19th century, today's globalization may falter.

Looking back to the history of what some historians call the 'first globalization' can be highly instructive. However, one problem is that people often tend to identify its end with the beginning of World War I in 1914. This is wrong, and contributes to historical misunderstanding that impedes understanding today's globalization.

The first globalization ended with the Wall Street Crash of 1929 and the ensuing Great Depression. That said, World War I was hugely significant because it permanently transformed political conditions. Consequently, when the economic order collapsed in 1929, the response was profoundly affected by the political conditions created by World War I. In the U.S., Britain, and France, the war created political and social conditions that fostered a turn to social democracy. In

Germany, the onerous economic burdens of the 1919 Treaty of Versailles fostered a turn to Nazism.

This history has enormous significance for understanding today's predicament. The first lesson is that politics did not bring down the first globalization, which suggests that politics will not bring down today's globalization. The economic crisis of 1929 brought down the first globalization, suggesting that economic crisis will bring down today's globalization. The second lesson is that whereas political developments preceding 1929 did not cause the crash, they mattered enormously for the international response. That too is critical for today.

Governments substantially recreated the pre-war economic system after World War I. Britain and France held on to their empires, and the 1920s saw a revival of international trade and investment whereby trade exceeded peak pre-1914 levels. Technological innovation flourished in the form of automobiles, airplanes, and consumer durables, and Britain returned to the gold standard in 1926.

However, as with the pre-1914 system, the reconstructed system distributed prosperity extremely unevenly. In the U.S., wealth and income inequality grew during the "roaring twenties." In Britain, the industrial midlands and north suffered from persistent stagnation because of an overvalued exchange rate. And prosperity simply bypassed Germany. Additionally, there was a popular turn to isolationism in response to the carnage wrought by the war. The system was therefore unpopular, and consequently it had few defenders when the crash came. That lesson holds for the current globalization, which is also unpopular and feared.

The first globalization crashed because of inherent financial fragility. Banking systems lacked modern safety nets such as deposit insurance and lenders of last resort, and the gold standard was also intrinsically fragile because countries could demand payment in gold. Consequently, the system was vulnerable to panics, and the danger increased as financial markets and banking systems grew because the supply of gold, the backing asset, was fixed. Once panic started, it was near impossible to stop. Banking systems collapsed, bankruptcy and deflation set in, and the rest is history.

This history suggests that if today's globalization crashes it will also be because of economic factors, but those factors will differ from the past because the system is different. The New Deal era created a system that remedied earlier financial fragility by restricting private ownership of bullion, and creating deposit insurance and lenders of last resort. It also created a new social democratic mass consumption economy in which income was more broadly shared owing to unionization, minimum wages, and social security provisions. However, a social democratic mass consumption economy is expensive for individual capitalists, giving them an incentive to evade its costs. That has been driving force behind globalization since 1980, and that is the contradiction in today's system.

Business has a private incentive to escape the system to countries with lower costs. Yet, it still needs mass consumption. The system needs a solid middle class, but is also driven to hollow out that middle class. This contradiction has been papered over by consumer borrowing provided by deregulated financial markets and a 25-year asset price boom. The problem is that such borrowing risks proving unsustainable if incomes are hollowed out, and if it stops the economic merry-go-round may also stop. If that stoppage produces an economic crash, globalization may crash, too. This is because it lacks political support, having been a primary cause of middle class hollowing out.

The pattern of retreat is difficult to predict. One possibility is a return to a world of tariffs and quotas. A second response may be the emergence of regional trade and investment blocs. A third response that would preserve globalization would be the establishment of new domestic and international rules that support a social democratic mass consumption economy. All three scenarios challenge today's elite's program.

Finally, if the global economy crashes, it will be important to correctly identify the economic causes. The Smoot-Hawley tariff was passed in June 1930. Its economic effects were minor for the U.S. given the pre-existing high tariff structure and the minimal extent of U.S. engagement in trade. Indeed, those effects may even have been beneficial to the extent that spending was switched from imports to domestically produced goods. Yet, for 75 years, free traders have sought to blame Smoot-Hawley for the Depression and thereby make a case for free trade. The rooster crows at dawn, but does not cause the sunrise. Smoot-Hawley did not cause the Depression. Likewise, trade stalemate and failure of the Doha trade round will not cause the next economic crisis. However, they may coincide, in which event rest assured that globalization boosters will argue causation.

Posted on April 26, 2006 at thomaspalley.com. Originally posted as "Could Globalization Fail?" by YaleGlobal Online on April 13, 2006.

VI THE POLITICS OF GLOBALIZATION

The political economy of globalization:
Why corporations are winning and workers are losing

♦

Fighting the flat-earthers

♦

Neoliberalism: A missing element in
America's conversation on globalization

♦

Globalization tames the left in Brazil

THE POLITICAL ECONOMY OF GLOBALIZATION: WHY CORPORATIONS ARE WINNING AND WORKERS ARE LOSING

November 20, 2005

Political economy has historically been constructed around the divide between capital and labor, with firms and workers at odds over the division of the economic pie. Within this construct, labor is usually represented as a monolithic interest, yet the reality is that labor has always suffered from internal divisions—by race, by occupational status, and along many other fault lines. Neoliberal globalization has in many ways sharpened these divisions, which helps to explain why corporations have been winning and workers losing.

One of these fault lines divides workers from themselves: since workers are also consumers, they face a divide between the desire for higher wages and the desire for lower prices. Historically, this identity split has been exploited to divide union from nonunion workers, with anti-labor advocates accusing union workers of causing higher prices. Today, globalization is amplifying the divide between people's interests as workers and their interests as consumers through its promise of ever-lower prices.

Consider the debate over Wal-Mart's low-road labor policies. While Wal-Mart's low wages and skimpy benefits have recently faced scrutiny, even some liberal commentators argue that Wal-Mart is actually good for low-wage workers because they gain more as consumers from its "low, low prices" than they lose as workers from its low wages. But this static, snapshot analysis fails to capture the full impact of globalization, past and future.

Globalization affects the economy unevenly, hitting some sectors first and others later. The process can be understood in terms of the hands of a clock. At one o'clock is the apparel sector; at two o'clock the textile sector; at three the steel sector; at six the auto sector. Workers in the apparel sector are the first to have their jobs shifted to lower-wage venues; at the same time, though, all other workers get price reductions. Next, the process picks off textile sector workers at two o'clock. Meanwhile, workers from three o'clock onward get price cuts, as do the apparel workers at one o'clock. Each time the hands of the clock move, the workers taking the hit are isolated. In this fashion, globalization moves around the clock with labor perennially divided.

Manufacturing was first to experience this process, but technological innovations associated with the Internet are putting service and knowledge workers in the firing line as well. Online business models are making even retail workers vulnerable—consider amazon.com, for example, which has opened a customer support center and two technology development centers in India. Public sector wages are also in play, at least indirectly, since falling wages mean falling

95

tax revenues. The problem is that each time the hands on the globalization clock move forward, workers are divided: the majority is made slightly better off while the few are made much worse off.

Globalization also alters the historical divisions within capital, creating a new split between bigger internationalized firms and smaller firms that remain nationally centered. This division has been brought into sharp focus with the debate over the trade deficit and the overvalued dollar. In previous decades, manufacturing as whole opposed running trade deficits and maintaining an overvalued dollar because of the adverse impact of increased imports. The one major business sector with a different view was retailing, which benefited from cheap imports.

However, the spread of multinational production and outsourcing has divided manufacturing in wealthy countries into two camps. In one camp are larger multi-national corporations that have gone global and benefit from cheap imports; in the other are smaller businesses that remain nationally centered in terms of sales, production and input sourcing. Multinational corporations tend to support an over-valued dollar since this makes imports produced in their foreign factories cheaper. Conversely, domestic manufacturers are hurt by an over-valued dollar which advantages import competition.

This division opens the possibility of a new alliance between labor and those manufacturers and businesses that remain nationally based—potentially a potent one, since there are approximately 7 million enterprises with sales of less than $10 million in the United States, versus only 200,000 with sales greater than $10 million. However, such an alliance will always be unstable as the inherent labor-capital conflict over income distribution can always reassert itself. Indeed, this pattern is already evident in the internal politics of the National Association of Manufacturers, whose members have been significantly divided regarding the overvalued dollar. As one way to address this division, the group is promoting a domestic "competitiveness" agenda aimed at weakening regulation, reducing corporate legal liability, and lowering employee benefit costs—an agenda designed to appeal to both camps, but at the expense of workers.

Solidarity has always been key to political and economic advance by working families, and it is key to mastering the politics of globalization. Developing a coherent story about the economics of neoliberal globalization around which working families can coalesce is a key ingredient for solidarity. So too is understanding how globalization divides labor. These narratives can help counter deep cultural proclivities to individualism, as well as other historic divides such as racism. However, as if this were not difficult enough, globalization creates additional challenges. National political solutions that worked in the past are not adequate to the task of controlling international competition. That further raises the solidarity bar as it calls for international solidarity supporting new forms of international economic regulation.

Originally posted as "The politics of globalization: Why corporations are winning and workers are losing" on November 20, 2005 at thomaspalley.com. Also published as "The globalization clock" in Real World Labor: A Reader in Economics, Politics and Social, edited by Ness, Offner, Sturr, and the Dollars & Sense Collective, 2009.

FIGHTING THE FLAT-EARTHERS

September 7, 2006

Progressives and trade unionists frequently complain about how globalization has tilted the playing field in favor of capital. By facilitating international trade and cross-border investment, globalization has enabled capital to go mobile. This has created multiple exit options for capital, and the credible threat of movement to other countries has raised capital's economic and political bargaining power. Corporations, who control capital, have then used this increased power to shift income distribution in favor of profits, roll back taxes, and challenge policies promoting social protection and inclusion.

There is also another way in which capital has gone global, and that is through ideas and language. Business schools and university economics departments have provided capital with a globally shared framework and language for talking about the economy. From Washington D.C. to Tokyo, from Berlin to Brasilia, neo-liberal economists share a common "free market" frame that quickly allows them to establish shared conversations.

The ability to communicate with each other is a powerful force driving the politics and policy of globalization. The shared conversation establishes shared cross-border policy priorities, and policymakers, politicians, and journalists brought up on this language are led to see the world in a particular way. The fact that all use the same language also creates a massive global echo chamber that drives global understandings.

This is how the rhetoric and misleading idealizations of the invisible hand and the "natural" rate of unemployment have come to dominate public discourse. Thomas Friedman's "flat world" smacks of a level playing field, yet globalization produces anything but. Workers do indeed compete internationally against each other, but that competition has been structured and designed by global corporations, not by an invisible hand.

Progressives and organized labor lack an equivalent simple framework for explaining the global economy, which is a huge disadvantage in the struggle for a fair and just globalization. When trade unionists from different countries get together this lack of a common analytical framework results in fractured conversations that obstructs the development of common understandings and policy priorities. It also obstructs the development of a global echo chamber to counter that of capital.

The lack of a shared language is a serious problem that hampers labor's efforts to counter the underlying problem of capital's newfound global mobility. Labor cannot go mobile, and nor should it. Moving machines and factories between countries is one thing: having workers uproot and migrate is another.

Instead, labor needs to establish international agreement and solidarity that can enable new strategies and policies that again corral capital and restore a human face to capitalism. Language is critical for this.

Proponents of corporate styled globalization use the metaphor of a sunny flat world to describe the economy. Advocates for workers should adopt an alternative metaphor: a box. The box describes how workers are being boxed in and squeezed from all sides by today's corporate inspired economic order. The box has four sides: globalization, less than full employment, small government, and labor market flexibility. These four sides describe the neo-liberal policy paradigm, which puts workers under continuous economic pressure that none can escape.

Private sector workers are pressured by globalization, which allows corporations to put them in international competition with oppressed low-wage workers in less developed economies. Public sector workers are pressured by the small government agenda that emphasizes privatization and places them in competition with private sector workers. Both groups of workers are pressed by policies that accept less than full employment and promote labor market flexibility. Less than full employment is where central banks enter the picture, as they keep interest rates high in the name of price stability, thereby preventing full employment. Labor market flexibility strips workers of employment and social protections, erodes the minimum wage, and makes union organizing near impossible.

The box can provide labor with a framework for a global economic conversation. Most importantly, it provides a compelling alternative to the metaphor of a flat world. Second, it provides a clear link between the economy and policy, driving a stake through the notion of a natural economy and emphasizing the significance of policy. Third, the box helps identify unities and disagreements between both northern (developed) and southern (developing) country workers. Among northern workers there is widespread agreement about the threat posed by the labor market flexibility, small government, and less than full employment pieces of the neo-liberal agenda. But there are differences about globalization and free trade. For instance, Canadian, Swedish, and German unions tend to be much more pro-free trade. Labor needs to understand the sources of these differences and what can be done about them if it is to offer a winning alternative to corporate globalization.

Canada is significantly a raw material exporter, which lends to classical comparative advantage arguments in favor of trade as it makes sense to get raw materials from the most abundant locations. Germany runs massive trade surpluses on the back of a relatively under-valued exchange rate. While Sweden has tended to have an under-valued exchange rate, and has several national industrial champions (think Volvo, Saab, Ericsson) that have given it a global edge. It also has labor market policies that assist workers displaced by trade. For northern unions the challenge is to negotiate whether these country-specific features are decisive, or whether there is better solidarity agenda that emphasizes fairly valued exchange rates and rules for global competition.

Globalization also divides northern and southern workers, a division that is repeatedly exploited by business-friendly policy elites. Developing country workers are familiar with the World Bank - IMF labor market flexibility, privatization, and small government agenda. They are also familiar with high interest rate policies that stifle growth. However, they frequently split on the issues of labor standards and export-led growth based on under-valued exchange rates. Here, they argue that cheap exploitable labor is a legitimate source of comparative advantage and that unbridled competition is the best path to development.

The box provides a simple framework for identifying both the extensive nature of agreement and where disagreement exists. The points of agreement provide an opportunity to build a robust global echo chamber, while identifying points of disagreement is the necessary first step to seeing if these can be resolved. The box neatly frames the problem and opens the way for a richer conversation that can identify coherent economic policy alternatives to the neo-liberal policy mix.

Finally, the box has one further political benefit. Using the box to describe the new global economic order highlights the support for anti-worker policies by the major political parties. In the U.S., both Republicans and "new" Democrats have pushed the box policy agenda. In Germany, the Social Democrats have also been drawn in this direction, as evidenced by their split over the "Agenda 2010" labor market flexibility debate. To paraphrase Rich Trumka, Secretary-Treasurer of the AFL-CIO, economic policy today is like a restaurant with one chef and two waiters serving the same meal – and it tastes like crow no matter who serves.

Originally posted on September 7, 2006 on TomPaine.com. Also posted at thomaspalley.com on September 17, 2006.

NEOLIBERALISM: A MISSING ELEMENT IN AMERICA'S CONVERSATION ON GLOBALIZATION

October 2005

Americans are widely familiar with the concept of globalization, defined as the international economic integration of countries. However, America's conversation about globalization suffers from lack of distinction between different types of globalization. It is as if we see the "physical" outline of globalization, but are unable to talk about its "character." This lack of language stunts our national conversation about globalization and is a huge problem.

Our linguistic deficit contrasts with Latin Americans, who widely use the term "neoliberalism" and refer to "neoliberal globalization." The reference to "liberalism" reflects an intellectual lineage that connects with 19th century economic liberalism associated with Manchester, England. The Manchester system was predicated upon *laissez-faire* economics, and was closely associated with the free trade movement of that era.

Contemporary neoliberalism is a more radical and broader philosophy about the nature and design of society. It emphasizes the efficiency of market competition, the role of individuals in determining economic outcomes, and the distortions associated with government intervention and regulation of markets. Whereas free trade was the core of 19th century liberalism, it is but an element of contemporary neoliberalism.

Though Americans do not use the word neoliberalism, they have contributed significantly to neoliberalism's rise. The modern neoliberal impulse begins with the work of the Austrian economists, Friedrich Hayek and Ludwig von Mises, both of whom deeply impressed former British Prime Minister, Margaret Thatcher. The American contribution has come through the Chicago school of economics, associated with Milton Friedman, George Stigler, Ronald Coase and Gary Becker. All four are Nobel prizewinners in economics, and their contribution has been twofold. First, these economists transformed the political economy claims of Hayek and von Mises into the mathematical language of idealized free markets that now benchmarks contemporary economics. Second, they exported this idealized free market version of neoliberalism to economic policy elites (especially in Latin America) through training of graduate students. In effect, the Chicago school has promoted neoliberalism while simultaneously obscuring its political and social character.

To talk of today's globalization without mention of neoliberalism is to miss the wood from the trees. Neoliberal globalization is a transforming political project that changes social and economic structures to empower wealthy elites, disempower workers, and disempower the state. It is full of ironies and paradoxes. Since the state is needed to implement the neoliberal project, this means the state cooperates in its own disempowerment. Moreover, because most large states are democracies, successful implementation requires electoral success. This means that some significant part of the working class must cooperate in disempowering itself. Finally, and most dangerously, neoliberalism creates economic structures of "lock-in." That is, once changes are made they are extremely difficult and costly to reverse. In this fashion neoliberalism cements its permanence.

Neoliberalism works by changing the regime of competition so that wages, work conditions, systems of social protection, and patterns of social and economic relations are subject to new forms of competition. It is not an issue of competition versus absence of competition: that is the misrepresentation Chicago school free marketers pull. The key to neoliberal regime change is free trade in goods and services, and free movement of capital – both financial and physical. Money is free to move across borders, while multi-national corporations are free to shift plant and equipment embodying the latest technology. This freedom of international movement enables arbitrage of wages, work standards and social codes across countries.

Such freedom of movement disciplines and disempowers governments by diminishing national policy effectiveness and curtailing policy space. These erosions in turn hollow out democracy. Though the form of democracy remains, the effective choice set is diminished. Social arrangements that were previously feasible become infeasible, and infeasibility then becomes the grounds for democratic rejection. What is never put to the vote is whether to shrink the choice set in the first place.

The lack of a word equivalent to neoliberalism means that Americans have no linguistic shorthand for engaging these vital issues. We need one. The term neoliberalism probably won't work because Americans associate liberal with the moral values agenda rather than economics. Corporate globalization is a good try, but it falls short of capturing the full phenomenon. Anyone have any suggestions?

Previously unpublished.

GLOBALIZATION TAMES THE LEFT IN BRAZIL

September 5, 2006

This October Brazilians will go to the polls in an election that constitutes a referendum on the presidency of Lula da Silva. As the candidate of the Workers Party, or Partido dos Trabalhadores (PT), Lula was elected in 2002 on a platform of progressive social democracy. Yet over the last four years, his macroeconomic policies have been marked by extreme caution and capitulation to the pressures of globalization. Consequently, Brazil has missed a golden opportunity provided by a robust global economy to chart a new and vibrant economic trajectory.

Lula's presidency provides another example of the timidity of the left in the era of globalization. Having fought so long and hard for power, his government has drawn back when the opportunity to govern finally arrived.

This timidity is the product of a combination of financial market intimidation and lack of intellectual confidence bred from the triumph of neoliberalism. Additionally, leftist politicians are also in the business of re-election, which means they often play it overly safe once in office.

Brazil faces a huge legacy of economic injustice that globalization has made even more difficult to remedy. This injustice is evident in Brazil's widely recognized massive income inequality, which a 1997 IMF working paper termed among "the most unequal in the world." Comparable statistics are hard to come by, but in 1989 the ratio of the top 20 percent's income share to the bottom 20 percent's share was 32.1, compared with an average of just 6.3 for industrial and high-income developing countries over the period 1960-90.

Remedying this inequality is a challenge requiring patience and good judgment for history imposes constraints, and poorly conceived attempts to rectify past injustices can do more harm than good. Overly aggressive policies can cause major economic dislocation by undermining property rights and business confidence upon which the economic system rests. The net result is that redistribution can shrink the economic cake so much that even though the poor get a larger share, they are worse off because the absolute size of their piece falls.

Globalization has amplified these difficulties since capital can now flee more quickly than ever before, when confronting governments in pursuit of redistribution policies. In financial markets, the threat of increased taxation can trigger a rush for the exits and financial crisis. With so many countries competing for foreign direct investment, corporations have a wide range of options and can readily redirect investment elsewhere. Moreover, tariff elimination has removed a powerful incentive for multi-national corporations to avoid tariff penalties by producing within a country.

All progressive governments must be sensitive to these dangers and Brazil especially so, because it has a high level of foreign indebtedness and a history of hyperinflation and financial crises. Indeed, in 1999 and 2000 Brazil experienced successive exchange-rate crises, and there was much talk prior to the election of 2002 of massive capital flight in the event of Lula winning. Though down as a result of recent robust exchange rate appreciation, Brazil's official foreign debt was still approximately 25 percent of GDP at the end of 2005.

Lula's administration has been rightly aware of these constraints. But it is one thing to be aware of constraints, and another to capitulate and be complicit with them. The fact that the possibilities for correcting past economic inequities are so limited requires the government to use the little space and few tools it has to good effect. It is here that Lula has failed Brazil.

Interest-rate policy, with its impact on the government budget and the economy, has been the source of that failure. Brazil has a large public debt on which it must pay interest. Yet, guided by neo-liberal financial policies, the Lula government has kept interest rates near twenty percent for its entire term. The result is that Brazil's government budget has become a giant machine for recycling scarce tax revenues back to Brazil's wealthy elites in the form of interest payments. In effect, the government's high interest-rate policy has created a situation whereby Brazil's scarce tax revenues, which should have been used to correct past inequities and promote growth, have instead ended back in the pockets of the wealthy.

High interest rates have also done serious harm by slowing economic growth and retarding job creation, thereby further injuring Brazil's workers. Though Brazil's headline numbers have looked good compared to the 1980s, growth has actually been significantly below par. The last four years have been a period of global economic boom during which world interest rates touched 40-year lows. On top of this Brazil entered the period with a highly competitive exchange rate, and it has especially benefited from the commodity price boom. Yet despite this once-in-a-generation fortuitous circumstance, Brazil has grown slower than the Latin American average because of self-inflicted high domestic interest rates.

The finance ministry's defense is that financial realities have compelled this policy, but such a defense rings hollow. The government has vigorously embraced tight monetary policy and never tested the possibility that interest rates could be lowered significantly without triggering higher inflation or financial crisis. Additionally, the government has consistently ignored other financial policies that can restrain inflation without imposing high interest rates on the public debt. Though trumpeting its early repayment of IMF loans, the reality is that the PT government has capitulated to financial markets, thereby reducing growth and undermining Brazil's already limited ability to correct past inequities.

104

Ironically, Lula's presidency has also witnessed a cementing of Brazil's role in the new neo-liberal global economic order, with Brazil increasingly reverting to its historical role as a supplier of primary products to the global market. In the second half of the 20th century Brazil looked to move away from that role by becoming a global manufacturing powerhouse. However, over the last four years it is commodity exports of iron ore and agricultural products that have increasingly become the engine of Brazilian economic growth.

This turn of direction has been promoted by the same neo-liberal financial policies that have so hamstrung Brazil's budget. High interest rates have made Brazilian financial markets highly attractive, causing large international inflows of financial capital that have appreciated the exchange rate by approximately 50 percent over the last four years. This appreciation has in turn diminished the international competitiveness of Brazilian manufacturing.

These developments are reflected in the rapidly growing trade relationship with China that has Brazil supplying agricultural products, particularly soy, in exchange for manufactured goods. Though the Brazilian government has celebrated growing trade with China, the emerging pattern of trade carries grave dangers. If China's impact on manufacturing in Mexico and elsewhere is a guide, then Brazilian manufacturing faces a potentially devastating competitive threat. Whereas Chinese policymakers have strategically engaged the global economy using an under-valued exchange rate and capital controls, Lula's neo-liberally inclined financial advisers have dismissed such policies.

Lula's 2002 victory was an historic event that broke with Brazil's past, with voters electing as president a trade union activist who was born in poverty. However, his government's lack of policy courage and imagination means that it has failed Brazilian workers. The root of this failure is the embrace of neo-liberal financial policies. Everyone recognizes that it is difficult to adopt progressive financial policies in times of economic crisis, but now the Lula government is saying such policies are also impossible in good times. That's a somber message about the implications of globalization for social democracy.

Posted on September 11, 2006 at www.thomaspalley.com. This article originally appeared in YaleGlobalOnline Magazine on September 5, 2006.

VII CHI-MERICA: HOW U.S. CORPORATIONS ABANDONED AMERICA

The profit vs. country dilemma

◆

The China effect: A reply to the China Business Forum

◆

Abandoning America: Corporate foreign direct investment

◆

U.S.-China trade: Pay now or pay more later

◆

Who's afraid of China?

◆

China's empty threat

◆

Death by renminbi

◆

Triangular trouble: The euro, the dollar and the renminbi

◆

Global implications of China's anti-inflation policy

♦

Investing in China: Fool's gold?

THE PROFIT VS. COUNTRY DILEMMA

June 5, 2007

Vladimir Ilyich Ulyanov, alias Lenin, was the leader of the 1917 Bolshevik revolution in Russia. One of his best known quotes is "The capitalists will sell us the rope with which we will hang them." Today, Lenin must be chuckling in his Moscow mausoleum as he watches U.S. business dealings with China.

Lenin's sarcastic quip identified how desire for profit can sometimes undermine class interest. In today's era of globalization a similar logic can hold for the national interest. Thus, with corporations looking to maximize their global profits, what is good for profit can sometimes be bad for country.

U.S. – China relations provide a case study of the "profit vs. country" dilemma. Current U.S. – China economic relations are marked by huge trade deficits and a steady migration of manufacturing to China. This structure was established in the 1990s at the behest of multi-national corporations and big retailers such as Wal-Mart. The former saw China as providing an unequaled low cost production platform from which to export to the U.S., while the latter saw China as a source of low cost imports.

Together, these business interests pushed permanent normal trading relations for China, and they also explain the U.S. Treasury's willingness to accept China's under-valued exchange rate. That is because an under-valued Yuan holds down the cost of goods sourced from China and increases profits on production exported from China.

For China, the new arrangements have contributed to spectacular economic success. Companies sourcing and exporting from China have also reaped handsome profits. However, for the U.S. economy it has been a different story. Manufacturing has steadily bled jobs as companies have closed factories in the face of low cost Chinese competition, and production and investment have shifted to China. That has tempered wages and investment spending, which helps explain the weak economic recovery and unsatisfactory expansion. It has also eroded the U.S. industrial base while expanding China's, thereby creating new national security problems

Through its trade surpluses, China has accumulated 1.2 trillion dollars of foreign exchange reserves – mostly held in U.S. treasury bills. Recently, China announced it will invest some of those funds in American equities, signaling the beginning of a new chapter that promises to further entrench existing policy.

This is because the new initiative will deepen Wall Street's support for current policy by offering the prospect of huge fees and capital gains from re-investing China's reserves. Consequently, Wall Street will now throw its full weight behind existing policy since the Street recognizes China needs continuing trade surpluses if it is to invest its foreign exchange holdings in risky assets such as equities. That augurs badly for the U.S. and Main Street.

Wall Street's greatest influence is at Treasury, which has been the leader in designing U.S. – China economic policy. The strong dollar policy originated at Treasury in the 1990s, and Treasury has persistently refused to label China a currency manipulator for fear of triggering irresistible public pressure for real action.

On top of this, Treasury Secretary Paulson - a Goldman Sachs alumnus - is actively advocating policies that risk compounding the damage to the U.S. economy. Thus, Treasury has consistently pushed China to open its financial markets and let money exit, and China has been doing just that. This benefits Wall Street since money flows there, but it reduces pressure on China to appreciate its currency. Worse than that, the Yuan could even depreciate if enough Chinese wealth holders decide to exit to diversify their portfolios against economic and political risk. That would be disastrous for the U.S. economy, but good news for Wall Street.

The profit vs. country dilemma is compounded by the political power of corporations, which has enabled them to capture policy. In earlier eras such capture promoted domestic monopoly and corruption in government procurement and tax policy. Today, it still does that (look at the Bush administration), but now it also enables corporations to push policies placing their interests ahead of country. That is the lesson of China.

Free market societies need separation between market and government, intermediated by constitutional democracy. In the 20th century many countries suffered from excessive government control over market activities, and they paid a heavy price. In the 21st century America risks paying a heavy price from the reverse problem of allowing excessive corporate influence over government.

This is a huge danger, yet it is off the political radar. One reason is that business funds both Republicans and Democrats, thereby silencing both. A second reason is that much of the public believes businessmen are smart and can run government well - after all they are rich. Put the two together, and it is easy to see why business executives move seamlessly from Wall Street and corporate boardrooms to top government policy offices on Pennsylvania and Constitution Avenues. That suggests the supply of rope will remain plentiful and Lenin may have the last laugh.

Posted on June 5, 2007 at thomaspalley.com and also posted as "The China dilemma" at TomPaine.com on June 5, 2007.

THE CHINA EFFECT:
A REPLY TO THE CHINA BUSINESS FORUM

February 3, 2006

The China Business Forum recently (January 2006) released a report titled "The China Effect" that claims "the long-term benefits to the United States of Trade with China are substantial and likely to endure (Executive Summary)." The top line conclusion of the report is that the average U.S. household stands to be one thousand dollars better off by 2010 as a result of lower prices and increased productivity in the U.S. due to the China effect. The bottom line take-away from reading the report is that it is flawed and misleading. Here is why.

The report seeks to dismiss the idea that China's trade deficit has been growing more rapidly than the U.S. deficit with other countries, and to this end it reports that China's share of the overall deficit has remained fairly constant at around 20 percent for more than a decade. This is misleading. The proper measure of what has been happening is the ratio of the U.S.-China trade deficit relative to the U.S. deficit with other countries. That tells us how trade with China has been evolving compared to trade with everyone else. That ratio has been growing fast. In 1994 the U.S.-China deficit was 24.4 percent of the U.S. deficit with the rest of the world. In 2004 it was 33.1 percent of the deficit with everyone else. And when they are released, the 2005 numbers will show that it has increased again since the China deficit grew by 25.8 percent through November 2005, while the deficit with the rest of the world (including OPEC) grew by only 15 percent.

A second claim is that Chinese imports have merely displaced imports from other East Asian economies: "...the deterioration in the trade deficit with China has come at the expense of other East Asian exporters to the United States (p8)." The reason given is that this displacement reflects a profound shift in production patterns by Asian and other multinational firms operating in the region. The logic of this claim is economically unsupportable. Businesses do not relocate to China because they like moo-shu pork. They relocate because costs are lower, and those lower costs enable them to export more to the U.S. Absent those lower costs they would have exported less.

Moreover, the displacement hypothesis assumes that other East Asian economies have the economic slack to produce what China produces. This is ludicrous. Other East Asian economies are operating close to capacity, and there is no way they could step in and replace China's exports. That means China's exports are substantially an addition to the steadily rising stream of exports that other East Asian economies have still been able to produce.

The central claim of the report is that the ordinary American worker and household will be significantly better off as a result of trade with China. The claim is pushed using the artifact of the average household, which the report claims will receive "an increase of around $1,000 in real disposable income" per year by 2010 because of trade with China. But the average household is a statistical figment created by dividing total GDP by the total number of households. What really matters is what happens to real hourly wages and median household income – which is the income of a real world household situated in the middle of the income distribution. Here, the data for the last four years are clear. Real hourly wages have been essentially flat, and median household income actually fell from $46,058 in 2000 to $44,389 in 2004 – a decline of $1,669. The reason is that all productivity growth is going to profits, and none to wages. Chinese wage competition, China induced manufacturing job loss, and the persistent threat of off-shoring are part of the explanation.

Additionally, the report fails to address the question of sustainability. Right now the U.S. is trading away manufacturing jobs and its manufacturing sector in return for cheap consumption goods. This trade involves racking up massive trade deficits, the proceeds of which China invests significantly in Treasury bonds. Interest on these bonds must be paid, which means that part of every tax dollar paid by Americans will in future be paid to the Chinese government. More importantly, there is the question of what happens if this arrangement breaks down. In that event, what will be the cost to the U.S. economy and standard of living of a high dependence on imports combined with an atrophied manufacturing sector? The report provides no estimate of this scenario.

Lastly, there is no acknowledgement of the long-term national security issues that must be part of any assessment of the U.S. – China economic relationship. These issues concern the implications of dependence on Chinese supplies and transfer of high technology and manufacturing capacity to China, a country that may yet turn out to be a geo-political threat to the U.S. These issues are undoubtedly hard to cost but that does not make them less real. By ignoring them, the report implicitly zero costs them. That is unrealistic.

Posted on February 3, 2006 at thomaspalley.com.

ABANDONING AMERICA:
CORPORATE FOREIGN DIRECT INVESTMENT

March 13, 2007

In recent years outward foreign direct investment (FDI) by U.S. corporations to other countries has been increasing rapidly, while inward FDI by foreign corporations into the U.S. has been trending down. Since investment in the U.S. is critical for future economic prosperity, these patterns are troubling and provide evidence of how globalization and flawed policy are encouraging corporations to abandon America.

Inward FDI is usually good for countries, though there can be legitimate national security and strategic industry caveats. Such investment has foreign investors either building new facilities or taking large ownership stakes in existing businesses. Their willingness to build new facilities expands productive capacity and creates jobs, while making large investments in existing businesses usually signifies an intention to grow them. The net result is that inward FDI benefits countries, especially since foreign investors bear the cost of financing these investments.

The benefits of outward FDI are less clear-cut. On one hand, it can expand the global reach of companies, thereby potentially increasing exports, and it can also give companies access to profitable foreign market opportunities. On the other hand, outward FDI may simply displace domestic investment and employment, as when corporations create offshore production platforms whose only purpose is to export back to home markets. In this case, outward FDI can be problematic.

These characteristics suggest that policy should aim to encourage inward FDI and discourage outward FDI that hollows the domestic economy. Yet, the U.S. appears set on the exact opposite course, with inward FDI trending down while outward FDI has trended up.

Having peaked at 321 billion dollars in 2000, inward FDI fell to 64 billion dollars in 2003 and then recovered somewhat to 110 billion dollars in 2005. Meanwhile, U.S. outward FDI rose from 159 billion dollars in 2000 to 252 billion dollars in 2004. Whereas in 2000 the U.S. had net FDI inflow of 162 billion dollars, by 2004 this had transformed into net FDI outflow of 145 billion dollars.

The volume and pattern of FDI can be viewed as indicating the degree of confidence business feels about U.S. economic prospects. Part of the decline of inward FDI between 2000 and 2003 can be attributed to the impact of recession. However, the subsequent weak recovery of inward FDI accompanied by the acceleration of outward FDI suggests deeper problems.

One policy problem is the over-valued dollar that raises the relative cost of producing in America, thereby discouraging investment. A second is policies that give incentives to corporations to offshore production. The net effect is to undermine the relative competitiveness of the U.S. economy, thereby making it a less attractive place to invest, especially in manufacturing.

With regard to outward FDI, part of the increase is attributable to affirmative improvements in emerging market economy prospects, but part is due to bad policy. The over-valued dollar has encouraged U.S. business to shift productive investments from the U.S. to both developing and other developed economies, while the lack of global labor and environmental standards encourages shifts to developing economies where standards are lower or even absent.

Another factor is the preferential tax treatment of foreign profits of U.S. corporations, which encourages outward FDI that displaces domestic investment. This speaks to repealing that provision.

Inward FDI is discouraged by the over-valued dollar and the extent to which U.S. corporation tax is higher than foreign country corporation tax. This connects to the problem of tax competition between economic jurisdictions. Such competition distorts investment decisions, strips the public purse of revenues, and contributes to shifting the tax burden from capital on to worker incomes. This is a global problem, to which the U.S. is also contributing, albeit through tax competition between the fifty states. That suggests need for stricter multilateral agreements on tax competition and the U.S. should also act unilaterally to prevent tax competition between the states.

Given the decline in inward FDI the U.S. Commerce Department recently launched an initiative to promote such investment, promising to actively court foreign companies. The initiative is welcome since inward FDI is generally beneficial, but it is also incomplete and inadequate. Cheerleading cannot substitute for fundamental policy change, while the exclusive focus on inward FDI is like one-hand clapping and completely misses the problem of investment off-shoring by U.S. corporations.

Posted on March 13, 2007 on thomaspalley.com.

U.S.-CHINA TRADE: PAY NOW OR PAY MORE LATER

May 2, 2007

After several years of patient negotiation, the U.S. appears embarked on a harder stance in dealing with its China trade deficit. In Congress there is talk of veto-proof legislation addressing China's under-valuation of its currency, while the Bush Administration has imposed tariffs on coated paper products to offset Chinese subsidies. Behind this shift is a dawning recognition that China is unwilling to reduce its surplus, and that reduces the policy choice to one of "pay now or pay more later".

Today's international trading system is a liberal order in which open exchange works well when all participants are market economies. However, it is widely recognized that individual countries can strategically game the system for their benefit at the expense of others. That is why the system needs rules and a spirit of cooperation. The problem is China has been admitted into the system but it is unwilling to play by the rules, in letter or spirit.

This unwillingness reflects political realities within China. China is strongly nationalist and prone to equate negotiation with external pressure. It remains an authoritarian country in which extensive state economic intervention is normal, and it is also beset by political divisions between hard and soft-liners that limit its ability to deliver on its WTO commitments.

In retrospect the U.S. decision in 2000 to permanently open its markets to China seems poorly conceived. That decision was driven by manic optimism about globalization that pushed a biased benefit - cost calculus that ignored economic and political reality. The Clinton Administration naively argued that simply exposing China to market forces would transform it into a democratically, while U.S. multinationals lobbied heavily on China's behalf seeing it as a profitable offshore production location.

The net result is the U.S. is now stuck between a rock and a hard place. Either it must live with China's gaming of the system that slowly erodes U.S. economic foundations, or it must adopt a tougher policy stance that even risks a costly trade war.

The downside of tougher policy is a trade war, which could be very disruptive. The upside is that it could spur a speedy negotiated settlement. Chinese policymakers are realists and likely recognize that China has more to lose from a trade war because it needs access to U.S. markets for its manufacturing sector and to attract foreign direct investment. Moreover, China is vulnerable to losses on its large holdings of U.S. financial assets.

Even if a trade war cannot be avoided, the U.S. still stands to benefit from tough policy because it is better to fix the problem now rather than later. Delay is costly. Larger trade deficits mean greater dependence on Chinese imports, along with further erosion of the U.S. manufacturing sector's ability to replace those imports. Had the U.S. acted firmly five years ago, the costs would have been smaller and manufacturing healthier. Another five-year delay means further erosion of manufacturing and larger costs to any future trade war.

Inevitably, the new tougher stance has triggered accusations that the U.S. is engaging in protectionism. These accusations are based on faulty economics and fail to distinguish protectionism from legitimate economic self-defense.

Opponents claim that the trade deficit stems from lack of U.S. saving, not exchange rates. This argument misunderstands market economics. Reducing the trade deficit requires increasing exports and decreasing imports. That requires inducing foreigners to buy more U.S. made goods, and inducing Americans to "switch" their spending from imports to domestic made goods. Market economies accomplish this through changed relative prices. That calls for exchange rate adjustment that makes foreign goods more expensive for U.S. consumers and U.S. goods cheaper for foreign consumers.

The opposition to tough policy also comes wrapped in faulty economic history that blames protectionism and the Smoot-Hawley tariff for the Great Depression. Yet, the fact is Smoot-Hawley was passed in June 1930, after the Depression had already begun. Moreover, its economic effects were minor given the pre-existing high U.S. tariff structure of 34 percent and small U.S. engagement in trade (less than ten percent of GDP).

The reality is that the U.S. has delayed addressing the China trade imbalance problem for five years. That delay has harmed manufacturing, distorted the current economic expansion, and raised the costs of remedy. Further delay will do further injury and further raise the costs of future remedy. That is the inexorable logic of "pay now or pay more later".

Posted on May 6, 2007 at thomaspalley.com. Originally posted as "China costs keep piling up" on May 2, 2007 on TomPaine.com.

WHO'S AFRAID OF CHINA?

February 9, 2006

In the early 1980s the U.S. suffered record trade deficits and severe de-industrialization as a result of an overvalued dollar. Those problems were tackled by the 1985 Plaza accord - an agreement between the U.S. and its major trading partners - which depreciated the dollar, reduced the trade deficit, and helped keep the economic expansion going.

Today, there is an urgent need for another exchange rate accord, but the changed composition of U.S. trade means it must involve new partners - particularly China. The problem is that China has refused to cooperate, while many U.S. policymakers are afraid of taking action to compel co-operation. They believe that either there is nothing the U.S. can do or that the costs of action outweigh the benefits. They are wrong on both counts.

The trade deficit matters because it drains spending from the economy. This has contributed to manufacturing decline, and it has also made for a weak and unbalanced economic expansion. Instead of creating investments and jobs at home, debt-financed spending leaks offshore leaving the U.S. financially burdened without any lasting capacity gains.

East Asia accounts for forty-five percent of the trade deficit, and China alone accounts for over twenty-five percent. Not only is the deficit with China the largest with any major industrial country, it is also the most unbalanced and fastest growing. Indeed, today's deficit with China substantially exceeds the peak total deficit of the 1980s. Yet unlike our trading partners back then, China refuses to recognize the problem. And fearing loss of international competitiveness to China, other East Asian economies also resist exchange rate adjustment.

China's refusal to adjust threatens the U.S.'s economic future. Near-term, there is a danger of a debt-driven recession; longer-term, the U.S. will have to compete globally with an atrophied industrial base. China is also placing unfair adjustment burdens on those that do play by the rules, including emerging Eastern Europe and Latin America. The global economic system is based on cooperation, but China has refused to adjust despite compelling evidence of gross imbalances. Put bluntly, China has become the mercantilist fox in the liberalized international trading coop.

One cost to the U.S. of an economic dispute with China stems from reliance on Chinese imports. These are predominantly consumer goods, and consumer price inflation would rise, lowering living standards. Big box discount stores like Wal-Mart that source from China, would be hurt and would scream. So would multi-nationals who produce in China. But global production is highly mobile and

117

can be shifted to other countries, which would quickly diminish costs to consumers.

A second concern is that China will sell its massive holdings of U.S. Treasury bonds, spiking interest rates. However, this can be avoided by having the Federal Reserve step in and buy the bonds, which the Fed can do because it has unlimited capacity to create money. The Treasury can also place a temporary hold on disruptive sales. Though there would surely be some financial turmoil, it can be handled by coordinated action involving the Federal Reserve and Wall Street as was done with the 1998 collapse of the hedge fund, Long Term Capital Management. And if China decides to repatriate its bond sale proceeds, that will lower the exchange rate, which is the name of the game.

For China, the costs of a dispute are much higher. One third of Chinese exports go to the U.S., whereas only four percent of U.S. exports go to China. Restricting U.S. market access for even a brief period would shut China's factories, causing massive unemployment. And massive unemployment could quickly trigger civil unrest, something China's Communist authorities deeply fear given their fragile control.

Moreover, restricting U.S. market access would also cause foreign direct investment in China to dry up. Such investment is key to China's growth strategy, providing jobs, manufacturing capacity, and technology transfer. Nor would it likely return to pre-dispute levels, since China's reputation for reliability would have been dented, making companies fearful of future repeat interruptions.

Make no mistake, trade wars are costly for all involved, and it is far better to resolve disputes by negotiation. But that said, a U.S. – China trade war would have far greater costs and consequences for China than for the United States. This is of critical significance. China's policymakers are rational and can do the math. It means they will quickly seek a negotiated settlement if confronted by a credibly exercised U.S. threat of a trade war that avoids national pride entanglements. Congressional trade legislation that sanctions China for its exchange rate manipulation by imposing tariffs is the perfect vehicle for this. Legislation along these lines has been proposed by Sens. Schumer and Gramm, and by Reps. Hunter and Ryan.

Today's cost-benefit equation decisively favors the U.S., but that balance is shifting. The U.S. is losing manufacturing capacity, and becoming more dependent on Chinese imports. In 2005, the U.S. trade deficit with China grew twenty-five percent. Meanwhile, China's manufacturing capacity and sophistication are increasing. Time is therefore on China's side.

Originally posted on February 9, 2006 on TomPaine.com. This version was posted on February 16, 2007 at thomaspalley.com.

CHINA'S EMPTY THREAT

September 3, 2007

The United States Congress is currently contemplating critical legislation aimed at remedying the huge U.S. - China trade deficit. China and businesses that benefit from Chinese imports oppose this legislation, and to discourage action China has hinted at retaliation – including possibly selling its U.S. Treasury bond holdings. That threat has prompted some to argue against legislative action on grounds that risks of a trade war are too large and costly. Such thinking is mistaken. The reality is China's threats are empty, whereas its currency manipulation is wreaking significant real damage on the U.S. economy.

The Ryan – Hunter bill (H.R. 1498), now before the Congress, proposes treating currency manipulation as a form of illegal subsidy that would be subject to countervailing duties. In this fashion Ryan – Hunter aims to offset China's under-valued currency and circumvent China's refusal to meaningfully revalue its exchange rate.

There is widespread agreement that China's currency is under-valued and harming the U.S. economy. This harm works through the trade deficit and imports that displace spending on domestically produced goods, thereby injuring manufacturers. Additionally, the under-valued currency displaces investment by encouraging business to invest in China rather than the United States. The challenge for the U.S. is how to respond in light of China's exchange rate intransigence.

Through its persistent trade surpluses China has accumulated over 400 billion dollars of Treasury securities and it is now the second largest foreign holder (after Japan) of government bonds. The fear is that China may retaliate against the U.S. by selling bonds, causing the price of treasuries to fall and interest rates to rise. That in turn could trigger financial disruption, which in conjunction with higher rates could topple the economy into recession.

Such reasoning is deeply flawed for several reasons. First, China has little incentive to engage in such tactics. If it starts selling bonds that will drive prices down, causing large capital losses on its holdings. More importantly, China has no interest in playing Russian roulette with the U.S. economy as that threatens its own economy. The reason China refuses to revalue its exchange rate is because it wants to retain a competitive advantage enabling it to sell in U.S. markets. Causing a U.S. recession would destroy the very market in which it wants to sell. Worse than that, a U.S. recession could trigger a global recession, thereby undermining markets in Europe and elsewhere that China also relies on.

Second, the Federal Reserve can always intervene to mitigate the effect of any Chinese selling. Thus, were China to irrationally start selling, the Fed could step in and buy those bonds in so-called "sterilizing operations". China would then be left holding lower-yielding bank deposits supplied by the Fed, and the Fed would hold the bonds sold by China. This would prevent interest rates from spiking and U.S. taxpayers would actually benefit by saving the interest that would have been paid to China.

Thereafter, China could decide to sell its bank deposits and buy foreign currency. If it were to try and buy renminbi and repatriate its dollar holdings that would quickly cause China's exchange rate to rise, which is exactly what U.S. policymakers desire. Alternatively, China could buy yen and euro, which would cause the dollar to depreciate against these currencies. That too would benefit the U.S., especially if the yen were to appreciate, as this would make U.S. producers more competitive versus European and Japanese companies.

Appreciation of the euro and the yen would then shift America's exchange rate dispute with China to Europe and Japan. This would expose China to risk of retaliatory action from these countries, which are much more administratively aggressive in protecting their markets than is the U.S. As a result, China could find itself at loggerheads with all its major customers (the U.S., Japan, and the European Union), suggesting it will not go this route.

Meanwhile, passage of Ryan – Hunter would enable U.S. manufacturers to seek countervailing duties offsetting the subsidy implicit in China's currency manipulation. That would raise Chinese product prices in the U.S. and reduce Chinese imports, yet the benefit of higher prices would go to the U.S. government rather than Chinese manufacturers. That again makes no sense for China, suggesting that Chinese policymakers would prefer exchange rate revaluation to tariffs. That way China at least gets the benefit of higher prices.

In sum, the U.S. and China are currently engaged in a policy struggle that resembles the game of "chicken". Policy analysis can help disentangle the likely outcome of such a game by examining the credibility of each country's postures. Such analysis shows China's threats are empty. China relies on export-led growth to provide demand for its products and attract foreign direct investment. That means it cannot afford to destabilize the U.S. economy or the global economy. And if it irrationally tries to do so, the Federal Reserve has the means to neutralize its actions.

Originally posted on September 3, 2007 in The Guardian, Comment Is Free. This version posted on September 4, 2007 at thomaspalley.com.

DEATH BY RENMINBI

November 9, 2009

Over the last several weeks, the dollar's depreciation against the euro and yen has grabbed global attention. In a normal world, the dollar's weakening would be welcome, as it would help the United States come to grips with its unsustainable trade deficit. But, in a world where China links its currency to the dollar at an under-valued parity, the dollar's depreciation risks major global economic damage that will further complicate recovery from the current worldwide recession.

A realignment of the dollar is long overdue. Its overvaluation began with the Mexican peso crisis of 1994, and was officially enshrined by the "strong dollar" policy adopted after the East Asian financial crisis of 1997. That policy produced short-term consumption gains for America, which explains why it was popular with American politicians, but it has inflicted major long-term damage on the U.S. economy and contributed to the current crisis.

The over-valued dollar caused the U.S. economy to hemorrhage spending on imports, jobs via off-shoring, and investment to countries with under-valued currencies. In today's era of globalization, marked by flexible and mobile production networks, exchange rates affect more than exports and imports. They also affect the location of production and investment.

China has been a major beneficiary of America's strong-dollar policy, to which it wedded its own "weak renminbi" policy. As a result, China's trade surplus with the U.S. rose from $83 billion in 2001 to $258 billion in 2007, just before the recession. So far in 2009, China's surplus has accounted for 75% of the total U.S. non-oil-goods trade deficit. The under-valued renminbi has also made China a major recipient of foreign direct investment, even leading the world in 2002 – a staggering achievement for a developing country.

The scale of recent U.S. trade deficits was always unsustainable, and the dollar has therefore fallen against the yen, euro, Brazilian real, and Australian and Canadian dollars. But China retains its under-valued exchange rate policy, so that the renminbi has appreciated relatively less against the dollar. When combined with China's rapid growth in manufacturing capacity, this pattern promises to create a new round of global imbalances.

China's policy creates adversarial currency competition with the rest of the world. By maintaining an undervalued currency, China is preventing the U.S. from reducing its bilateral trade deficit. Furthermore, the problem is not only America's. China's currency policy gives it a competitive advantage relative to other countries, allowing it to displace their exports to the U.S.

Worse still, other countries whose currencies have appreciated against the renminbi can look forward to a Chinese import invasion. China's currency policy means that dollar depreciation, rather than improving America's trade balance and stanching its leakage of jobs and investment, may inadvertently spread these problems to the rest of the world. In effect, China is fostering new imbalances at a time when countries are struggling with the demand shortfall caused by the financial crisis.

The dollar is part of an exchange-rate Rubik's cube. With China retaining its under-valued currency policy, dollar depreciation can aggravate global deflationary forces. Yet a mix of political factors has led to stunning refusal by policymakers to confront China.

On the U.S. side, a lingering Cold War mentality, combined with the presumption of U.S. economic superiority, has meant that economic issues are still deemed subservient to geo-political concerns. That explains the neglect of U.S.-China economic relations, a neglect that is now dangerous to the U.S., given its weakened economic condition.

With regard to the rest of the world, many find it easy to blame the U.S., often owing to resentment at its perceived arrogance. Moreover, there is an old mentality among Southern countries that they can do no wrong in their relationships with the North, and that they should exhibit solidarity with each other regarding those relationships.

Finally, all countries likely have been shortsighted, imagining that silence will gain them commercial favors from China. But that silence merely allows China to exploit the community of nations.

The world economy has paid dearly for complicity with and silence about the economic policies of the last 15 years, which have culminated in the deepest and most dangerous recession since the 1930's. It will pay still more if policymakers remain passive about China's destructive currency policy.

Distributed by Project Syndicate on October 30, 2009. Also posted at thomaspalley.com on November 9, 2009.

TRIANGULAR TROUBLE:
THE EURO, THE DOLLAR AND THE RENMINBI

October 14, 2007

For the last several years the euro has been appreciating steadily against the U.S. dollar. Given the Chinese renminbi and other East Asian currencies are pegged to the dollar that means the euro has been appreciating steadily against all. This spells trouble for Euroland, and it suggests European policymakers should join with the U.S. to address the global problem of under-valued currencies.

The euro has now appreciated approximately seventy percent relative to its historic low against the dollar, set on October 26, 2000. This appreciation has been economically justified given Europe's large trade surplus with the United States. That surplus peaked in 2005 and is now gradually coming down as the Euro appreciates, which is the exactly how a market based global economy is supposed to correct international financial imbalances.

Some in Europe are beginning to raise red flags regarding this appreciation, but the reality is it is still within the bounds of reasonableness. Though the euro has appreciated seventy percent against its historic low, it has only appreciated twenty percent relative to its January 1999 introductory parity.

That said, European concerns about exchange rates are justified, but the focus should be East Asia's currencies, not the dollar. The key player is China, which has the largest surplus. Additionally, other East Asian countries are rationally reluctant to adjust their currencies absent a Chinese revaluation, as they fear losing competitiveness. This means China's refusal to significantly revalue its currency against the dollar is forcing a lop-sided adjustment process that places the burden of rebalancing the U.S. trade deficit exclusively on Europe. That is imposing a deflationary burden on Europe that could easily undermine the European economy.

Europe is now experiencing double trouble as its surplus with the U.S. begins to fall while its deficit with China is large and growing. Between 2002 and 2006 the European Union's deficit with China rose from 54 billion euros to 128 billion euros. At current exchange rates the 2006 deficit was 179 billion dollars, and the EU Chamber of Commerce expects that deficit to hit 260 billion dollars in 2007.

In a sense, Europe now finds itself involuntarily on the same path that the U.S. voluntarily locked itself into in the late 1990s. That path is characterized by rising trade deficits, weakened manufacturing investment spending, and loss of manufacturing jobs.

The renminbi's under-valuation stands to lower European exports and increase imports from China as spending is redirected from European produced goods to cheaper Chinese goods. The resulting increased trade deficit will directly cost jobs, and reduced demand and profitability of European manufacturing companies will reduce investment spending. Furthermore, European manufacturers will have an incentive to close plants and shift production and new investment to China, just as happened in the U.S.

These effects are likely to be especially disruptive from a regional perspective. Whereas Germany's high value-added capital goods exporters may still be able to prosper, the economies of Italy, Spain, and other Mediterranean countries stand to be badly impacted. Additionally, manufacturing in Central Europe's new member states stands to be severely affected, making their integration into the European economy more difficult.

The bottom line is that by all reasonable standards China's currency is under-valued against both the dollar and the euro. China is running huge and growing trade surpluses with both Europe and the U.S.; it has a growing global trade surplus; and on top of that it has an even larger current account surplus since its trade surplus is supplemented by massive foreign direct investment inflows.

These conditions suggest Europe and the U.S. have a common interest in closely cooperating to pressure China to adjust its currency. Yet, so far, that has not happened. One reason is that until recently the euro was under-valued so that Europe had no grounds for or interest in pressuring China to revalue. A second reason is that Europe and the U.S. are in competition for sales to China and each may fear antagonizing the Chinese government. This has triangulated Europe and the U.S. to their disadvantage and to the benefit of China. The implication is that fixing the structural problem of triangulation and remedying the failure to cooperate on the China currency question should be urgent policy priorities for both sides of the North Atlantic partnership.

Originally posted on October 14, 2007 in The Guardian, Comment Is Free. This version posted on October 15, 2007 at thomaspalley.com.

GLOBAL IMPLICATIONS OF CHINA'S
ANTI-INFLATION POLICY

September 19, 2007

China's government recently announced inflation hit a ten-year high of 6.5 percent in August. This increase in inflation is directly related to global trade imbalances, yet China is trying to control inflation without addressing that problem. That carries two consequences. First, it is doubtful this strategy can work, which likely augurs rising Chinese inflation. Second, the strategy aims to shift the onus of global trade adjustment on the U.S., which may come back to haunt China and the global economy.

China's current inflation is a textbook case of prolonged under-valuation of a fixed exchange rate in tandem with export-led growth. As such, significant exchange rate revaluation should be a central element of its anti-inflation policy. However, instead of making such an adjustment, China's authorities are hoping to control inflation by exclusive reliance on tighter domestic monetary policy. It is doubtful this strategy can succeed because it leaves intact the inflationary impulse from China's trade surplus and under-valued exchange rate.

One important contributing factor in China's inflation is the rise in global commodity prices, including oil and base metals, which are now feeding through into prices. Food prices are also on the rise owing to increased global prices for wheat and corn. Furthermore, China has been hit by a virulent outbreak of swine flu that has decimated its hog population, driving up the price of pork, which is China's favored meat.

In coastal areas, which have been the hub of China's export-led growth, wages have started rising in response to rising living costs and in response to the gradual elimination of extreme surplus labor conditions.

Most importantly, China is beset by significant asset price inflation that borders on an asset price bubble. This asset price inflation is the product of massive expansion of the money supply caused by China's trade surplus and foreign investment inflows. Dollars earned by Chinese exporters have flowed back to China and been converted into local money by the central bank, which has bought them at the fixed exchange rate to prevent appreciation. Holders of these money balances have then bought stocks and real estate to gain higher returns and to protect against potential inflation. This has driven up real estate prices, triggering a massive construction boom that has in turn caused inflation.

The implication is clear. China is suffering from imported inflation caused by higher global commodity prices, domestic demand inflation caused by excess demand in export industries, and asset price inflation due to an increased money supply caused by China's trade surplus.

125

The under-valued exchange rate is a key culprit since it contributes to excess demand in export sectors and it is also drives money supply increase via the trade surplus – which has hit new record highs in 2007. That suggests significant exchange rate revaluation should be a central component of China's anti-inflation strategy. Moreover, revaluation would also diminish the impact of global commodity price inflation because commodities are priced in dollars so that a revaluation lowers their domestic price in renminbi.

Instead, China has chosen to rely exclusively on monetary tightening, raising interest rates and reserve requirements on bank deposits. This strategy is unlikely to work. First, there is already significant asset inflation and extensive debt-financed speculative investment, which means the monetary authorities are constrained from sufficiently meaningful tightening for fear of triggering a financial collapse.

Second, raising reserve requirements on bank deposits lowers the return on deposits and makes them less attractive. That provides an incentive for depositors to spend their money or invest elsewhere, which spurs more inflation.

Third, and most importantly, continuation of China's under-valued exchange rate means continuing trade surpluses and large foreign direct investment inflows, which means further monetary expansion in China.

Putting the pieces together, the picture is one of rising Chinese inflation, and with that comes the risk of inflation-triggered social and political problems. In this regard it is worth recalling that the Tiananmen Square disturbances of May 1989 were in part caused by industrial worker unrest over erosion of living standards by inflation.

As for the global economy, China's anti-inflation policy and continued refusal to adjust its exchange rate places the burden of trade imbalance adjustment squarely on the U.S. This adjustment will likely happen via recession and there are signs that process may already be underway. This is a sub-optimal approach that could potentially injure all.

Originally posted September 19, 2007 as "Inflation, Chinese Style" on The Guardian, Comment is Free and on thomaspalley.com.

INVESTING IN CHINA: FOOL'S GOLD?

January 15, 2008

Americans tend to disregard history. Henry Ford declared bluntly, "History is bunk," while Gore Vidal calls the U.S. "the United States of Amnesia." Usually, this disregard has few consequences, but sometimes not. That may be so with investing in China, where history suggests profits will be far below expectations, possibly making those investments fool's gold.

China's history is completely different from that of the United States and it has left deep imprints on China's politics. Therein lies the trap for investors and policymakers who ignore history and wishfully think market forces will inevitably make China just like the United States.

One critical factor is China's attitude to foreigners. That attitude is captured by the Great Wall of China, which provides a metaphor for China's long history of isolationism and xenophobia. A second critical factor is the legacy of China's humiliating defeats in the unjust 19th century opium wars with Great Britain. At the time, Britain was importing large amounts of tea and silks from China, and demanded the right to sell Indian opium in exchange. As the opium trade grew, not only did it cause massive addiction, it also caused a damaging monetary outflow of silver from China. That prompted China to stop the trade, and Britain then turned to military force to keep China's market open.

This historical experience has made China nationalistic and profoundly averse to foreign exploitation, which is why history is so relevant for investing in China. As a result, China will never allow itself to be exploited by foreigners. For investors, the trouble is that China views making profits from the Chinese market as a form of exploitation.

When foreign investments are for exports, China has viewed the profits as being earned abroad. Difficulties only arise when the goal is production for the domestic market. This explains why profitability on such investments has historically been so low, and why so-many joint-venture investments with Chinese partners have failed. It also helps explain China's persistent refusal to enforce foreign owned patents and copyrights that apply to medicines, movies, and music.

The lesson is that companies are likely to be disappointed regarding hopes of profiting from China's massive domestic market.

That has special relevance for American banks and insurance companies. China will allow these companies to invest and modernize its financial services infrastructure, but the profit pay-off is questionable. The same holds for auto companies, which China will allow to transfer technology and build modern plants. As long as the production is for export, those plants will be allowed to earn large profits. But once they start selling in the Chinese market, profits will likely shrivel under burdensome restrictions and theft of technology, ideas, and designs.

Stock market investors face a different case of fool's gold, with stock prices being artificially inflated by China's under-valued exchange rate and capital controls. That makes prices vulnerable to changes of policy.

The under-valued exchange rate has contributed to China's massive trade surpluses, and China has had to buy dollars and sell yuan to prevent its exchange rate appreciating. That has expanded China's money supply, and Chinese investors have bought stocks to earn higher returns and protect against inflation, which has driven up stock prices. Capital controls have also played a critical role by limiting investments available to Chinese citizens. Since money cannot leave the country, they have been forced to buy local stocks. Hence, the explosive appreciation of the Shanghai stock market, which has spilled into the Hong Kong market.

China's government has profited from this bubble, as it has been able to sell state-owned companies at high prices. Wall Street has also bought into the bubble, telling Main Street investors that the appreciation of Chinese stocks reflects China's growth prospects rather than its artificial market. However, come the day that China allows external investment by Chinese citizens, Chinese stock prices are likely to suffer as local investors move to diversify outside of China. That potentially makes long-term investing in China's stock market another case of fool's gold.

The bottom line is that when it comes to China, investors would be wise to remember all that glistens is not gold.

Posted on January 15, 2008 at thomaspalley.com. Also posted on Asia Times Online on January 16, 2008.

VIII THE EURO ZONE CRISIS: NEOLIBERALS RUN AMOK

Euroland is being crucified upon its own cross of gold

♦

Europe's debt crisis and Keynes' green cheese solution

♦

Euro bonds are not enough:
Eurozone countries need a government banker

♦

The euro lacks a government banker, not a lender of last resort

EUROLAND IS BEING CRUCIFIED UPON ITS OWN CROSS OF GOLD

February 10, 2010

The last quarter of the 19th century witnessed a period of sustained global deflation. In the 1896 U.S. presidential election, William Jennings Bryan famously attacked the gold standard as the cause of deflation, declaring "You shall not press upon the brow of labor this crown of thorns. You shall not crucify mankind upon a cross of gold."

Today, Euroland is being crucified upon its own cross of gold that is the institutional arrangements behind the euro. Those arrangements have distorted the monetary – fiscal balance, creating deflationary central bank dominance. That balance needs correction and failure to do so could even risk the viability of the euro in its current form.

The euro was introduced in 1999, the high-water mark of neoliberal economics. As such, its institutional design embeds neoliberal monetary theory which in many regards rests on the same economic principles as the gold standard. These principles are that fiscal policy is ineffective; inflation is caused exclusively by money supply growth; and the real economy quickly and automatically returns to full employment in response to negative shocks.

Principles discredited

All three principles have been fundamentally discredited by the current recession. Around the world, countries have turned to fiscal policy to offset the collapse of private sector spending, and the recession would have been far deeper absent that fiscal response. Money supplies have risen dramatically almost everywhere without matching increases in inflation, showing that the money – inflation link is highly contingent upon economic factors such as unemployment, capacity utilization, commodity prices, and business expectations of profits. Finally, rather than rebounding to full employment, the global economy looks set for high unemployment that will last years. This possibility was Keynes' message in his 1936 *General Theory*.

Owing to its neoliberal monetary arrangements Euroland has run smack into these economic realities. The European monetary union (EMU) establishes central bank dominance through an independent central bank that is prohibited from providing financial assistance to member country governments. Thus, whereas the U.S. and UK have been able to finance their fiscal and financial market rescue plans with assistance from the Federal Reserve and Bank of England respectively, euro zone governments have received no equivalent assistance. Instead, they have had to fend for themselves in private capital markets, which has raised the costs of policy and dissuaded more aggressive action.

Not only do these monetary arrangements contribute to sub-optimal fiscal policy, they are also aggravating fissures within Euroland. The periphery economies of Greece, Italy, Portugal, and Spain, suffer from high public debt, large budget deficits, high unemployment, and lack of competitiveness. Capital markets are therefore driving up periphery country bond rates and aggravating their financial distress. Meanwhile, these economies no longer have their own exchange rate or interest rate to restore full employment and financial balance. Consequently, their sole internal adjustment mechanism is deflation, which is counter-productive in a situation of high indebtedness.

Embrace expansion

Given this, the stronger European economies must embrace expansion and act as an economic locomotive for the periphery economies. But instead, the European monetary system imposes a deflationary bias by restricting fiscal space, while Germany has shown persistent recalcitrance toward expansionary policies and exports deflationary pressures.

Part of escaping this trap requires rebalancing monetary – fiscal relations and increasing access to money-financed fiscal policy. To this end the European Central Bank (ECB) should establish annual country loan quotas set according to each country's economic size and output gap, making them a form of automatic stabilizer. This would create a mechanism for countries to monetize part of their budget deficits. In the current environment it would provide a flow of low cost deficit financing that would facilitate periphery country rebalancing, while also providing an expansionary impulse in Europe's core economies.

Additionally, the ECB should establish emergency stand-by country loan facilities that would be governed by pre-determined policy conditionality. In effect, the ECB would act as an analogue International Monetary Fund (IMF) for euro member countries.

The Greek crisis

This has direct relevance for Greece's current financial crisis. Having Greece borrow from private capital markets at exorbitant interest rates only compounds Greece's financial burdens. Alternatively, having the IMF bail-out a euro-member country will damage the euro's standing as a reserve currency and it too makes no sense. Greece needs euros to refinance its debt and the ECB is the logical source given it is the ultimate creator of euros.

Lastly, to counter potential inflationary consequences, the ECB could be given discretion regarding distribution of seignorage dividends resulting from issue of currency and bank reserves.

Monetary reform alone will not bring prosperity to Euroland. That will also require breaking with the neoliberal approach to labor markets and macroeconomic policy. However, monetary reform is a necessary ingredient and absent such reform Euroland faces stagnation and protracted high unemployment. Moreover, some financially weaker member countries may be forced to exit the euro because of financial market pressures or domestic political discontent. Either way, this could have potentially devastating global economic consequences, which means all countries have an interest in EMU reform.

Posted in the FT Economists' Forum, February 10, 2010. Also posted at thomaspalley.com on March 18, 2010.

EUROPE'S DEBT CRISIS AND KEYNES'
GREEN CHEESE SOLUTION

May 23, 2010

The great German physicist Max Planck remarked that "Science advances one funeral at a time." The situation is worse in economics which is subject to regress, as happened when the valuable but imperfect insights of Keynesianism were supplanted by the ideological blinkers of neoliberalism.

The effects of this regress have again been on display in the confused discussions and policy responses to Europe's sovereign debt crisis. The fact is countries who borrow in their own currency and control their money supply will never default because they can always issue the money needed to repay their debts.

For such countries, central banks should respond to speculative debt crises with "bear squeeze" tactics that have them buy existing debt. In this fashion, countries can buy back debt below par value, effectively repaying it on the cheap. It is what the European Central Bank should have been doing on behalf of its member countries.

Not only does a bear squeeze assist debt reduction, it also punishes speculators and lowers interest rates, enabling countries to refinance on favorable terms. In a sense, this is what the Bank of England and the Federal Reserve have been doing on behalf of their respective governments by buying Gilts and Treasuries. Though such policy does increase the money supply, this is desirable at a time of massive demand shortage and excess capacity when inflation is a distant danger.

The eurozone has cheated itself of these benefits because of the neoliberal design of the European Central Bank. That design ignores the fact that having central banks act as the government's banker and help manage the national debt was one of the original reasons for the establishment of central banks. This is no accident as neoliberalism intentionally aimed to sever the fiscal – monetary policy link, but in doing so it discarded an essential tool of macroeconomic management.

The most damaging aspect of the crisis is the global boost it has given to the arguments of those advocating fiscal austerity. That is a cure which will almost certainly kill the patient by causing deep recession that lowers tax revenues and aggravates budget difficulties, while also causing bankruptcies that threaten an already weakened banking sector.

It is true that governments cannot limitlessly increase debt and the money supply without cost. If such policies were continued, once the economy was back to normal there would eventually be a price to pay in the form of higher inflation and reduced confidence in money as a store of value. That means there is need to

136

design policies and institutional arrangements that guard against such an outcome. But that is a wholly different proposition from saying governments and central banks should not use their powers to create money to address problems of excessive debt, speculation, financial panic and deep recession.

Central banks were slow to adopt quantitative easing to address the run on the financial sector in 2008 when money markets froze and banks could not refinance. That cost the global economy dearly. Now, the mistake is being repeated in Europe with the slow embrace of quantitative easing to address the run on public debt.

Europe, and perhaps the global economy, again confronts the possibility of a run for liquidity. In such circumstances there is only one thing for central banks to do: supply it. Keynes wrote of this in his masterful *General Theory*:

"Unemployment develops, that is to say, because people want the moon; -- men cannot be employed when the object of desire (i.e. money) is something which cannot be produced and the demand for which cannot be readily choked off. There is no remedy but to persuade the public that green cheese is practically the same thing and to have a green cheese factory (i.e. a central bank) under public control."

Yet, policy continues to respond with too little, too late, and then goes on to compound the damage with inappropriately timed austerity and doubling-down on policies of wage suppression that have already wrought such havoc.

The root problem is the dominance of flawed neoliberal economic thinking. This problem is particularly acute in the European Central Bank and European finance ministries which are dominated by economists trained in Chicago School neoliberal macroeconomics. Ironically, social democratic Europe has been much more virulently infected by this strain of thinking than the U.S. where politicians' pragmatism has moderated economists' extremism.

The Great Recession may have lowered economists' public standing but it has not yet changed their thinking or swept away the top policy appointees who have failed so disastrously. When it comes to economics, Max Planck was too optimistic about scientific progress.

Posted in the FT Economists' Forum on May 23, 2010. Also posted at thomaspalley.com on May 26, 2010.

EURO BONDS ARE NOT ENOUGH: EUROZONE COUNTRIES NEED A GOVERNMENT BANKER

August 31, 2011

The eurozone's public finance crisis continues to fester, reflecting both political and intellectual failure. The intellectual failure is the crisis has been interpreted exclusively as a debt crisis when it is also a central bank design crisis resulting from the euro's flawed architecture. The flaw is the inability of eurozone governments to harness the central bank's power to assist government finances. This systemic weakness explains why U.S. and U.K. government bonds are weathering the storm, whereas Spain confronts default rumors despite having roughly similar debt and deficit profiles.

The euro solved the problem of exchange rate speculation by creating a single currency but in doing so made countries vulnerable to bond market speculation. That is because European Central Bank (ECB) support buying of member country bonds is prohibited under the "no bail-out" provision. This prohibition is appropriate as buying one country's bonds would subsidize it relative to others. However, it means country governments lack access to central bank help to ward off speculative bond market attacks; to finance budget deficits; and to conduct quantitative easing (QE) programs of the sort conducted by the Federal Reserve and Bank of England.

One proposal to address the crisis is the idea of a "blue bond". Countries would have the right to issue blue bonds up to sixty percent of their GDP that would be guaranteed collectively by euro member countries. This would significantly lower interest rates charged to troubled countries, helping them attain solvency. In effect, financially strong countries would *de facto* lend their creditworthiness to weak countries.

The blue bond proposal would undoubtedly help solve the current crisis. However, there are two problems. First, it relies on an implicit transfer from the strong who take on a guarantee liability but get nothing in return. That is a political non-starter. Second, it does not solve the structural problem of lack of a government banker. That leaves eurozone governments vulnerable to future crises, and it also maintains persistent market pressure on government finances that will ultimately destroy Europe's social democratic project.

A second proposal is a "euro bond". The ECB would issue euro bonds and countries could elect to have the ECB use the proceeds to buy their existing debt up to sixty percent of their GDP. Individual countries would then be responsible for their share of the interest on euro bonds. This proposal would also help solve the current crisis but it too has problems. First, it would violate the "no bail-out" clause because all countries would pay the same interest rate on euro bonds but the ECB would be responsible for the higher interest rate on debt it purchased.

Second, perversely, higher income countries could transfer relatively more debt under the sixty percent of GDP rule. Third, and most importantly, the scheme fails to address the government banker problem.

I have advanced a third proposal that solves both the debt crisis and government banker problems. Stage one would have eurozone countries establish a European Public Finance Authority (EPFA) that would be governed by member countries, with votes allocated on a per capita basis. EPFA would then issue bonds that the ECB can buy and sell through standard open-market operations. These bonds would be collectively guaranteed and countries would cover EPFA's interest on a per capita basis. Bond proceeds would be used to buy existing country debt, again on a per capita basis. Countries with low levels of existing debt (like debt-free Luxembourg) would simply receive their share of EPFA proceeds as cash and they could buy EPFA bonds to cover their EPFA interest obligation. This debt swap would solve the debt crisis; create conditions for the ECB to engage in open-market operations to manage government bond interest rates; and create conditions for QE policies.

Stage two would have EPFA annually issuing new bonds to help finance government budget deficits. The amount issued would be democratically decided by EPFA's governing council, presumably acting on instructions from national governments. New issue proceeds would be deposited with governments to spend as they wish. Those wishing to run surpluses could retire debt or create a sovereign wealth fund. Three features are important. First, EPFA would never spend money and all spending would be determined by governments. Second, the ECB could assist budget financing by managing bond interest rates just as the Federal Reserve and Bank of England do. Third, the eurozone would have a democratic financial union but no fiscal transfer union.

The critical feature is EPFA bonds have no taint of "national identity", enabling the ECB to trade them without violating its "no bail-out" clause. Moreover, there are no financial transfers between countries and the per capita rule means all countries are treated equally.

The EPFA proposal solves both the debt crisis and government banker problem, and it does so without imposing unfunded obligations or unilateral transfers on any country. It therefore meets all German objections. Moreover, the EPFA proposal creates the financial space for eurozone countries to grow and continue with their social democratic projects should voters choose. This makes it more democratic than existing arrangements which impose financial constraints that restrict space for democratically determined social and economic policy.

Posted in the FT Economists' Forum on August 31, 2011. Also posted at thomaspalley.com on September 6, 2011.

THE EURO LACKS A GOVERNMENT BANKER, NOT A LENDER OF LAST RESORT

December 9, 2011

In his novel, *The Jungle*, the American muckraking author Upton Sinclair wrote about the horrendous work and sanitary conditions in the Chicago meat packing industry of the early 20th century. It is sometimes said Sinclair aimed for the heart but hit the stomach. That is because he aimed for progressive social and economic change but instead prompted the founding of the Food and Drug Administration.

The same problem of aiming for the heart and hitting the stomach confounds current discussions of the euro zone's problems. What the euro lacks a government banker, not a lender of last resort as is widely claimed.

The euro has a lender of last resort in the European Central Bank (ECB) which has dutifully performed that function. Lenders of last resort provide liquidity in financial panics, which is exactly what the ECB did in the financial crisis of 2008-09 and has continued doing via its Lombard lending facility. According to Bagehot's rule, lenders of last resort should lend without limit, to solvent firms, against good collateral – though Bagehot also recommended lending at high rates whereas today's practice is (sensibly) to lend at low rates.

The euro lacks a government banker, like the Federal Reserve or Bank of England, which helps finance budget deficits and keeps rates low on government debt. This explains why the U.S. and U.K. can borrow at low rates and remain solvent, whereas Spain, which has a roughly similar deficit and debt profile, is under speculative attack.

The lack of a government banker reflects the euro's neoliberal birthmark. Neoliberalism aims to diminish the role of the state and enhance the power of the market, and this goal is reflected in neoliberal monetary theory which guided the euro's design. The theory argues central banks should control inflation, but there should be complete separation between the central bank and government finances.

By adopting this theory, the euro's architects intentionally changed the monetary/fiscal balance. Whereas previous national monetary systems ensured "fiscal dominance" as central banks served governments, the euro instituted "central bank dominance" by stripping governments of access to central bank help managing public finances. This was done by creating a "detached" central bank that is prohibited from buying government debt. This is fundamentally different from an "independent" central bank which distances its decision making from government, but is allowed to purchase government debt. The Federal Reserve and the Bank of England are both independent but they are not detached. The ECB is detached by design.

The consequences are enormous. Prior national banking systems made governments masters of the bond market. The euro's architecture makes bond markets master of national governments, and that is the problem.

The solution is to create a European Public Finance Authority (EPFA) that issues collectively guaranteed debt on behalf of euro zone governments which the ECB is allowed to buy. That would enable the ECB to manage governments' interest rate via open market operations, as does the Federal Reserve and Bank of England. Proceeds from EPFA debt issues would be distributed to countries on a per capita basis so that national governments would control all spending decisions. Country liability for EPFA debt would also be on a per capita basis, and EPFA decision-making would be governed by member countries with voting rights again granted on a per capita basis. That would render EPFA democratic.

The critical feature is EPFA's power to issue debt would be used immediately to finance the roll-over of existing debt at lower rates, and it would also be used on a permanent basis to finance current and future budget deficits. EPFA would therefore be a solution to both the current crisis and the euro's design flaw regarding absence of a government banker.

The great psychoanalyst Sigmund Freud claimed everything we say has psychic sense. That holds for economics too. Characterizing the problem as lack of a lender of last resort obscures the euro's fundamental neoliberal design problem regarding lack of a government banker and subservience of fiscal policy. That is a structural flaw which creates financial fragility and permanent budgetary pressure that shrinks social democratic policy space. Failure to frame the problem accurately blocks identification of the proper resolution, so that policy reform – the intended solution - misses the mark and hits the stomach instead of the heart.

This article was originally posted in the FT Economists' Forum on December 9, 2011.

IX ECONOMISTS AS THEOLOGIANS OF NEOLIBERALISM

Breaking the neoclassical monopoly in economics

♦

The capture of Keynesianism

♦

The knowledge police in economics

♦

Economics education (for the masses)

♦

Milton Friedman: The great conservative partisan

BREAKING THE NEOCLASSICAL MONOPOLY
IN ECONOMICS

January 31, 2008

For the past 25 years, the so-called "Washington Consensus" – comprising measures aimed at expanding the role of markets and constraining the role of the state – has dominated economic development policy. As John Williamson, who coined the term, put it in 2002, these measures "are motherhood and apple pie, which is why they commanded a consensus."

Not anymore. Dani Rodrik, a renowned Harvard University economist, is the latest to challenge the intellectual foundations of the Washington Consensus in a powerful new book titled *One Economics, Many Recipes: Globalization, Institutions, and Economic Growth*. Rodrik's thesis is that though there is only one economics, there are many recipes for development success.

Rodrik has rendered a major service by stating so openly the claim of "one economics." A critic who made the same claim that economics allows only one theoretical approach would be dismissed as paranoid, whereas Rodrik's standing creates an opportunity for a debate that would not otherwise be possible.

The "many recipes" thesis is that countries develop successfully by following eclectic policies tailored to specific local conditions rather than by following generic best-practice formulas designed by economic theorists. This challenges the Washington Consensus, with its one-size-fits-all formula of privatization, deregulated labor markets, financial liberalization, international economic integration, and macroeconomic stability based on low inflation.

But, while the many recipes thesis has strong appeal and empirical support, and suggests a spirit of theoretical pluralism, the claim of "one economics" is misguided, for it implies that mainstream neoclassical economics is the only true economics.

Part of the difficulty of exposing this narrowness is that there is a family split among neo-classical economists between those who believe that real-world market economies approximate perfect competition and those who don't. Believers are identified with the "Chicago School," whose leading exponents include Milton Friedman and George Stigler. Non-believers are identified with the "MIT School" associated with Paul Samuelson. Rodrik is of the MIT School, as are such household names as Paul Krugman, Joseph Stiglitz, and Larry Summers. This split obscures the underlying uniformity of thought.

The Chicago School claims that real-world market economies produce roughly efficient (so-called "Pareto optimal") outcomes on which public policy cannot improve. Thus, any state intervention in the economy must make someone worse off.

The MIT School, by contrast, argues that real-world economies are afflicted by pervasive market failures, including imperfect competition and monopoly, externalities associated with problems like pollution, and an inability to supply public goods such as street lighting or national defense. Consequently, policy interventions that address market failures – as well as widespread information imperfections and the non-existence of many needed markets – can make everyone better off.

None of this is about fairness, which is a separate issue. Indeed, neither the Chicago School nor the MIT School say that market outcomes are fair, because actual market outcomes depend on the initial distribution of resources. If that distribution was unfair, current and future outcomes will be unfair, too.

However, Chicago economists seem to believe that real-world outcomes are acceptably unfair and, more importantly, that attempts to remedy unfairness are too costly, because tampering with markets causes economic inefficiency. Moreover, they believe that government intervention tends to generate its own costly failures because of bureaucratic incompetence and rent-seeking, whereby private interests try to steer policy to their own advantage.

MIT economists tend to espouse the opposite: fairness is important, the real world is unacceptably unfair, and government failure can be prevented by good institutional design, including democracy.

These differences reflect the intellectual richness of neo-classical economics, but they provide no justification for the claim that there is one economics. On the contrary, heterodox economists like Thorsten Veblen and Joseph Schumpeter long ago raised many of today's cutting-edge issues in neoclassical economics, including the role of social norms and the relationship between technological innovation and business cycles.

More importantly, heterodox economics includes core theoretical concepts that are fundamentally incompatible with neoclassical economics in either of its two contemporary forms. These concepts result in significantly different explanations of the real world, including income distribution and the determinants of economic activity and growth. Moreover, they often result in different policy prescriptions.

The late Robert Heilbronner – one of Schumpeter's most renowned students – viewed economics as "worldly philosophy." Just as philosophers are divided on the nature of truth and understanding, economics is divided on the workings of the real world. Paradigms should co-exist in economics, just as in other social sciences. Yet, in practice, the dominance of the belief in "one economics,"

146

particularly in North America and Europe, has led increasingly to a narrow and exclusionary view of the discipline.

This reality is difficult to convey. One reason is that liberal neo-classical economists like Stiglitz and Krugman share values with heterodox economists, and shared values are easily conflated with shared analysis. Another reason is that heterodox and MIT School economists also often agree on policy, even if their reasoning is different. Finally, most people are incredulous that economists could be so audacious as to enforce one view of economics.

The "many recipes" thesis enriches neo-classical economics' contribution to the development debate, and many of its policy proposals will find support from heterodox economists. However, it fails to engage the deep intellectual divisions regarding economic development, trade, and globalization, because it refuses to admit the legitimacy of such disagreements.

By repeating the claim of "one economics," Rodrik inadvertently reveals the censorship embedded in contemporary economics. The great challenge is not to admit that there are many recipes, but rather to create space for other perspectives on economic analysis and policy.

Distributed by Project Syndicate on January 31, 2008.

THE CAPTURE OF KEYNESIANISM

April 14, 2008

Communist revolutionary Che Guevara rapidly became an inspirational figure for revolutionary socialist change after his execution in Bolivia in 1967. Forty years later, Che lives on but his image now adorns t-shirts that have become popular fashion statements. This transformation reflects the extraordinary power of markets to capture and transform, turning an avowed enemy of the market system into a profit opportunity.

The process of capture also holds for economic policy, which has witnessed the conservative capture of Keynesianism. This capture is now on display as U.S. policymakers struggle to contain the effects of a collapsing house price bubble that was recklessly funded by Wall Street. The sting is that the full powers of Keynesian policies are being invoked to save an economy that no longer generates Keynesian outcomes of full employment and shared prosperity.

The political economic philosophy of Keynesianism emerged after World War II following the catastrophic experience of the Great Depression. The new paradigm advocated an economy with full employment and shared prosperity, and gave government the critical role of regulating markets and adjusting monetary and fiscal policy to ensure levels of demand sufficient to generate full employment.

These Keynesian tools are now being applied forcefully. The Federal Reserve has dramatically cut its interest rate target in response to financial sector weakness. Its goal has been to shore up asset prices, prevent further financial losses, lower mortgage rates to make houses more affordable and prevent further defaults, and to stimulate spending by lowering the cost of capital. Moreover, the Fed has done this despite consumer price inflation being above four percent.

Simultaneously, the Bush administration has pushed for fiscal stimulus, albeit with its usual preference for tax cuts benefiting business and the rich that deliver little bang for buck. The Democratically controlled Congress has also gotten in on the act with stimulus packages that are better designed, but still contain plenty of expensive and relatively ineffective tax cuts.

On one level, policymakers are absolutely right taking these measures, as the costs of a financial and economic meltdown are so large. But true Keynesian policy would also address the failure to generate full employment and shared prosperity. The current U.S. economic expansion looks like being the first ever in which median household income fails to recover its previous peak. Job growth has been tepid for much of the time, and the employment-to-population ratio has remained well below its previous peak. This dismal experience comes on top of three decades of wage stagnation during which household income only grew because of longer working hours and having both household heads work.

The capture of Keynesianism has been a gradual process. In the 1950s military Keynesianism became the hallmark of American policy, with defense spending becoming a huge and permanent component of government spending, to the benefit of the war industry. President Reagan continued the process of capture, pushing rhetoric and policies that undermined working families while simultaneously running budget deficits that kept the lid on unemployment. In the last recession of 2001, the Bush administration again invoked Keynesian stimulus for tax cuts that contained minimal stimulus and were closer to looting of government finances.

In 1971 President Nixon famously declared "We are all Keynesians now." Nixon was half-right. Everyone recognizes the need and efficacy of Keynesian policy instruments, including conservatives who are happy to promote tax cuts and interest rate reductions to support asset prices. However, most have forgotten the Keynesian goals of full employment and shared prosperity.

The result is Keynesian policy instruments remain, but Keynesian policy goals have been abandoned. Both Democrats and Republicans are quick to push for Keynesian stimulus policies when financial stability is threatened, but most (including too many Democrats) are silent when the economy fails to deliver shared prosperity.

Keynesian full employment stimulus policies must be accompanied by Keynesian structural policies that ensure wages grow with productivity, thereby ensuring sustainable demand growth. These structural policies include labor and social insurance laws supportive of unions and worker bargaining power, and international economic policies that prevent inappropriate competition and unsustainable trade deficits. The conservative capture of Keynesianism has both obliterated these structural policies and put a brake on reaching for full employment.

Posted on April 14, 2008 at thomaspalley.com. Originally published as "In name only" on The Guardian, Comment Is Free on February 7, 2008.

THE KNOWLEDGE POLICE IN ECONOMICS

December 12, 2006

It is often said that knowledge is power. One implication of this is that the powerful have an incentive to police what gets called knowledge. Nowhere is this truer than in economics since how we describe the economy has vital consequences for economic policy, providing a clear motive to police the production of economic knowledge. Unmasking this reality is critical for a democratic equal opportunity society. However, it is extremely difficult to do.

The policing of knowledge is often done through professions, and unmasking the process is difficult for two reasons. First, the very idea that knowledge might be policed in the interests of the rich and powerful creates a cognitive dissonance since we like to think of knowledge in terms of truth. Second, to the extent that professions serve a *bona fide* quality control function, it is easy to camouflage policing as quality control.

One function of professions is to oversee and ensure the quality of services that members provide. However, professions also work to bolster the social and economic standing of their members, and this private economic interest creates a permanent tension with their role as guardians of quality. It is easy to justify supply restrictions (such as licensing) in the name of professional standards and quality, when the real reason is to drive up pay. Likewise, technical professional discourse can suffer from the same tensions. On one hand it is needed to articulate specialized ideas and concepts, but on the other hand it excludes the public. Put bluntly, private language is a barrier to entry that confers ownership of the secrets of the temple, and it is not for nothing that professions have been described as a conspiracy against the laity.

The pursuit of self-interest by professions is unsurprising, being normal economic behavior. Economists are also professionals. Ironically, that means the economic logic of economists applies as much to themselves as it does to other professionals. The difficulty with acknowledging this is that it creates a huge dissonance with the rhetoric of academic economics, which is cast in terms of pursuit of "scientific truth." The reality is that the practices and rules governing economic enquiry may also be partly about promoting self-interest. As with other professions, this can take the form of licensing requirements and private languages that restrictively shape discourse.

Such self-interest provides a point of entry for spotlighting far more important concerns about the role of social forces in the production of economic knowledge. Economic research is a job, and who pays the bills has an impact on the research produced. An economist working at the Federal Reserve or International Monetary Fund (IMF) will tend to produce research and advice consistent with the political and ideological alignment of those institutions. This is the route to promotion and

150

an easier life, and institutions also tend to select economists who share their alignment. That is just a complicated way of saying that employers affect what workers produce. The only thing surprising about this is that it applies to the production of economic knowledge.

Economists are also members of society. That means they too are affected by trends and influences in society, just like everyone else. When society drifts left, economists drift left too. When society drifts right, so too do economists. Nothing surprising here except that it has consequences for economic knowledge. In the decade after the Great Depression, society drifted left and the economics profession became more progressive. The late 1940s inaugurated the Cold War, which pitted the ideology of central planning against free market capitalism, and American economists began to drift right in the wake of this struggle. Again, nothing surprising once it is recognized that economists are also members of society.

All knowledge is produced in a social context of politics, values, institutions and employment relations. This context exerts important influences on the knowledge that is produced, and this social context also influences economics. Once again, nothing surprising – unless one subscribes to the science myth in economics, in which case it is hard to reconcile these social impacts with the idea of true objective knowledge.

To become accepted, knowledge claims are subject to screening processes that warrant these claims. Tests of passage include logical coherence of the ideas and compatibility with selected facts. They also usually include a requirement that ideas are presented using the appropriate professional language, and have some degree of conformity with the political values and ideology of the professional community. Values are therefore part of the screen for warranting ideas as knowledge.

Sociologists term this screening process "gatekeeping" – which is the professional sociologist's way of saying policing. This gatekeeping process varies with political and social climate. In some eras gatekeeping may be more open, in others more closed. Like all knowledge, economic knowledge is also screened and subject to gatekeeping. However, gatekeeping in economics is stricter than in comparative literature. It is easy to understand why. Wealth, income, and power are at stake in the former, since how we explain the economy affects law and policy governing markets.

Interestingly, the gatekeepers may not even be aware of their gatekeeping activities if they share the values embedded in the dominant knowledge paradigm. Here, the "science myth" can prove especially useful. This is because it can provide the gatekeepers with a justification for their activities that is constructed in terms of error and truth. Consequently, they can use the notion of "truth" to advance one point of view and suppress another.

This is not a conspiracy theory. It is simply the consequence of the fact that people produce knowledge, and people live and work in social contexts defined by values, institutions, and power relations. At one level, all of this is obvious. At another level, it is very disconcerting because it challenges widely held beliefs about the relation between knowledge and truth.

The important practical lesson is that we should be open-eyed about conventional economic knowledge claims, and open-minded about economic ideas that the gatekeepers have consigned to the underground. That has relevance for debate surrounding such issues as the economic impact of minimum wages, the employment effects of trade unions, the determination of income distribution, the consequences of job off-shoring, and the existence of a natural rate of unemployment.

Beyond that there is a serious problem because the policing of university economics has become so one-sided that only one view is admitted. Consequently, it is as if we have two economic policy waiters – in the U.S. they are the Republicans and so-called "new" Democrats – but only one chef. What we need is another chef in the economic policy kitchen, working from another economic cookbook and producing another economic policy menu.

Posted on December 12, 2006 at thomaspalley.com.

ECONOMICS EDUCATION (FOR THE MASSES)

November 13, 2007

Some U.S. academic economists express concern about low levels of economic literacy among the general public. There is also concern that undergraduates remember little from their college economics courses. Together, these concerns are being used to motivate an agenda for making economics mandatory in college and high school.

That agenda obscures important complexities. The question of literacy may be driven as much by the public's disagreement with economists over important policy matters, such as free trade, as it is by concern about public understanding. If the public agreed with economists it is likely the question of public understanding would be a non-issue.

This suggests the promotion of mandatory economics education may be an attempt to force feed economists' views. Ironically, one could say that despite its intellectual monopoly, orthodox economics is failing in the market for ideas. However, rather than breaking that monopoly and opening economics education to competing perspectives, some in the profession prefer compulsory purchase.

With regard to what students remember, recent research suggests non-majors (i.e. those not specializing in economics) learn and retain little in the way of key economic concepts. They also have a largely negative view of the quality of economics teaching, captured in the derisive student description of economics as "graphs for laughs".

For students majoring in economics the picture is different. These students have a strong positive impression of economics and remember much of what they are taught. Furthermore, casual observation suggests economics majors are impressed by the use of math, which in their eyes renders economics "hard knowledge" that can be called a science - albeit not quite on par with the natural sciences. This promotes belief that economists know the truth, which confers authority on economics and also justifies excluding ideas that are not part of the paradigm. The implication is length of exposure impacts attitudes toward economics.

The campus disrepute of economics and the general public's willingness to challenge its ideas are troubling for the economics profession. The former means economics is not a popular major on campuses where a business major is offered. Ironically, that means economics departments may even need subsidies out of fees paid by students enrolled in the humanities and other social sciences. The latter means the public may not accept economists' policy prescriptions, which challenges both the profession and the broader economic power structure.

Making economics education mandatory and extending its reach into high schools would solve these problems. First, it would guarantee a large pool of students, as would the need to train high school economics teachers. Second, pushing the curriculum into high schools would lengthen exposure to economics and the evidence suggests that impacts beliefs.

The importance of this low profile issue is illustrated by the fact that the Federal Reserve has an extensive high school economics outreach program. That program promotes orthodox economics, and includes giving away free teaching kits and publishing economics pamphlets in cartoon form.

However, there is another interpretation of student resistance to economics, which is that the stories students learn in economics classes do not tally with their real world lives. Thus, real world experience shows phenomena such as norms and power matter for who gets paid what, and tastes and preferences are subject to important social influences contrary to economists' accounts. This real world experience conflicts with the free market story and creates a divided-self that is simultaneously respectful and dismissive of economics. That divided-self leaves people open to ideas and policies not recommended by orthodox economists. It also leads people to look for understanding in places other than economics classrooms.

This suggests rather than making economics mandatory, teaching of economics should be reconfigured. If understanding is the real goal, economics should be taught in terms of ideas and competing visions of the economy. That fits with the late Robert Heilbronner's notion of economics as "worldly philosophy." Philosophers are divided on the nature of truth and understanding, and so too economics is divided on the workings of the real world.

Unfortunately, a worldly philosophy approach is the very opposite of current teaching practice and professional thinking. The great challenge is how to get it on to the table since many economists are not trained in worldly philosophy, and they are likely intellectually threatened by it.

Previously unpublished.

MILTON FRIEDMAN:
THE GREAT CONSERVATIVE PARTISAN

November 27, 2006

Milton Friedman died on November 16, 2006 at the age of 94. Without doubt, Friedman was one of the most influential – perhaps the most influential - economists of the second half of the twentieth century. Not only did he contribute to reviving belief in the economic efficacy of the market system, he also had a profound political impact by linking capitalism with freedom.

Friedman's treatment of capitalism and freedom colored understandings so that many among America's elite now see a simplistic identity between the two. However, the reality is a complicated tango whereby free markets promote certain dimensions of freedom but can also bruise others – including democracy, meritocracy, and equality of opportunity. To paraphrase George Orwell, in market systems we are all free but some are (a lot) freer than others.

In 1976 Friedman was awarded the Nobel Prize in economics for his contributions to scientific economics. These contributions are marked by two characteristics. First, they are imbued with an underlying conservative partisanship characterized by profound animus to government. Second, Friedman achieved public standing through his macroeconomic work, much of which has been discredited. In a sense, Friedman is the economist who lost the battle but ended up winning the war, convincing society to adopt his view of the world.

One of Friedman's most widely recognized contributions is monetarism, which recommends that central banks target money supply growth. Monetarism flourished in the late 1960s and 1970s and was briefly adopted by central banks as a policy framework in the late 1970s and early 1980s. That experiment produced devastating interest rate volatility, prompting central banks to revert to their traditional practice of targeting interest rates.

Monetarism was supported by Friedman's joint work with Anna Schwartz in which they argued that the Federal Reserve caused the Great Depression through mistaken monetary tightening. This was Friedman's first major salvo in his crusade against government, implicitly blaming government for the Depression. Friedman's claim has always smacked of the tail wagging the dog since the Fed's tightening was modest and brief, suggesting an underlying instability of the 1929 economy. The 1929 stock market was characterized by feverish speculation, and the Fed would indeed have done better to provide easy liquidity when investors rushed to exit. However, that also proves the dangerous instability of financial markets and makes the case for an active government regulatory presence, the very opposite of Friedman's philosophical perspective.

At the theoretical level, monetarism asserts that central banks control the money supply and should aim for steady money supply growth. Friedman even recommended replacing the Fed with a computer that would mechanically manage the money supply regardless of the economy's state. Furthermore, he suggested the Fed aim for a zero nominal interest rate. If the equilibrium real interest rate is three percent, that policy implies steady deflation of three percent.

These monetarist propositions reflect a flawed understanding of money. Money is a form of credit - an IOU. If central banks try to control the narrow money supply, the private sector just moves to create other forms of credit. That is why the Fed was unsuccessful in targeting the money supply, and why predicating economic policy on the relationship between the money supply and economic activity is a will o' the wisp. With regard to deflation, Japan's recent experience has confirmed the lessons of the Great Depression. In a credit-money economy generalized deflation is catastrophic and should be avoided.

Monetarism's most famous aphorism is that "inflation is always and everywhere a monetary phenomenon." This saying reflects Friedman's polemical powers, capturing for monetarists what all sensible economists already knew. Inflation is about rising prices, and prices are intrinsically a monetary phenomenon since they are denominated in money terms.

Sustained inflation requires that the money supply grow in order to finance transacting at higher prices. For Friedman, this made villainous central banks the exclusive cause of inflation because of his belief that they control the money supply. However, the reality is that the private sector can also inflate the money supply through its own credit creation activities. Additionally, central banks (viz. the Bernanke Fed) may be compelled to temporarily accommodate inflationary private sector pressures to avoid triggering costly recessions. The implication is that inflation can have different causes, something Friedman denied. Sometimes inflation is caused by excessively easy monetary policy or large budget deficits financed by central banks. Other times it is due to private sector forces, including speculative booms and conflicts over income distribution.

Monetarism asserts that monetary policy is all-powerful. Subsequently, Friedman changed his view and argued that monetary policy had no long-run real economic impacts. Friedman cleverly termed his later theory the natural rate of unemployment, thereby enlisting nature on his side.

His new theory supported an extreme conservative policy agenda that still lives. According to the theory, the minimum wage increases unemployment by driving up wages, and should therefore be done away with. The same holds for unions. No consideration is given to the possibility that these institutions create an income distribution that promotes mass consumption and full employment. Finally, since central banks supposedly have no long run effect on unemployment and wages, they are not responsible for labor market outcomes. Natural rate theory thereby allows the Fed and European Central Bank to take full employment policy off the table while protecting them from charges that their policies may contribute to wage suppression.

Close inspection reveals natural rate theory to be akin to a religious doctrine. This is because it is not possible to conceive of a test that can falsify the theory. When predictions of the natural rate turn out wrong (as they repeatedly have), proponents just assert that the natural rate has changed. That has led to the most recent incarnation of the theory in which the natural rate is basically the trend rate of unemployment. Whatever trend is observed is natural – case closed.

Since natural rate theory cannot be tested, a sensible thing would be to examine its assumptions for plausibility and reasonableness. However, Friedman's early work on economic methodology blocks this route by asserting that realism and plausibility of assumptions has no place in economics. With most economists blindly accepting this position, the result is a church in which entry is conditional on accepting particular assumptions about the working of markets.

The theory of consumption is another area in which Friedman contributed. His permanent income theory of consumption sensibly argues that household consumption and saving decisions are made on the basis of households' assessments of their long term sustainable income, and not just on the basis of today's income. However, Friedman also asserted that all households save the same proportion of their sustainable income. This proposition is manifestly false, as shown by the behavior of the super-paid. It also has clear conservative implications. Since all save the same proportion, transferring income from higher paid to lower paid households generates no economic stimulus. Progressive taxes can still be justified on ethical grounds, but not on economic stimulus grounds.

Lastly, Friedman was an early proponent of flexible exchange rates. Whereas the argument that flexible exchange rates facilitate macroeconomic adjustment has worn well, Friedman's arguments against the dangers of destabilizing speculation have not. In line with his ideological predisposition for markets and against government intervention, Friedman ruled out destabilizing speculation. His argument was there exists a fundamental equilibrium price and if prices depart from this equilibrium, speculators see a profit opportunity and drive prices back. However, experience has shown that exchange rates and asset markets are prone to speculative bubbles, and it has been extremely difficult to find a relation between exchange rates and fundamentals – whatever they are.

While such findings do not support fixed exchange rates, they do support a case for sensible exchange rate management by well-informed officials who can do a better job than speculative casino markets. Yet, the triumph of Friedman's anti-government economics means that this sensible policy approach has been ignored by U.S. policymakers.

In sum, Milton Friedman's political economy helped provide a corrective to the excessive disregard of markets and the price system engendered by the Great Depression, and his advocacy of the power of economic incentives abides. However, Friedman was not a lone defender of markets. Keynes, himself, always held an enormous regard for the market system – what he termed the Manchester System. Leading American and British Keynesians also shared that regard. However, whereas these Keynesian economists understood the limits of the market and the importance of government in making capitalism work for ordinary people, Friedman did not. By all accounts, Milton Friedman was a considerate and compassionate person, and he was a revered teacher. However, his fame rests on his ideas, and those ideas suffer from an excess of conservative partisanship.

Posted on November 27, 2006 at thomaspalley.com. This article also appeared as "The great conservative partisan" on November 29, 2009 in The Guardian, Comment Is Free.

X REPUBLICAN LOOTERS AND DESTROYERS

Sabotaging government: The new politics of the radical right

♦

Social origins of the American corporate predator state

♦

Scapegoating regulation

♦

In defense of Sarbox

♦

Manipulating the oil reserve

♦

Iron grip

SABOTAGING GOVERNMENT:
THE NEW POLITICS OF THE RADICAL RIGHT

November 20, 2005

Thirty years ago the economic debate between Democrats and Republicans was framed in terms of the case for bigger versus smaller government. Democrats emphasized market proclivities toward monopoly and inequality, failure of markets to efficiently provide public goods, market incentives to pollute, and above all the tendency of markets to produce less than full employment. Republicans countered that such market failures were over-stated. More importantly, using government to solve market failures could lead to even worse problems of government failure associated with bureaucratic inefficiency, policy misjudgments, and private capture of regulatory agencies. In an imperfect world, Republicans argued that it is better to live with the problem of market failure and opt for small government, than try and solve it by resort to big government.

This bigger versus small government debate was one of real substance, with strong arguments on both sides. Though differences were sharp, all agreed on the need for "good" government. But a funny thing happened on the way to the forum. Over the last three decades the Republican Party has morphed from a party of "small government" into an "anti-government" party. This morphing has had profound political consequences. Whereas the party of small government favored good government, the anti-government party actively promotes bad government knowing that it feeds popular anti-government sentiment.

The drift toward bad government began with the Reagan budget deficits of the 1980s. Conservatives had historically been against large budget deficits, calling themselves fiscal conservatives. Indeed, a core complaint against bigger government was that it promoted over-spending and large deficits. However, the Reagan era introduced a new political line whereby massive budget deficits could finance short-term political gains while simultaneously imposing long-term financial handcuffs on government.

In the short-term, large spending programs (such as weapons procurement and highway construction) reward the political base. At the same time, large deficits rack up large government debts on which interest must be paid. These interest payments continue long into the future, thereby pre-committing future tax revenues and leaving less room for future discretionary spending. Moreover, the interest accrues to bondholders who belong disproportionately to the Republican base. Lastly, such pre-commitment is especially potent if deficits are racked up at a time of high interest rates, as happened in the 1980s.

The same logic that encourages anti-government advocates to push irresponsible spending policy holds with even greater force for tax policy. Tax cuts usually go predominantly to the well to-do because they have the income and pay top tax rates. However, this skewing is profoundly worsened when the focus is cutting taxes on unearned income (interest and dividends) and wealth transfers (the estate tax). Additionally, tax cuts worsen the budget deficit by reducing revenues, thereby tightening the financial handcuffs on future spending policy. Most pernicious of all, there is an incentive to push bad tax policy, and even the most complicated poorly designed tax cuts are deemed desirable. They too reward the political base and handcuff future policy. But they also fuel resentment of the tax system, strengthening popular anti-government sentiment.

All of the above features have been clearly visible under the Bush administration. It has pushed grossly inequitable tax cuts and created large structural budget deficits. At this stage of the business cycle the budget should be close to balance. Instead, it is stuck around three percent of national output, which promises to sabotage future government finances. The budget has become a pork barrel, exemplified by the Medicare drug benefit. Rather than looking for the simplest most cost effective way to provide a drug benefit for seniors, the administration chose a complicated costly scheme that bars government from using its size to get discounts, limits price competition, and rewards the pharmaceutical companies who are part of their political base. If one were absolutely cynical, it is even possible to view incompetence and misconduct in high places as logically fitting in with the anti-government agenda. Such behaviors discredit government and undermine public trust.

Restoring the sensible bigger versus small government debate of the past calls for outing the "soft treason" of the anti-government agenda. But there is a strange irony to this unhappy tale. While the small government Republican Party was morphing into an anti-government party, an important segment of the bigger government Democratic Party was morphing into small government Democrats. That means the old small versus big government debate between Rockefeller Republicans and Kennedy Democrats is now played out between right and left of the Democratic Party, which explains why Democrats are so divided. It also means that Democrats need to recapture confidence in their historic political identity as much as do Republicans.

Posted on November 20, 2005 at thomaspalley.com. Also posted as "Sabotaging government: How the right shifted from a "small government" stance to a radical "anti-government" one" on Mother Jones on January 10, 2006.

SOCIAL ORIGINS OF THE AMERICAN CORPORATE PREDATOR STATE

August 12, 2008

Jamie Galbraith's recent book describes modern (Bush-Cheney) Republicanism as creating a "predator state". Its predatory aspects are starkly visible in the gangs of corporate lobbyists who roam Washington D.C., the Halliburton Iraq war procurement scandal, and the corruption and incompetence that surrounded the Hurricane Katrina relief effort.

However, the broad concept of a predator state needs qualification as we are really talking of an "American corporate" predator state. Thus, the predatory nature of contemporary U.S. governance is quintessentially linked to corporations, and it is also a uniquely American phenomenon.

Kleptocratic predator states, like Mugabe's Zimbabwe or Mobutu's Zaire in Africa, are fundamentally different. There is no equivalent in Europe, and none in East Asia where ruling elites have a sense of obligation to the nation even as they often enrich themselves illicitly. Nor too is there an equivalent in Latin America because government there never reached an economic size proportional to that of government in the U.S.

It is important to understand the social origins of the American corporate predator state because understanding is a necessary part of developing responses for caging the predators and replacing them with another better order. Those origins clearly trace back to the military – industrial complex that President Eisenhower warned about in his final televised address to the nation on January 17, 1961.

That complex has captured politics and corrupted the business of government, including of course the conduct of national security policy. The fact that it has wrapped itself with the flag and entwined itself with the military makes it impossible to confront without being charged as unpatriotic. Worst yet, its enormous enduring profitability has provided a model for imitation by other industrial complexes like Big Pharma and Big Oil.

The political success of these predators is clearly linked to money's role in politics. Money gives the power to buy the political process, and that power is defended by a gospel of free speech that takes no account of the fact that out-shouting someone is qualitatively equivalent to silencing them. Economics also comes to money's defense with its absurd myth of a market for ideas in which participants compete on a level playing field and truth is effortlessly sorted from error.

The American worship of business and businessmen, which Sinclair Lewis (*Babbitt*, 1922) wrote about long ago, also plays a role. This worship privileges business over thought and other activities, and is behind the dismissive sneer "if you're so smart how come you are not rich?" As a result, Americans are all too willing to hand over their government to business predators. Today, it is in Goldman Sachs we trust.

Another feature of business worship is a tendency to conflate profit with free markets. That means the distinction between fair competition (which is good) and fat profits (which are bad) is lost, thereby providing cover for predators.

Lastly, there is the legacy of the Cold war which contributed to economic dumbing-down and suppression of awareness of class and class conflict. This suppression was seen as necessary for blunting the dangerous appeal of Soviet communism, but a consequence was to create blindness to the predators in our midst.

All of this reveals a deep deficit in America's social and economic understanding (some deficits really do matter). And as long as this deficit remains, the predators will have a starting gate advantage in the game of political persuasion.

Yet, how to close the deficit and insert another understanding is an enormous challenge. There are deep institutional obstructions in the academy, the media, and the Democratic Party. Moreover, raising these issues may create unsettling cognitive dissonance that pushes voters into denial and a closer embrace of the predators.

In effect, there is a paradox to be solved. Lasting progressive political victory requires transforming understanding, but the immediate political incentives are aligned to discourage engagement with such a project.

This article appeared as part of a discussion of James Galbraith's book, The Predator State, on TPMCafé on August 12, 2008 and at thomaspalley.com.

SCAPEGOATING REGULATION

August 8, 2008

Many progressives now believe the age of Milton Friedman may be drawing to a close. Their hope is the current financial crisis has shown the costs and dangers of inadequate market regulation, thereby discrediting the anti- regulation philosophy of Milton Friedman and his Chicago School colleagues.

Evidence of the changing times is supposedly provided by Treasury Secretary Paulson's and Federal Reserve Chairman Bernanke's public admissions about the need for regulatory change.

Yet the reality is far more complex, and economic conservatives will not roll-over and surrender just because of a financial crisis. Instead, if history is a guide, they will blame regulation for the crisis. That was Milton Friedman's *modus operandi* when he launched the modern era of deregulation and animus to government with his false claim that the Fed caused the Great Depression.

This tried and tested conservative tactic is already surfacing in the debate surrounding Fannie Mae and Freddie Mac, the giant mortgage financing companies. The conservative argument is government's provision of an implicit guarantee to Fannie and Freddie distorted the market by giving them subsidized finance. The implication is that this enabled them to pump up the housing bubble, while simultaneously making them the dominant players in the securitized mortgage market.

This conservative tactic scapegoats Fannie and Freddie, making them the fall guys for the bubble's financial excesses, when the true cause was inadequate regulation of mortgage lending and failed macroeconomic policy.

The insinuation that Fannie and Freddie were primary movers of the housing market excesses of 2004 – 2006 lacks even superficial merit. This is because since 2003 both Fannie and Freddie have had limited asset growth, and Fannie's assets actually fell significantly after 2003.

Moreover, the roots of the crisis lie in the sub-prime market. That is where "no doc" and "zero down" mortgages proliferated, where loan originations exploded in volume, where losses started, and where the bulk of losses have been so far. Yet, Fannie and Freddie are prevented from financing such mortgage products by their charters.

These facts should make clear that Fannie and Freddie did not cause the crisis. Instead, it was driven by loose and negligent lending by banks and Wall Street. That behavior was due to lack of regulatory oversight, combined with a failed incentive system that rewards management and mortgage brokers for pushing loans rather than prudent lending.

Such loan pushing was even promoted by conservative animus to Fannie and Freddie, as Wall Street was encouraged to muscle in on the formers' business. That is why the Bush administration sought regulatory limits on Fannie and Freddie's asset holdings. However, unlike Fannie and Freddie, Wall Street has no legal restrictions on loan quality and opted for gorging on sub-prime.

The bubble's origins lie in the combination of a flawed economic growth paradigm that prompted the Fed to push interest rates too low for too long, plus loose lending by banks and Wall Street. This combination inflicted a huge negative "pecuniary externality" on Fannie and Freddie, driving up house prices in the normally sound mortgage markets they serve. Consequently, they too have been battered by the bubble's implosion.

The bottom line is Fannie and Freddie had little to do with the bubble. That said conservatives raise a legitimate question of how to organize the securitized mortgage market.

Fannie and Freddie's implicit government guarantee has helped them lower the cost of mortgage finance, making home ownership more affordable to millions. In effect, the guarantee has made government's lower borrowing cost available to the public, which is good. The downside is it has made Fannie and Freddie overwhelmingly dominant in the securitized mortgage market.

This suggests that in addition to tighter mortgage lending regulation, there is a case for nationalizing Fannie and Freddie on grounds that they are natural monopolies. That is the very opposite of conservative arguments opposing need for tighter regulation and proposing disbanding Fannie and Freddie. That would leave Wall Street unreformed, and make home ownership more expensive by removing the assist provided by access to government's lower borrowing cost.

Posted on August 8, 2008 at thomaspalley.com. Also posted on August 11, 2008 at ourfuture.org.

IN DEFENSE OF SARBOX

February 7, 2007

The economics of regulation teaches that regulation only matters if it is binding and compels people to change their behavior. It also teaches that because binding regulation compels change, those subject to it oppose it. After all, they preferred doing what they were doing before the regulation was passed. That carries an important political lesson: those subject to binding regulation will want it repealed.

These academic musings have direct relevance to business's attack on the Sarbanes-Oxley Act (Sarbox) regulating capital markets. The story being told is that Sarbox has raised the cost of doing business in America's financial markets, thereby undermining America's competitive position. However, close inspection reveals that there is little foundation for these charges. Instead, they provide a case study of business's anti-regulation scare tactics.

From its inception, Sarbox has faced strong opposition. The initial argument was that the frauds associated with Enron (Lay and Skilling), MCI-Worldcom (Ebbers) and Tyco (Kowalski) were just a "few bad apples" and the "barrel" remained fundamentally sound.

That argument has been scotched by the CEO stock options backdating scandal that may extend to many hundreds of companies, with Boards of Directors also apparently implicated. The media has focused on the money involved, but the money is actually chump change relative to what CEOs are already paid. The real story is the illustration of just how corrupted much of corporate America has become. That means the "few rotten apples" story is no longer credible, and the "barrel" really is the problem.

Unable to invoke the rotten apples defense, business groups have now shifted to their traditional anti-regulation line that regulation costs jobs. Top business economists, such as Glenn Hubbard, Dean of Columbia University Business School, have been engaged to come up with arguments for diluting Sarbox.

The self-styled, "blue ribbon" Committee on Capital Markets Regulation funded by Wall Street money and co-chaired by Hubbard, recently issued a report recommending making shareholder class action suits more difficult to bring, lowering the legal liability of auditors and directors and easing accounting certification requirements. All this is in the name of making America's financial markets more competitive.

The committee's central piece of evidence was that U.S. markets have seen a decline in foreign listings, and that there has also been a decline in the U.S share of initial public offerings (IPOs). This is supposedly proof of regulatory excess.

But there is a very different and more plausible explanation: Foreign financial markets are catching up in quality of technology and regulatory governance.

With foreign stock markets becoming better, deeper and more liquid, there is less incentive to list in the usual places, including the U.S. Thus, since 2000 London's main stock market has seen foreign listings decline 23 percent since 2000, the Deutsche Börse is down 58 percent and Tokyo is down 39 percent.

With regard to IPOs, these have fallen in part because comparison is made with 1999 when the market was in the throes of a speculative bubble. When the NASDAQ was at 5,000, firms had an incentive to bring offerings to market as quickly as possible. It also explains why the premium received by foreign companies for listing in U.S. markets has fallen. In 1999 U.S. investors were paying bubble prices, giving foreign companies a premium relative to what they could get in home country markets.

Another committee argument is that there has been significant de-listing of equities through private equity takeovers, which is supposedly indicative of Sarbox increasing the cost of public listing. However, the reality behind the private equity boom is the mainstreaming of junk bond finance combined with increased income and wealth inequality. These features have driven private-equity funds in which the super-rich pool their wealth and leverage it to take companies private. That is the explanation behind the activities of the Carlyle Group, the Blackstone Group, KKR and the Texas Pacific Group. It has little to do with public listing costs.

William Niskanen, another leading conservative economist from the Cato Institute, claims that declining stock market price-to-earnings (PE) ratios are further proof of Sarbox's adverse effects. His argument is that Sarbox has made companies less valuable to investors, which is reflected in lower PE ratios. However, it is well known that PE ratios are counter-cyclical, being highest at the end of recessions when actual profits are low but prices are high because profits are expected to increase with future recovery. As recovery sets in, PE ratios fall as profits rise. They have remained low during the current expansion because it has been so generous to profits.

The Hubbard Committee's report is one-sided. It also illustrates the phenomenon of "deep lobbying" by conservative business groups. These well-funded groups commission "expert" reports that contain unbalanced views. Those reports then get covered extensively in the media, thereby becoming the reference point for debate. In this fashion, the policy playing field is tilted in favor of business - something we are now seeing in the run-up to Treasury Secretary Paulson's high-profile conference on capital markets planned for spring 2007.

Posted on February 7, 2007 at thomaspalley.com.

MANIPULATING THE OIL RESERVE

January 26, 2007

2006 was the year that oil prices came close to breaching $80 per barrel. This was despite the fact that there were no significant supply interruptions and oil demand actually fell in industrialized countries. That raises the question of what caused the spike.

It turns out there is good reason to believe that record oil prices may be due to our own strategic oil reserve, which the Bush administration may have been manipulating to drive up prices for the benefit of its clients. This is something Congress must investigate, and here is some preliminary evidence.

Any finding of manipulation would go far beyond corruption and be close to economic treason. That is because when oil prices increase America must pay more for its imported oil. That increases the trade deficit and our foreign debt. Alternatively, one can think of price manipulation as the equivalent of a tax increase on American families that is paid to foreign governments, including Iran.

While some small energy scandals are under investigation by Congress, the big enchilada is the strategic oil reserve, which may have been "strategically" manipulated to drive up oil prices. The key to understanding this manipulation is demand and supply and oil storage capacity.

The last three years have seen rapidly rising oil prices, and a tight oil market has meant that even small increases in demand have had large price impacts. During this period the Bush administration purposely expanded inventories of the strategic oil reserve, which rose from 600 million barrels in May 2003 to 700 million barrels in August 2005. The administration therefore increased demand by 125,000 barrels per day, and oil prices rose from $30 per barrel to $70.

As oil prices rose, Wall Street became increasingly engaged in commodity speculation (the destructive effects of which is a story for another day), and this is where storage matters. As speculators entered the market the spot price of crude oil rose above the futures price. However, buying spot oil means taking delivery, which requires storage capacity. By adding to the strategic reserve, the administration not only increased oil demand but also increased storage capacity because the oil it bought was stored in the strategic reserve's caverns. That helped speculators by adding storage capacity vital for cornering the market.

That brings us to today. Over the last month spot oil prices have been tumbling. The reason is that the market has finally run out of storage capacity, which means that all oil produced must now be immediately sold – and that has driven oil prices down. This suggests there has never been a supply shortage warranting $75 oil, and absent the administration's dealings oil prices might not have risen as they did.

171

The story does not end here. With private sector oil storage capacity exhausted, the administration has now announced its intention to double the size of the strategic oil reserve from 700 million barrels to 1.5 billion barrels, and it plans to start purchasing 100,000 barrels of oil per day.

The result has been predictable, with the price of oil jumping from $50 to $55 per barrel over the last week (01/19/07 – 01/24/07). Not only will these purchases increase oil demand, they will also provide new storage capacity needed to re-corner the market.

One last piece of evidence concerns Hurricane Katrina and the oil loan program. Following Katrina, gulf oil production was interrupted causing shortages of crude for refineries. The administration's response was to loan crude to refiners who were to pay it back in-kind. That was a huge gift to refiners who got the oil they wanted and then made a killing on the processed gasoline that was in short supply after Katrina. The proper way to handle the situation would have been to auction the oil, in which case taxpayers would have got the windfall disaster rent (excess profit) resulting from Katrina. This is because refiners would have been willing to pay a high price knowing that gas prices were high.

But there's yet more damage. If government had auctioned the oil, it could have chosen when to buy it back. Instead, companies paid it back in-kind in late 2005 and early 2006, and these repayments tightened market demand and also freed up private storage capacity facilitating further market cornering.

The oil market is full of smoke that provides perfect cover for corruption. Every price blip calls forth explanations in terms of Chinese demand, more violence in Nigeria's delta region, cold weather, threats from Venezuela's Hugo Chavez, or heightened tensions over Iran's nuclear program. The strategic reserve is the perfect vehicle for corruption since transactions can be cloaked in the veil of national defense. But the facts are clear. A motive exists, the bad character of the administration is known, and the circumstantial evidence is strong.

Congress must investigate the strategic oil reserve, how it has been managed and what its purpose is. The recently announced expansion serves no real national security function (though that will be the justification) and will only drive up oil prices and add to the budget deficit and national debt.

One last factoid. A recent IMF study documented that oil prices in the U.S. appear to be politically manipulated, falling prior to elections – as they did in 2002, 2004, and 2006. If you are an economist you ask how that is done. The answer is the strategic oil reserve.

Posted on January 26, 2007 at thomaspalley.com.

IRON GRIP

July 3, 2008

Iron ore prices have recently been in the headlines, having jumped eighty-five percent. This news is troubling as such price increases threaten to raise steel prices, which will add to cost inflation and further undermine economic activity.

Behind these price increases lies the unusual structure of the iron ore market which is best characterized as bi-lateral oligopoly. That structure makes enormously troubling the Bush administration's decision to give regulatory clearance to a combination of the number two (Rio Tinto) and number three (BHP Billiton) ore producers.

Unlike other commodity markets, iron ore prices are set through annual negotiations between the ore producers (Big Iron) and the ore users (Big Steel). Recent contractual negotiations have resulted in huge price increases that reflect the ore market's structure.

On one side is Big Steel, consisting of an increasingly few large steel producers. On the other side is Big Iron, made up of an even fewer number of ore producers. Thus, the top three producers – Vale do Rio Doce, Rio Tinto, and BHP Billiton – account for seventy-five percent of total global production. Moreover, the oligopolistic power of the producers is reinforced by geography. Vale do Rio Doce is Brazilian and located in the western hemisphere, while Rio Tinto's and BHP Billiton's operations are in Australia. That creates a geographic split that helps Big Iron's profits.

In recent years steel production has been marked by significant mergers and right-sizing of capacity, combined with growth of state-directed steel capacity in China. The result has been a huge boom in steel profits that is reflected in steel company stock prices. For instance, consider U.S. Steel that traded at twelve dollars a share five years ago, and in June 2008 peaked at one hundred and ninety-six dollars a share.

Big Steel's earnings rolled in first, being at the end of the production chain. Now, Big Iron is trying to muscle in on the action and grab a share of those profits for itself. It is able to do so because of its bargaining power, and it would be no surprise if there also were some informal collusion among ore producers given their small world.

With limited alternatives, Steel has been forced to cough up some of its oligopoly profits, turning them into Iron's mining rents. That is a bad switch. Higher earnings in iron ore mining will have negligible impact on their economic plans as the industry was already earning large excessive profits. However, higher ore prices will raise steel prices, undermining manufacturing and causing inflation. Meanwhile, lower steel profits will reduce steel investment.

Lastly, speculation may also have contributed to the jump in ore prices, albeit not the speculation associated with other commodity markets in which speculative trading is rampant. Since iron ore is not traded on global commodity markets, financial speculators cannot be responsible for higher prices.

Instead, iron ore speculation is best characterized as 'joint speculation" by the ore producers and users about the continuation of steel profits and the ability of steel companies to pass on higher costs. In this light, the jump in ore contract prices can be viewed as a combination of profit capture by the ore producers plus a big bet on future macroeconomic conditions.

Such user – producer speculation is hard to argue against, but one can argue against an oligopolistic market structure that amplifies speculation's destructive effects. That makes the Bush administration's decision to approve a Rio Tinto – BHP Billiton combination another terrible public policy decision.

The approval of combination reveals the worst proclivities of the Bush administration, which is peppered with extractive industry pirates, particularly from oil. The quest for combination shows that the much maligned Karl Marx was right about capital's proclivity to combine.

Posted on July 3, 2008 at thomaspalley.com.

XI FAILURE OF DEMOCRATS AND PROGRESSIVES

Silent spring: How the Democrats lost their economic policy voice

♦

Deep thinking and economic policy: Why it matters

♦

Why progressives keep losing

♦

Old Democrats vs. New Democrats

♦

Third way, wrong direction

♦

The flaws in fiscal austerity (Rubinomics)

♦

Economics for contenders

♦

Beyond red and blue

♦

Deaf to history's rhyme: Why President Obama is failing

SILENT SPRING: HOW THE DEMOCRATS LOST THEIR ECONOMIC POLICY VOICE

January 5, 2006

In 1962 Rachel Carson published her environmental epic, *Silent Spring*, which documented how chemical-based agriculture was killing the bird-life and birdsong of America's countryside. Over the last forty years the Democratic Party has also slowly lost its voice and fallen silent on the economy, with Democrats substituting a laundry list of program plans for economic vision.

What happened to mute the Democrats' voice on the economy? The academic ascendance of the *laissez-faire* vision of an economist named Milton Friedman. Friedman's vision benchmarks modern economic theory and it thereby benchmarks policy. Put another way, most economists are singing the same hymn---Friedman's 1968 classic, proclaiming a "natural rate of unemployment" that is worsened by minimum wages, unions, and labor standards.

For Rachael Carson, restoring America's birdsong called for banning the chemical DDT. For Democrats, recovering their voice calls for rediscovering an earlier economic paradigm now extinguished in policy discourse. The problem is that contemporary economics has been captured by Friedman's Chicago school construction of free market economics, leaving little room for alternative interpretations of economic reality.

As a result of the dominance of the Chicago school, both Democratic and Republican economic advisers are trained to occupy a common intellectual space, which tends to limit differences to values and support for an egalitarian society. This has huge policy implications, but it is a difficult issue to convey to pragmatic worldly politicians. Seventy years ago, John Maynard Keynes acerbically captured this reality:

"(T)he ideas of economists and political philosophers, both when they are right and when they are wrong, are more powerful than is commonly understood. Indeed, the world is ruled by little else. Practical men, who believe themselves to be quite exempt from any intellectual influences, are usually the slave of some defunct economist. (J.M. Keynes, *The General Theory of Employment, Interest and Money*, 1936, p.383.)

And so it remains today. The current cohort of Democratic policy advisers unconsciously uses the same analytical framework as their Republican counterparts.

Mentioning names can appear churlish, but not doing so invites charges of vagueness. Consider the following. Professor Greg Mankiw of Harvard University (famous for his observation that flipping hamburgers is a manufacturing job) was

Chairman of President Bush's Council of Economic Advisers (CEA). Mankiw made his name in the 1980s as a new-Keynesian, a school of thought that maintains unemployment exists because of inflexible prices and wages. This intellectual background readily qualifies him to serve in a Democratic administration. The same holds for Ben Bernanke of Princeton University, who was recently confirmed as the next Federal Reserve Chairman. Like Mankiw, he too made his name in the 1980s as a new-Keynesian, writing about the Great Depression.

Alan Blinder of Princeton University is the very best of Democratic economic advisers, being deeply sensitive to problems such as income inequality and out-sourcing. Yet, Blinder shares the same analytical views of the economy as Mankiw and Bernanke. Specifically, he shares their views regarding the conduct of monetary policy and the economic logic of free trade and globalization, though his values lead him to have different positions regarding progressive taxes and the need for social insurance

Bernanke is from Princeton; so is Blinder. Mankiw is from Harvard; so is Lawrence Summers. All got their Ph.Ds. from Harvard or MIT. No doubt, all are virtuous people, but virtue is not the issue. The issue is that all share the same invisible hand paradigm, albeit each may see varying degrees of arthritis. How this state of affairs came about is a complicated story. One important factor is the science myth in economics, whereby economists tolerate only one "core" theory about how the economy works.

Given this common shared analytical framework, what distinguishes economic advisers is their level of "compassion." Ironically, this makes the Democrats the true "compassionate conservatives." However, within the *laissez-faire* paradigm, compassion usually reduces economic efficiency. Consequently, Republicans own the market efficiency franchise, while Democrats own the fairness franchise. Meanwhile, efficiency appears to trump fairness with the American electorate, which explains Democrats relative disadvantage in public economic debate.

This pattern is evident across an array of issues. The Clinton administration consistently ducked on trade and labor standards. To the extent that there was support, it was for reasons of compassion and political expediency. The same holds for elite Democratic policy thinking about trade unions and the minimum wage. The one area where elite Democratic policymakers have made an upfront economic efficiency argument is the budget deficit, but this poorly conceived foray has merely risked turning the party of FDR into the party of Herbert Hoover.

What is needed are Democratic economic advisers that challenge the flawed economic assumptions of Friedman's *laissez-faire* school. Three generations ago Keynes identified the economic challenge as one of optimizing capitalism so that it delivers for all. That challenge continues in the era of globalization. Meeting it

180

requires unashamedly and openly making the economic efficiency case for labor standards, trade unions, minimum wages, corporate accountability, and financial market regulation. Additionally, today's advisers must confront the environmental challenge posed by the industrial economy itself. That's a big ticket, but it's a ticket that can own both the efficiency and fairness franchises, and that's a politically unbeatable combination.

Posted on July 3, 2008 at www.thomaspalley.com.

DEEP THINKING AND ECONOMIC POLICY:
WHY IT MATTERS

January 22, 2007

Deep thinking involves going to the root of ideas, analyzing core assumptions and the logic upon which arguments are built. In a sense it is analogous to the Research component of R&D. Research represents deep thinking, while Development takes the product of that thinking and turns it into something that can be marketed profitably. In like vein, physicists distinguish between pure and applied physics, while economists distinguish between theory and policy.

Progressives like to flatter themselves that they are the party of ideas, the party of deep thinking. However, when it comes to economics it is the *laissez-faire* right that has been the party of deep thinking. This has had enormous consequences and helps explain the weakness of progressives in shaping and moving the economic policy debate over the last generation.

Across the board – think tax policy, trade liberalization and globalization, the Federal Reserve and monetary policy, labor market policy, pension and health policy, public investment and the budget deficit debate – progressives have been losing. The best that can be said is that on occasions they have been able to stop the right, as in the battle over privatization of Social Security. However, even here the right may yet largely get its way by shrinking Social Security, although it will remain a public program.

This economic policy weakness of progressives is often explained in terms of "the country moved right." An alternative explanation is that "the country was moved right", a simple re-phrasing that carries huge implications. First, it implies that the other side did something right. Second, progressives may have done things wrong. Most importantly, it strips away the too easily adopted victimization defense, and compels progressives to look inward regarding their own contribution to the current state of affairs.

Lack of deep thinking by progressives is an important part of the story. The consequences can be illustrated in terms of a football metaphor. Proponents of *laissez-faire* have had permanent home-field advantage and have been taking possession of the ball on the progressive twenty-yard line. This advantage derives from the right's engagement with deep thinking, the result of which is that its free market model dominates public understanding and frames public policy analysis. Indeed, many Democratic policy makers often share the same analytical understanding having been schooled in it, though their values lead them to look for more compassionate policies.

The fact that the public and policymakers often subscribe to simplistic free market economics allows the right to readily propose policy initiatives that need little additional selling. This compares with progressive policy initiatives that must first expose the inadequacies of the free market story, next provide an alternative story of how the economy works, and only after that is space created for debating specific policy proposals. That's like getting the football behind one's own goal line, and it makes scoring policy touchdowns a lot harder.

There are numerous examples of issues where the right's deep thinking frames the economic policy debate. A first example is the saving shortage argument that claims America's number one problem is a shortage of saving. The saving shortage hypothesis rests on doubtful theory that maintains saving is the cause and engine of economic growth. That in turn frames the budget deficit debate, promotes tax policy that privileges capital income relative to labor income, and pushes tax exemptions for saving that favor upper income groups and strip government of revenue.

A second example is the labor market flexibility agenda that is anti-union, anti-minimum wage, and anti-worker protection. This agenda emerges from theoretical claims that price flexibility can restore full employment, and it rests on a false analogy comparing the labor market with the market for peanuts.

A third example is income distribution where *laissez-faire* proponents argue that wages and incomes are tightly related to productivity, which determines what people are worth. *Ergo*, there's no problem with the CEO explosion because CEO pay merely reflects the stellar productivity contribution of these super-stars. Likewise, if some workers are being paid less it is because their productivity has diminished.

A final example is the international trade agenda asserts that trade is based on comparative advantage, which ensures we are all better off. Despite the fact that the world does not conform to the assumptions of comparative advantage, that does not stop comparative advantage being invoked as a hammer to close debate.

These assumptions about the role of saving, labor market flexibility, the determination of income distribution, and the role of comparative advantage in trade, frame economic policy debate in ways that favor *laissez-faire* policy prescriptions. This situation is the product of the right's engagement with deep thinking, and it constitutes an enormous obstacle blocking a progressive economic policy agenda.

The difference in importance attached to deep thinking is visible in the different character of conservative and progressive economic policy think-tanks. *Laissez-faire* inclined think-tanks such as the American Enterprise Institute, the Cato Institute, and the Institute for International Economics devote considerable energy to linking economic policy and deep thought. Thus, they push policies that rest on established theoretical stories about the economy, and these institutions continuously invest in re-telling and re-selling these stories. This contrasts with progressive think-tanks, where the focus has been on score-keeping the economy – that is monitoring what is happening to employment, wages, income distribution, and the trade deficit.

Conservative policy dominance rests on having won the war of ideas. For progressives, that means policy success now only comes when the economic body count from conservative policies gets too high. That is a costly way of winning. Score-keeping the economy is and will remain an essential ingredient in the war over economic policy, but numbers are far more effective when they are mobilized in support of ideas. That is where deep thinking enters and why progressives must invest in it.

Money also matters, and business clearly has an advantage today. But money is not decisive. Progressives are still able to raise lots of money. History also shows that money is not enough. Trade unions were once one of the most powerful and well-funded segments of the American political spectrum, yet they have still suffered a steep loss of power.

The Great Depression sparked an era of powerful deep thinking by progressives, exemplified by the Keynesian revolution in economics. In the twenty-five years after World War II that deep thinking moved a tremendous progressive policy agenda that contributed significantly to the prosperity of the period. However, in the late 1960s the progressive well of deep thinking ran dry, and since then progressive leaders seem to have lost sight of the significance of deep thinking for economic policy. That has cost working families dearly.

Looking to the future, the lesson is that progressives must invest in political activism, scorekeeping, AND deep thinking. That's a tall order, but it is also the only way to start with the ball at the opposition's twenty-yard line – as against relying on occasional fumbles and turnovers, as is now the case.

Posted on January 22, 2007 at thomaspalley.com.

WHY PROGRESSIVES KEEP LOSING

August 15, 2008

Jamie Galbraith is an optimist, or maybe I'm just a pessimist. According to his latest book conservative economics is exhausted, burnt out, finito, kaput. All that is needed is for liberals to recognize this, abandon their lily-livered kowtowing to conservative economics, and start pushing on an open door by advocating a return for grand progressive policy action – i.e. long range policy planning and economic standards with government at the wheel.

That is an audacious strategy, but I beg to differ. I do not disagree with his policy recommendations (the chapters on planning and standards are two of the best), only his premise. Not only is conservative economics alive and well, but progressives have hardly begun the job of convincing the world that they have a better understanding of the economy.

I'm all for boldness, and there's always a possibility Jamie's strategy could succeed. History allows for flukes. The economy could also experience another "Great Depression", causing a turn to progressive policy out of desperation. That is an awful thought, but it signals the extent of progressive weakness on economics.

The sad fact is progressives need "bad economic times" to win the policy debate. No, it's worse than that. They need "terrible economic times", and even then it is not clear they win.

In good times progressives sound hollow. In bad times they get a hearing and occasionally manage a win in the form of an extension of unemployment insurance or a small increase in the minimum wage. In terrible times there might be a turn to real progressive policy a la Galbraith. But it is only a chance. Remember the 1930s. Fascism won out in Europe, and the U.S. also had a strong fascist movement that showed its strength in 1940 with America First. The popularity of the Bush-Cheney administration in 2004 and widespread public disregard for its attacks on *habeus corpus* leave me worried crypto-fascism could easily win out if the U.S. experienced a really tough time.

Am I overstating the economic weakness of progressives? I don't think so. Take a look at the five grand areas of policy debate Galbraith focuses on – the market, supply-side economics, monetarism and the natural rate of unemployment, fiscal responsibility, and free trade. In each of them there remains strong policymaker support for the underlying economic ideas, and the public also holds a mostly conservative stance.

Galbraith rightfully scorns the "free to shop" construction of the economy as grossly inadequate, but it is a widely held position that progressives do not have a sharp pithy counter to. Besides progressives should be in favor of "free to shop", but it should be "free to shop plus a lot more".

With regard to supply-side economics, it still has significant academic and professional policymaker support, but tax cut rhetoric has lost traction with the public. However, the public has not migrated to gung-ho support of a progressive alternative.

With regard to budget balance, that still has support among both policymakers and the public. The technical support is based on nonsense claims about budget deficits and interest rates. The deeper support rests on budget balance being code for small government, which is still popular.

Monetarism (control of the money supply) has been totally discredited as an operating philosophy for monetary policy, but it has been replaced by the even more odious doctrine of the natural rate of unemployment. While it is true the natural rate does not guide day-to-day policy, the underlying construct remains completely intact and guides long term policy thinking. The public also implicitly buys into its logic. Thus, most people believe higher wages will cause some unemployment, and there is no popular conception of full employment as an alternative to the natural rate of unemployment.

Finally, there is free trade (and globalization). Elite policymakers remain strongly attached to free trade, support of which is the test for joining the elite. However, the public has become increasingly skeptical. That said, the public lacks an affirmative alternative so its skepticism is more likely to turn into isolationist protectionism than internationalist progressivism.

Comprehensively winning the economic policy debate requires two things: (1) imaginative logically consistent policies; (2) control of the frame for understanding the economy and its underlying problems. To use a sports metaphor, not having control of the frame always gives the opponent home field advantage. With control, policy is an easy sell and it is also easy to introduce new policy arguments. Without control, selling policy is an uphill struggle that leaves one saddled with an increasingly stale agenda that is not up to the challenge of changing times.

I have worked in Washington D.C. for twelve years and have seen zero interest among Democratic politicians, labor unions, and progressive think-tanks in engaging in a sustained war for control of the frame of understanding. Compare that with the American Enterprise Institute (AEI) that was set up in 1943 to explicitly defend *laissez-faire* capitalism from FDR's New Deal, and which brought Milton Friedman to Washington thereby launching the "Age of Friedman".

Instead, the Washington progressive establishment persistently thinks it can win by cobbling together ever longer lists of policy proposals. It may eventually do so, but if it does win it will be because working men and women have been put through the economic wringer.

That is a terrible indictment. There is a smarter way of winning. In this war of ideas Jamie Galbraith is on the side of the angels, so I whole heartedly support the audacity of his declaring victory and marching in. However, my sense is his declaration is premature.

Posted as part of a discussion of James Galbraith's book, The Predator State, on August 15, 2008 in TPMCafe.

OLD DEMOCRATS VS. NEW DEMOCRATS

March 2, 2006

Jeff Faux and Gene Sperling are two titans of democratic economic policy. Last week (February 23, 2006) they debated the core economic policy differences that define and divide old Democrats from new Democrats.

Jeff Faux is the founder and former President of the progressive Washington think-tank, the Economic Policy Institute. Gene Sperling was the head of President Clinton's National Economic Council from 1996 to 2000. Both have just published new books. Faux's book is titled "The Global Class War: How America's Bipartisan Elite Lost Our Future – and What It Will Take to Win It Back." Sperling's book is titled "The Pro-Growth Progressive: An Economic Strategy for Shared Prosperity."

The two books provide a marvelous window on today's Democratic Party. Faux is an old labor Democrat, Sperling a new Democrat. It is striking that two leading Democrats could come up with such fundamentally different accounts of the American economy. This suggests that the Democrats are really two parties when it comes to the all-important economic agenda.

Faux is a political economist, and therefore emphasizes politics in his analysis. Political power lies behind economic policy. His core thesis is that America's elite, drawn from both Republicans and Democrats, has abandoned America and joined a new global political party - the Party of Davos. Globalization therefore represents a new class war. On one side is a new global uber-capitalist class. On the other side are the rest of us, which is workers everywhere – not just the United States.

Sperling is a policy economist, and accordingly his outlook emphasizes policy – fiscal responsibility, policies to help workers adjust to trade related job losses, public investment in education, and tax incentives to help people save and accumulate wealth.

These are the bright eye-catching differences between Sperling and Faux. However, there are deeper analytic differences rooted in competing assessments of today's economic policy mix. Faux seeks a reconfiguration that is nothing short of paradigm change. Sperling accepts the current paradigm and is content with small adjustments. These foundational economic differences have not been adequately framed. Democrats must come to grips with them, so here is a stab at framing them.

Ron Blackwell, Chief Economist at the AFL-CIO, talks of how working families are boxed in by economic policy. This metaphor can be used to dissect the old (Faux) versus new (Sperling) Democrat debate. Imagine a square whose sides are labeled globalization, less than full employment, privatization and government spending cuts, and labor market flexibility. Standing inside this square are working families who are impacted from all four sides.

The old labor Democrat interpretation of the box sees workers pressured from all four sides. Globalization is more about competition than trade---exerting massive pressure on private sector workers that drives down wages and benefits. Manufacturing has borne the brunt thus far, but the larger service sector is now increasingly in play because services can be provided over the Internet. Globalization brings lower prices, but it does so at the high cost of lower wages and job insecurity. Public sector jobs and wages are threatened by the privatization and government spending cuts side of the box which puts them in competition with private sector workers.

Both private and public workers are pressured from the other two sides. Less than full employment is where the Fed enters. Because the Fed puts a floor to the unemployment rate in the name of price stability, it contributes to weakening workers' bargaining position. Meanwhile, 'labor market flexibility' is code used by conservative business leaders for eroding the minimum wage and employee protections, and attacking unions. This shifts bargaining power to business and lowers wages for all workers, not just union members.

New Democrats (Sperling) have a dramatically different take on the box. For them, globalization benefits working families by providing cheap imports that raise the standard of living, improve productivity via heightened competition, and provide jobs in the export sector. Sperling recognizes this creates losers as some jobs are eliminated, and therefore calls for programs like worker trade adjustment assistance that can supposedly be paid for from the gains of globalization.

In the new Democrat economy, working families benefit from the Federal Reserve's less-than-full employment approach because it brings low inflation which brings down interest rates, thereby spurring investment and growth. This is why new Democrats were okay with Alan Greenspan, except when he strayed into Social Security or tax policy as in 2001. Indeed, Alan Blinder – another highly respected new Democrat economic adviser – calls Greenspan "the greatest central banker ever."

When it comes to privatization and cutting government spending, there is some agreement among new and old Democrats that these policies need resisting. Thus, Sperling supports public spending on education and childcare. However, in the background lurks "Rubinomics", which means that budget constraints and fiscal responsibility can always put the kibosh on these plans.

Finally, new Democrats are largely silent on the labor market flexibility agenda, and appear uncomfortable confronting it. This is the case with Sperling's book. While he does support the minimum wage, he says nothing about the right

189

to organize unions or strengthening the minimum wage by indexing it to wages so as to create a true floor that can rise with growth. This silence reflects new Democrats' discomfort with questions of power as the labor question has always been one of power in capitalist economies. This contrasts with Faux's interest in politics.

Republicans argue that all four sides of the box benefit working families. In many ways, that makes new Democrats closer to Republicans than to old Democrats. New Democrats are essentially on board with the corporate globalization and less than full employment agendas. At the same time, new Democrats are largely silent on the question of minimum standards and protections for workers. Additionally, Rubinomics and its focus on deficit reduction, provide an escape from public investment commitments.

From an old Democrat perspective, new Democrats persistently seek to deal with "effects", and refuse to deal with "causes". In other words, new Democrat policy solutions are simply not proportionate to the scale of the problem facing America's working families.

That inevitably leads back to Faux's focus on politics, money, and power. Dealing with causes challenges the political and economic power structure. However, power pays the bills, and new Democrats want the money that the powerful currently give them. *Ergo*, new Democrats refuse to challenge the power structure, and hence their band-aid approach to working family economic woes.

Originally posted as "Old Democrats vs. New Democrats: Faux vs. Sperling" on March 2, 2006 at thomaspalley.com.

THIRD WAY, WRONG DIRECTION

February 21, 2007

In anticipation of 2008, a potentially historic debate is shaping up within the Democratic Party. On one side are progressive Democrats whose lineage reaches back to FDR and the New Deal. On the other side are New Democrats, who emerged in the 1980s and embraced Ronald Reagan's critique of big government.

The economy is the central point of contention between the two groups. Thus, New Democrats maintain the economy is headed in the right direction, and they deny progressive Democrat claims about income stagnation and corporate excess. This denial was recently on display in a report (*The New Rules Economy*) issued by Third Way, an influential New Democrat think-tank in Washington D.C. The report denies America's working families have been short-changed. In doing so, it misrepresents economic reality, undercuts working families and gives comfort to supporters of corporate excess. That makes the Third Way the wrong way. Here are the facts.

Denial #1: family income has not stagnated. The report begins by claiming America's middle class has been doing well. According to Third Way, incomes for married couple households half way up the income ladder (the fiftieth percentile) rose twenty-two percent between 1979 and 2004. That seems pretty good - except tucked away in a footnote is the fact that adjusting for increased hours worked by wives, income only rose nine percent. Over a twenty-five year period that translates into an average increase of about one-third of one percent per year – which is not the economy American families once knew.

The situation is far worse for those lower down the income ladder. Families near the bottom (the tenth percentile) saw their incomes rise just one percent over twenty-five years. If hours worked had not increased, their incomes would have fallen. For families at the thirtieth percentile (America's historic blue-collar middle class), the twenty-five year income gain was fourteen percent. Strip out increased hours worked and we're talking income stagnation.

Sizeable family income gains only kick in higher up the ladder: a thirty-one percent increase at the seventieth percentile and forty-two percent at the ninetieth percentile. But claiming these top-end families represent the middle-class is like believing we all have above average income.

Denial #2: executive pay not a problem. A second denial concerns the CEO pay explosion, which Third Way describes as "maddening" but just a "drop in the bucket" and of no major economic consequence. Reality says otherwise, with corporate executive excess now reaching such proportions that it is like a tax on all of us.

Harvard Law School Professor Lucian Bebchuk and Yaniv Grinstein of Cornell report that between 2001 and 2003 the aggregate compensation paid by public companies (about 2000 of them) to their top-five executive officers equaled ten percent of company profits. In a sense, these executives are implicitly claiming their productive contribution equals the contribution of ten percent of their companies' net equity capital.

The raw numbers show that between 1993 and 2003 total top-five executive compensation paid by public companies totaled 350 billion dollars. That averages 35 million dollars per executive, or 3.5 million dollars per executive per year. This is not a drop in the bucket; it's a hole.

Even worse, executive excess is a like cancer that ripples down and distorts organization pay structure, creating massive top-heavy pay inequality and leaving less for ordinary workers.

Denial #3: trade deficits not a problem. Next, Third Way casually dismisses the trade deficit as not a cause for concern. The trade deficit has caused job loss, and while it is true that the economy eventually creates new jobs, those replacement jobs tend to pay significantly less. Displaced workers therefore first suffer the injury of unemployment, and then find inferior jobs.

Moreover, it is widely known that companies use the threat of job off-shoring to suppress pay and benefits. This helps explain why family incomes have stagnated. Jobs don't need to be lost for current trading arrangements to do harm.

The trade deficit has also contributed to the erosion of the U.S. manufacturing base. Unable to compete because of unfair foreign trade practices and our own flawed policies, many manufacturing firms have either shut shop or moved offshore. That has shrunk manufacturing, which threatens future living standards because manufacturing is key to productivity growth.

It has also made the U.S. dependent on imported manufactured goods to accompany our dependence on imported oil. That is an economic and national security threat, which is compounded by the financial vulnerability that goes with growing foreign indebtedness. The trade deficit is the funnel through which these effects stream, yet Third Way recommends turning a blind eye.

Denial #4: no household debt or saving problem. Lastly, the report claims families have no debt problem because most debt is mortgage debt. However, data shows that households are paying a record share of income as interest, and debt is at record levels relative to income.

This has increased household financial vulnerability but that has been obscured by rapid house price inflation. Should house prices start falling or merely stall, as speculation evaporates or adverse demographics and income stagnation grind away, mortgage debt could quickly become a problem, Moreover, any problem will be amplified by increased income volatility since debt makes families more vulnerable to income shocks, be they due to sickness, outsourcing, or parenthood.

As for retirement saving, here too Third Way tries to hide behind house price inflation. The claim is that increased house prices have solved the saving problem. That is like saying we can take care of saving through inflation.

Higher house prices have benefited those who bought early enough, but prices must be sustained. Even if they are, owners' gains come at the expense of buyers whose own saving is eaten up by large mortgage interest payments. And if someone sells their home because they need retirement income, where do they live? On top of that, what about the thirty-plus percent of people who do not own?

House price inflation is a one-time wealth transfer that at best solves the saving problem of one generation of owners. Put bluntly, price inflation that robs Peter to pay Paul does not solve families' long-term problem, which is one of wages and income.

Posted on February 21, 2007 at thomaspalley.com.

THE FLAWS IN FISCAL AUSTERITY (RUBINOMICS)

May 2, 2007

With Senator Hillary Clinton firmly cemented as the front-runner for the Democratic Party's nomination, Rubinomics—named after former Treasury Secretary Robert Rubin, who shaped economic policy under President Clinton— has re-emerged as a critical issue. This is because Senator Clinton has firmly embraced it. Rubinomics rests on faulty economics and embodies bad politics. Progressive Democrats and the nation need to understand this. Here's an explanation.

The central proposition of Rubinomics is that budget deficits reduce saving and increase interest rates, thereby reducing investment and lowering future living standards. However, the record shows that interest rates fell to historic lows over the past several years, a time of large deficits. That fits the common sense observation that the Federal Reserve largely determines interest rates contingent on economic conditions. Meanwhile, a flood of savings has poured into financial markets from wealthy individuals and pension funds, and corporations have been net buyers of stock on the back of record profits.

Nor does the "twin deficit" argument — that budget deficits cause trade deficits — make sense, as evidenced by the fact that in the late 1990s the United States ran record trade deficits as the budget moved into record surplus. Japan and Germany also disprove the argument as they have run large trade surpluses and budget deficits for many years. Rather, the U.S. trade deficit is due to undervalued foreign currencies and export-led growth strategies by many countries that look to grow by selling to the United States while restricting purchases of American-made goods.

Despite these logical failings, Rubinomics still has great appeal because Rubin's tenure as Treasury Secretary coincided with the 1990s boom. That appeal is misplaced. The rooster crows at dawn but does not cause the sunrise. Rubin was Treasury Secretary during the boom, but budget surpluses did not cause it.

The political origins of Rubinomics trace back to the 1970s, when conservative charges about big government and "tax and spend" liberals took deep hold on America's political consciousness. Throughout the 1980s Democrats struggled to respond, eventually settling in the 1990s on a strategy of "fiscal responsibility." That strategy was always transitional and defensive, aimed at blunting Republicans' relentless attack on government and plutocratic tax cuts. The long-term goal was always an alternative narrative to free-market mythology.

The tragedy is that once a myth takes hold it must be lived out to be disproved. That is the price paid for losing the war of ideas. This process has now worked itself out, and America is finally grasping the fallacies of market fundamentalism. That creates a historic opportunity, but Rubinomics risks a tragic second act. Rubinomics worked brilliantly as a political strategy in the 1990s. But its success was political, not economic. However, its supporters have lost sight of this and now credit it with causing the late-'90s boom. Consequently, they argue for sticking with Rubinomics, thereby missing the opportunity created by the dismal failure of Bush's presidency.

Instead of continuing down a mistaken path that focuses on the budget deficit, proponents of a progressive economic policy should focus on increasing investment, which is key to productivity growth and full employment. Rising wages and full employment, in combination with a fairly valued dollar, create a favorable investment climate. That sets the stage for a virtuous circle of shared prosperity. Investment raises productivity, which raises wages and profits, thereby increasing demand and drawing more investment. This is the real basis of a rising tide that lifts all boats. With regard to the trade deficit, the solution is to revalue exchange rates, raise wages abroad so that foreign workers can consume more of what they produce and have countries adopt coordinated policies that stimulate the global economy. That would benefit all, and it is why labor standards and exchange rate provisions must be in all trade agreements.

Rubinomics is not only bad economics but also bad politics. First, by arguing that the problem is a shortage of saving Rubinomics promotes a conservative tax agenda privileging saving and profits, which primarily benefits the rich. Second, by placing budget deficits at the center of the saving problem, it sets government up as a problem and makes a case for shrinking it. Furthermore, by promising to lock Democrats into a path of fiscal austerity, it exposes future Democratic Administrations to the charge of "flip-flopping." This is because fiscal stimulus will inevitably be needed when the current unbalanced boom ends.

The greatest tragedy of all concerns the potentially disastrous consequences for Social Security and Medicare. These programs are more vital than ever, given America's aging population and retirement wealth inequality. Yet Rubinomics establishes the premise for dismantling them. By claiming the budget must be balanced to increase savings, it sets up a political deal whereby Republicans suspend their unjustifiable tax cuts in return for Democrats putting Social Security and Medicare on the table. This would be the ultimate conservative triumph, the evisceration of the crown jewels of FDR's New Deal and Johnson's Great Society.

The cruel irony is that Democrats would be the agent of this destruction at the very moment when history is proffering the opportunity for a great reversal of market fundamentalism. At a time of significant productivity growth, due to the maturation of the Internet and other technologies, Rubinomics establishes the premise that America cannot afford these great programs. Most bitter of all, once institutions like Social Security are dismantled, they are hard to resurrect, whereas tax cuts can be easily restored. This means dealing Social Security benefit cuts in return for repeal of the Bush tax cuts is both unjustified and a political trap. All of this is worth thinking about if you're thinking about voting for Hillary Clinton.

This article appeared originally as "The flaws in Rubinomics" in The Nation, 284 (20), May 2007 and at www.thenation.com. Also posted on October 9, 2007 at thomaspalley.com.

January 8, 2007

MEMO

TO: Progressive Presidential Candidates:
RE: Framing a Winning Economic Policy
FROM: Thomas I. Palley

The unbalanced U.S. boom that has followed the 2001 recession provides a real window of opportunity for progressive Democrats to reverse the laissez-faire extremism of the last 30 years. This window may open still wider if the economy suffers a recession in the next two years. If progressives are to take full advantage of this opportunity, they will need a new economic policy frame. Here's a suggested road map.

(1) The roots of past failure. As a rule, progressive economic policies have played well in slumps, but their traction has tended to weaken with recovery as it becomes more difficult to argue for change of direction. This pattern has been a recurrent problem over the last 25 years, especially since the so-called good times have often not been that good for many working families. Once recessions have ended, policy has quickly reverted to the laissez-faire model. The result has been globalization without standards, persistent erosion of worker bargaining power, and expansion of the economic power of corporate and financial elites.

Behind this political failure lies a progressive economic policy framed in terms of unemployment, fairness, and, more recently, budget deficits. This triptych—unemployment, fairness, and budget deficits—is deeply flawed as it lacks staying power, rests on an essentially negative message that clashes with America's economic optimism, and is prone to economic confusions.

Though unemployment resonates deeply in recessions, it loses traction once the economy moves into recovery stage. That means progressive critique can sound off-key for the greater part of the business cycle.

Economic fairness has more lasting appeal. However, it seems to be a secondary economic value for many Americans and is usually trumped by concerns with efficiency, enterprise, and growth. This public attitude is reinforced by laissez-faire economists who regard a trade-off between equity and economic efficiency as unavoidable

Finally, focusing on budget deficits makes it look as if government itself and lack of saving—conservative positions— are the problems. That, in turn, pushes tax policies that privilege saving and profits and increases both the deficit and inequality. Additionally, focusing on the deficit produces message confusion since

197

budget deficits can be desirable to counter recessions or finance public investment. That adds the further complication of distinguishing "good" deficits from "bad" deficits due to tax cuts for the wealthy and wasteful spending.

(2) A winning economic policy frame. Despite their failings of framing, progressives have considerable traction on economic issues because of deep-seated public anxiety about the economy.

These anxieties have only deepened during the unbalanced boom of the last four years—a boom marked by slow job growth, hidden chronic unemployment, wage stagnation, stagnant poverty rates, and further increased wealth and income inequality. The only upside has been robust consumption spending, but even that is superficial since its source was a housing price bubble.

These unhealthy features provide the key to a winning progressive economic policy frame. That frame must restore the link between wages and productivity growth, combined with full employment. In addition, the budget and trade deficits should be discussed in terms of long-haul sustainability.

Linking wages and productivity growth focuses on the entire business cycle, rather than just recession. That fills the gap afflicting existing policy messaging in booms, and booms that fail to deliver rising wages can be rightly criticized. Moreover, emphasizing productivity growth makes it an explicitly pro-growth message. Lastly, the message is anchored in economic history, the "golden age" of the American economy being 1945—'73 when wages and productivity rose together and the rising economic tide lifted all boats.

A winning strategy substitutes full employment for unemployment. Words matter. Full employment is an affirmative concept, whereas unemployment is a negative one. Full employment also resonates with self-help, whereas unemployment can suggest welfare. And spotlighting full employment also fits with tying wages to productivity since tight labor markets help workers win a share of their productivity. Of course, what constitutes full employment is open to debate, but that is a debate worth having and one that conservatives have shuttered since the late 1960s.

Finally, the budget and trade deficit should be reframed in terms of sustainability. That escapes the prison of the lock-box and balanced budgets by recognizing that deficits can be both good and bad. As with full employment, sustainability is also open to debate, but once again that's a debate worth having.

A productivity based wages, full employment, sustainable deficits frame embodies a powerful affirmative logic. Moreover, it provides an easy funnel for showcasing the "hot-button" discontents of today's economy. Rising inequality and the CEO pay explosion are simply the flipside of today's wage-productivity disconnect. The trade deficit drains demand from the U.S. economy, undermining

198

full employment and manufacturing, which is key to future productivity-wage growth. And George Bush's tax cuts have promoted bad unsustainable deficits.

Most importantly, such a frame invites questions of what caused the disconnection between wages and productivity, and what can be done to remedy that disconnect, That opens the way for deeper discussion about the economy, and in particular the role of economic power. Once that door is open, it's easy to understand the role of unions in tying wages to productivity and limiting CEO excess. It is also easy to see why globalization will not work unless accompanied by global labor standards.

By way of example, consider the debate over the minimum wage. The existing progressive policy frame emphasizes fairness, with the minimum wage helping low-paid workers make a living. Compare that with a wage-productivity frame in which the minimum wage is part of the system for tying wages to productivity growth. That suggests not only should the minimum wage be increased, it should also be indexed to the median wage (say at 50 to 60 percent). Whereas the former approach relies on charitable sentiments, the latter approach gives everyone a vested interest in the minimum wage. That's a winning political strategy.

(3) Lessons from history. History contains some encouraging parallels with the current moment, but it also shows that winning will require more than just a wish list of progressive policies. In the 1940s, Keynesian economics swept through the halls of academe and policymaking, transforming the way that people thought about the economy. Absent the Great Depression, it is unlikely this revolution in thought would ever have happened.

Likewise, in the 1970s, the stagflation induced by the OPEC oil price increases created a window of opportunity for Milton Friedman's laissez-faire idea of a natural rate of unemployment that returned economics to pre-Depression modes of thought. George Bush's sick and unbalanced boom provides progressives with a similar opportunity.

However, history also illustrates that crisis alone is not enough to change thinking. Ideas must also be ready to fill the vacuum that opens. That has important strategic implications for progressive presidential candidates.

Put bluntly, a laundry list of policy proposals is not enough to transform thinking about the economy. That is a deeper task requiring policy be connected to a convincing vision of how the economy works.

Posted on January 8, 2007 at thomaspalley.com.

BEYOND RED AND BLUE

May 18, 2007

It is widely recognized that the debacle in Iraq has contributed importantly to disenchantment with the Bush administration and Republican Party. However, less recognized is the potential long-term political impact of Iraq, which has opened the door to moving beyond the red state – blue state division that has marked U.S. politics for the past generation. That in turn could create a lasting progressive majority.

American electoral politics has operated historically along two dimensions of "values" and "economics". The values dimension concerns issues of abortion, guns, religion and flag. The economics dimension concerns the perceived efficiency of markets, corporate power, income inequality and trade. For the past twenty-five years economics has played second fiddle to the values dimension, which has dominated electoral politics and defined the division between red and blue states.

This political ordering reflects the triumph of Ronald Reagan and Milton Friedman, who captured middle America's political imagination and established a new *laissez-faire* consensus. That consensus lowered the electoral traction of economic argument and raised the traction of values, which helps explain the convergence of New Democrats with Republicans on matters of economic policy and globalization.

Now, America's searing experience in Iraq has unexpectedly opened the door to reversing this ordering. The brutal intolerance of Islamic fundamentalism has provided a mirror for reflecting upon Christian fundamentalism and what it might mean for American society. In a sense, Iraq has discredited all religious fundamentalisms by showing what happens when religions try to enforce their views on all. That stands to reduce support for the Christian right's agenda and strengthen support for separation of church and state and the right to privacy.

A second plank of the right's values agenda has been the construction of patriotism in terms of muscular militarism. That construction grew out of the humiliations of U.S. defeat in Vietnam and the 1979 Iran hostage crisis, and it is reflected in the popular "Rambo" fantasy. This neo-con fantasy has been permanently discredited by the dismal military outcome in Iraq. Despite easily defeating Saddam Hussein, the U.S. has been unable to achieve victory. That failure stands to diminish the appeal of framing patriotism and national security in terms of unilateralist militarism.

At the same time that Iraq has exposed these failings of the right's values agenda, economic issues have increased in salience. Globalization, wage stagnation, and rising income inequality and economic insecurity have all become major public concerns in both red and blue states. When values ruled the political roost these economic concerns were trumped, but now they are surfacing and redefining the political terrain.

These changes are captured by the "new populism" associated with the likes of Senators Jon Tester of Montana, Claire McCaskill of Missouri, and Jim Webb of Virginia. All won election in 2006 in red states running on messages that contained a strong economic component.

The success of new populism is driven by two factors. First, growing willingness of red state voters to see through the veil of values-based identity politics. Second, recognition that red states share common economic challenges with blue states. Once the veil of identity is pierced, it becomes clear that farmers, factory workers, and urban white-collar workers share many similar problems.

Those problems are loss of livelihood, be it the family farm or a manufacturing job; economic insecurity, be it due to outsourcing or agricultural price volatility; and exploitation due to unequal economic power. Manufacturing workers must negotiate with multi-national corporations and face low wage competition from the global sourcing practices of retail firms like Wal-Mart. Service sector workers also increasingly confront global out-sourcing.

Farmers face similar problems. Corn and grain farmers confront the power of Archer Daniels, Cargill and Monsanto; beef, chicken and pork growers must deal with Smithfield and Tyson; dairy farmers confront Dean Foods, while all purchase equipment from John Deere and use the railroads to ship product to market. Up and down, the farm economy is dominated by economic power concentrated in massive agro-businesses.

Just as global sourcing has squeezed manufacturing workers and shifted profits to large retailers and brands such as Nike, so too small farmers are receiving less of the value created in the farm-to-food production chain. In effect, workers, small manufacturers and farmers all compete on a tilted playing field, which calls for new policies restoring a balance of power.

Growing recognition of this reality has created the possibility of a new politics spanning red and blue states, auguring well for a future progressive majority. Iraq has played an important role by lifting the political fog generated by the right's divisive values agenda.

Originally posted as "From quagmire to progressive victory" on May 17, 2007 in TomPaine.com. Also posted at thomaspalley.com on May 18, 2007.

DEAF TO HISTORY'S RHYME:
WHY PRESIDENT OBAMA IS FAILING

December 2, 2010

The great American novelist Mark Twain observed "History does not repeat itself but it rhymes." Today the rhyme is with the 1930s, and if you don't hear it read FDR's great Madison Square Garden speech of October 1936:

"For twelve years this nation was afflicted with hear-nothing, see-nothing, do-nothing government. The nation looked to government but the government looked away. Nine mocking years with the golden calf and three long years with the scourge! Nine crazy years at the ticker and three long years in the breadlines! Nine mad years of mirage and three long years of despair! Powerful influences strive today to restore that kind of government with its doctrine that that government is best which is most indifferent."

Despite this clarity, the Obama administration insists on hearing a rhyme with the 1990s. That tone deafness has its roots in political choices made at the administration's outset and explains why the administration has stumbled so badly in its first years. If continued, the economic and social consequences will be grave.

In 2008 President Obama captured the nation with a message of change, yet in office he has chosen to deliver change of style rather than change of substance. At the headline level this choice was reflected in his call for bi-partisanship that looked to split the difference with Republicans. In economic policy, it was reflected in the wholesale reappointment of the Clinton administration team led by Larry Summers and Timothy Geithner, a case of continuity not change.

Now, the administration is sinking under failure of its economic policy. That failure is due to its attempt to revive a 1990s paradigm that never worked as advertised and can only deliver stagnation. Painful though it is for Democrats to acknowledge, the reality is the economic policies of President Clinton were largely the same as those of President Bush. On this the record is clear for those willing to see. The Clinton administration pushed financial deregulation; twice reappointed Alan Greenspan; promoted corporate globalization through NAFTA and China PNTR; initiated the strong dollar policy; spoke of the "end of the era of big government"; contemplated privatization of Social Security; and struck down a core element of the New Deal by ending the right to welfare.

The main difference between the Clinton and Bush administrations was the former's willingness to offer some helping-hand policies to cushion the harsh effects of the invisible hand. Differences in outcomes were not policy driven but reflect the fact the Clinton administration enjoyed the good fortune of the Internet investment bubble. It also benefitted from the beginning of the housing bubble when American families had plenty of untapped home equity and credit.

President Obama's fateful decision to go with Clintonomics meant the recession was interpreted as an extremely deep downturn rather than a crisis signaling the bankruptcy of the neoliberal paradigm that has ruled both Republicans and Democrats for thirty years. That implied the recession could be fully addressed with stimulus, which was the same response as the Bush administration to the recession of 2001.

The current recession is the deepest economic downturn since the Great Depression of the 1930s, inviting comparisons with President Franklin Delano Roosevelt. FDR had the advantage of taking office three years into the Depression when the unemployment rate was near 25 percent. The verdict was in: the system needed change. President Obama took office as the crisis was deepening. Those who had designed the system could still argue it could be revived and as establishment insiders they had the upper hand. But that argument is done and today the prospect is of long stagnation.

The New Deal was a break with both the politics and economic policies of the past. Its economic policy innovations like Social Security, the Securities and Exchange Commission, the Fair Labor Standards Act, and the Wagner Act granting the right to organize, are still celebrated. However, it was FDR's new politics of solidarity and compassion that created the necessary political space: solidarity that recognized the country was in the Depression together and compassion that recognized many were suffering through no fault of their own. That is the political rhyme President Obama must hear, while the New Deal is the policy rhyme.

The President's failure to deliver on the country's desire for change of substance has left a vacuum that is being filled by dangerous unstable forces. This is the tale of the Tea Party, which is a tale that has resonance for Europe. The economic risk, already more advanced in Europe, is a doubling-down of disastrously failed hardcore neoliberal economic policies. The political risk is a rise of intolerance and xenophobia.

These are not normal times. If the administration persists with its deafness to history it will surely hit the rocks and an historical opportunity for progressive change will be squandered. Worse yet, its deafness will leave the field open to the extreme right whose "blame-the-victim" social message and "liquidationist-austerity" economic policies clearly confirm today's rhyme is with the history of the 1930s.

Posted on December 2, 2010 in the FT Economist's Forum and on thomaspalley.com.

XII RESTORING SHARED PROSPERITY

Economics for the real world

♦

Keynesianism: What is and why it still matters

♦

Plan B for Obama on the economy

♦

Income distribution: A question of power

♦

A global minimum wage system

♦

The immigration debate: Worker rights are missing

♦

Expand Sarbox, not shrink it

♦

A better way to regulate financial markets:
Asset based reserve requirements

♦

A new trade agenda:
Tropical trade liberalization plus labor standards

◆

Exchange rates: There is a better way

◆

Exchange rates, labor standards, and democracy:
Why China must change

◆

Markets and the common good

ECONOMICS FOR THE REAL WORLD

January 25, 2006

Many Americans have rightly identified China, uncontrolled trade deficits, and Wal-Mart style competition as looming threats to the American economy. However, they remain hard-pressed countering the free market/free trade story of mainstream economists that these are all for America's long run benefit.

In a previous piece I explained how mainstream economics has been captured by laissez-faire idealizations that are heavily peppered with ideology. Now it is time to present an alternative real world economics. America's economic problems can only be solved by good policy rooted in sound economic analysis. And to find that analysis Americans must look to their own past.

The Great Depression of the 1930s was an era of tumultuous economic debate. Though now largely confined to history books, those debates have vital relevance for today's challenge of globalization. The economy of that earlier era was marked by callousness, gross inequalities of wealth, and vicious boom – bust cycles. These problems were ultimately solved by a combination of New Deal institutional reforms and Keynesian economic stabilization policies. While some of the reforms of that period may have aged, the economic principles that motivated them remain intact. This is a cruel irony, since the thinking that can help address our present malaise has been forgotten by many who once championed such thinking.

The policies that emerged from the Depression provided the foundation of the prosperity that followed World War II. But familiarity and success tend to breed forgetfulness. As a result, the thinking forged on the anvil of those hard times has been gradually expunged, and replaced by revived pre-Depression era free market thinking. Carried by this intellectual tide, policymakers have created a modern variant of the Victorian economy under the rubric of globalization.

Today's economic conditions hint of the 1920s, a period when America experienced a credit boom and a speculative bubble while the rest of the world experienced relative stagnation. Hopefully, enough post-Depression era policy thinking remains to avoid another great slump. But simply avoiding a slump is not sufficient. The challenge is to design policies that will once again engender the broadly shared prosperity that defined the early post-war decades. That, in turn, will require recovering economic thinking that has been relegated (by mainstream economics) to the history books.

One lasting contribution from the Depression came from the British economist John Maynard Keynes, who identified the importance of total demand for determining employment. Total demand is defined as the aggregate of household, business and public spending within the economy. Unemployment can result from reduced spending by business and households. At best, markets are painfully slow in dealing with such declines, and at worst they can get trapped with permanent high unemployment.

Keynes recognized that the market economy price system does not automatically ensure adequate total demand, and what works for an individual product market does not automatically work for the economy as a whole. In individual markets, lower prices make goods relatively cheaper, providing an incentive for households or businesses to switch expenditures away from other products. However, for the economy as a whole, this mechanism does not work since all prices (including wages) are falling so that there is no ability or incentive to increase spending. Worse than that, the mechanism may operate in reverse as falling prices increase the burden of debts and interest payments, which reduces demand and can also bankrupt the banking system.

Consequently, there is reason for policy to step in and stabilize demand to avoid such outcomes. This is classic Keynesian policy, sometimes referred to as counter-cyclical spending. The essence of the principle is that when household and business demand falls off, policymakers should step in and, through federal spending on infrastructure and lower interest rates, stop the downward spiral and prime the economy.

A second vital contribution, now forgotten, came from American "institutional" economists who emphasized the significance of the nature of competition. The most famous living proponent of this American school is John Kenneth Galbraith. Whereas Keynes's analysis gave birth to the modern field of macroeconomics, American institutionalists focused on the microeconomic failings of the system. These failings were framed in terms of the "competitive menace," a notion that echoes today's concept of the race to the bottom -- epitomized by Wal-Mart.

Institutionalists did not challenge the idea that self-interest and profit are major motives for economic action, but they did recognize that their pursuit could lead to sub-optimal outcomes. What appears to maximize well-being from an individual perspective can be sub-optimal once the competitive inter-play of actions is taken into account. Thus, when Wal-Mart refuses to pay health benefits, other retailers are forced to go in this direction to remain competitive and survive. Likewise, when Wal-Mart sources globally, so too must other retailers. The result is erosion of American manufacturing jobs and wages. Nor do wages rise in developing countries because Wal-Mart plays them off against China.

Such a perspective leads to the idea of "regimes of competition," and policy should aim to create a competitive environment in which working families prosper. The challenge is to design regulatory institutions (regimes) that balance the Keynesian need for stable flows of demand and income with the capitalist need for economic incentives. Such market regulation prevents excessive price fluctuations, and also prevents the kinds of pre-Depression monopoly and exploitation that weakened America's income and spending base.

The New Deal embodied much institutionalist policy in the form of laws establishing a minimum wage, the forty-hour week, the right to overtime, and the right to join unions. These labor laws complemented consumer product safety laws. The New Deal also introduced law regulating financial markets, which paired with earlier legislation establishing the Federal Reserve as regulator of the banking system. Together, these regulations established an economic regime that excluded destructive competition, ensured a "Henry Ford" distribution of income whereby workers could buy the things they produced, and prevented market tendencies to deflation.

Viewed in this light, American institutionalism provided a new microeconomic thinking that paired logically with Keynes' macroeconomic analysis. Keynesian monetary and fiscal policies stabilized the business cycle, while institutionalist market regulation built the middle class, and together they underwrote the great prosperity of the post-World War II era.

However, even as these policies were being put into practice, they were being driven out of economics classrooms and textbooks. Whereas Keynesianism won mainstream standing, its microeconomic counterpart never did. One reason was institutionalism's focus on capitalism's crueler failings, which was politically unacceptable in the Cold War era of geo-political competition. This meant institutionalism was driven out of classrooms by the end of the 1950s, which meant it was driven out of policy shops and legislative chambers by the end of the 1970s.

Globalization has again raised the specter of destructive competition, calling for a resurgence of institutionalist thinking. However, such thinking is now barred and obliterated by post-Cold War, free-market triumphalism.

This has enormous practical and political consequences. Absent the one-two combination of Keynesianism and institutionalism, globalization will likely stumble badly. Similarly, well-intentioned progressive politicians in America and Europe, looking to tackle the problems of globalization, will find themselves lost as long as they adhere to the laissez-faire thinking that dominates universities.

This risks making progressives irrelevant for economic policy. In the 1930s, the economics of the day proved not up to the challenge of the Great Depression, forcing the development of new economic ideas. The same holds today for globalization.

Originally posted as "Back to Basics: Progressive Economics for the 21st Century" on January 18, 2006. Also posted as "Back to the future: Economics for the real world" in Mother Jones on January 25, 2006.

KEYNESIANISM:
WHAT IS AND WHY IT STILL MATTERS

September 18, 2005

For the last three decades *laissez-faire* conservatives have sought to systematically discredit the ideas known as "Keynesianism." This assault has had deleterious consequences for economic policy and public economic understandings. It is time for Keynesians to fight back.

Keynesianism refers to the set of ideas associated with the great British economist John Maynard Keynes, who published his *magnum opus, The General Theory of Employment, Interest and Money*, in 1936. *The General Theory* provided a framework for understanding the Great Depression. But far more than that, it provided a framework for understanding the "big picture" operation of modern capitalist economies. In a sense, it was to economics what Einstein's general theory of relativity was to physics.

Keynesianism rests on the simple compelling insight that, subject to capacity limits, the level of economic activity is determined by demand for output. This principle explains a wide range of phenomena in capitalist economies. If demand is insufficient, firms will reduce production and employment and the economy will fall into recession. That is why we worry about consumer and business spending.

Most importantly, Keynes explained why market economies do not automatically generate sufficient demand to ensure full employment. In fact, demand is usually slightly less than that needed for full employment, which means market economies spend most of the time with unnecessary unemployment that is economically wasteful, socially destructive and the cause of great individual suffering. Moreover, on occasion the employment shortfall can be large, as during the Great Depression. However, though recognizing that market economies usually fail to produce full employment, Keynes was not anti-market. Markets work well for those that are employed; the problem is they tend to create insufficient employment.

This failing means that there is a role for government in ensuring full employment. Thus, government can affect demand through taxes, social security and unemployment insurance, and through spending on infrastructure and government services. Government can also affect demand through labor and minimum wage laws that impact wages and income distribution. Finally, central banks affect demand through their control over interest rates.

The period 1945 – 1975 is widely regarded as having been a golden age of mass prosperity, and it was a time when Keynesian ideas dominated policymaking. In 1971 President Nixon famously declared "We are all Keynesians now." Since then Keynesianism has been in retreat, though owing to its outstanding earlier success policymaking still remains subject to Keynesian influences. This influence is evidenced by Federal Reserve interest rate policy and by the acceptance of larger budget deficits in recessions. However, there has been a retreat in politics and academic teaching, with important consequences.

This retreat is the result of both attack by the right and over-selling by the left. With regard to the right, it always opposed Keynesianism's identification of an important policy role for government and it disliked progressive taxation. The right also opposed labor market institutions and financial regulations that promoted robust stable demand at the expense of their economic and political power. With regard to the left, it tended to overstate the extent of Keynesian market failure, to understate the effectiveness of market prices and incentives in driving economic action, and to stretch the case for government replacing market production. Finally, Keynesian success in achieving full employment aggravated the perennial problem of conflict over income shares, thereby causing higher inflation. This problem needed a political solution that was never forthcoming, and the right skillfully used the inflationary OPEC oil shocks of the 1970s to blame Keynesianism for the resulting economic disruption.

The political, intellectual and rhetorical retreat from Keynesianism has had enormous consequences. First, there has been a retreat from true full employment, which means that we live today with unwarranted unemployment. Second, the pre-Keynesian ideology of self-adjusting economies has reasserted itself and been used to rollback financial regulation, labor market protections, trade unions and the minimum wage. This has worsened income distribution and created a proclivity to boom-bust cycles. Third, the case for progressive taxes and a more equal income distribution have been rolled back as this is no longer viewed as part of the demand management policy agenda. Fourth and finally, the relevance of Keynesianism for globalization has been suppressed. Keynes was always cautious about free trade and skeptical about international mobility of financial capital because of the impacts on employment and the ability to conduct national economic policy. These concerns speak to the 21st century relevance of Keynesianism and the need for a Keynesian counter-revolution.

Posted on September 18, 2005 at thomaspalley.com.

PLAN B FOR OBAMA ON THE ECONOMY

September 6, 2010

TO: President Obama
FROM: Thomas I. Palley
RE: How to avoid stagnation and restore shared prosperity
DATE: Labor Day, 2010

Mr. President,

With hopes of a V- or U-shaped recovery fading, there is the increasing prospect of an L-shaped future of long stagnation, or even a W-shaped future in which W stands for something worse.

The reason for this dismal outlook is economic policy is trapped by failed conventional thinking that can only deliver wage stagnation and prolonged mass unemployment.

Your administration's current economic recovery program has been marked by four major failings:

1. Inadequate fiscal stimulus.
2. Failure to cauterize the housing market.
3. Failure to neutralize the trade deficit.
4. Failure to restore the link between wage and productivity growth.

If your policy team remedies these four failings our economy will quickly begin robust recovery. However, the longer you wait the greater the challenge, because recession creates new facts in the form of bankruptcies, foreclosures, destroyed credit histories, job losses and factory closures.

Suggested remedies

1. Let the Bush administration tax cuts expire and use the savings for additional targeted stimulus

The economy needs a further demand boost to establish recovery momentum. The majority of the Bush tax cuts were an income redistribution program favoring the wealthy rather than a stimulus or growth program. That makes extending them bad policy.

The Bush 10 per cent bracket and marriage provisions should be retained, while everything else should be allowed to expire with the savings used to fund new temporary fiscal stimulus.

Half the funds should be directed to state and local governments to help avoid another round of job losses, this time in state and local government. The other half should fund an immediate lump sum non-taxable payment to all individuals earning less than $50,000 ($100,000 for married couples). This means 80 per cent of households will continue benefiting and the total paid to these households will actually increase.

Moreover, the lump-sum design will increase the benefit going to those at the bottom, which will further stimulate demand and also lower income inequality. This temporary stimulus should be repealed once self-sustaining recovery is underway.

2. Cauterize the housing market

The second critical measure is to cauterize the housing market. Throughout the crisis, policy has disproportionately benefited banks and corporations. It has largely failed to help households directly and has instead relied on hopes of trickle-down effects from banks, combined with expensive tax subsidies to attract new home buyers.

The failure to directly help households has been a grievous policy error. Along with banks and corporations, households have needed debt relief but this has not been forthcoming. Banks have resisted meaningful loan modifications, while many households have been unable to refinance mortgages at lower interest rates because of zero or negative home equity. Consequently, the household sector has remained distressed and trapped in a foreclosure tsunami that has traumatized the economy.

Policy must immediately put a floor under existing homeowners. The solution is use the Federal Housing Administration to refinance Fannie Mae and Freddie Mac mortgages with low or even negative equity and then have Fannie and Freddie repay some of their federal government borrowings. The test criteria should be whether the mortgage is viable once refinanced at low rates.

Additionally, the Federal Reserve must continue with purchases of mortgage-backed securities to ensure that mortgage rates stay low until the housing market has stabilized.

Refinancing such mortgages will yield a huge boost to the distressed corner of the household sector that is currently unable to refinance. It would reduce foreclosures; boost consumer demand by lowering mortgage payments; and it is urgent because adjustable rate mortgages issued late in the bubble are still resetting upward.

The problem has always been inability to service interest costs, and the foreclosure wave could have been avoided if lower interest servicing had been made immediately available to households. Policy did this for the business sector via the TARP and various Federal Reserve rescue facilities but failed to do so for households.

3. Neutralize the trade deficit

The third critical measure is to neutralize the trade deficit. The adverse effects of the trade deficit can be understood through the metaphor of a bathtub. Fiscal and monetary stimulus is being poured into the tub but that demand is leaking out through the plughole of the trade deficit. Moreover, it is not just demand that leaks out, but also jobs and investment due to off-shoring.

The trade deficit and off-shoring are significantly attributable to China's under-valued exchange rate, which also forces other countries to under-value their exchange rates to stay competitive. This has resulted in an over-valued dollar which makes the U.S. economy internationally uncompetitive.

As China refuses to correct its under-valued exchange rate, it is long past time for the U.S. to take protective action. That can be done via administrative interventions and legislation to make countries with under-valued exchange rates subject to countervailing duties.

There may be trade disruption and retaliation, but the costs of inaction and appeasement are far worse. The problem of under-valued exchange rates was visible a decade ago yet policymakers have failed to take action with devastating consequences.

The choice has always been pay now or pay more later. Inaction means working families have already paid enormously and continued inaction will compound their devastation.

4. Restore the wage – productivity growth link.

Finally, policy must address the central problem of the last 30 years: the destruction of the income generating process and severing of the wage – productivity growth link.

Rebuilding that link is critical to recovery and shared prosperity, and it requires rebuilding worker bargaining power. One immediate measure is passage of the Employee Free Choice Act that will enable unions to organize on a level playing field.

A second measure is to index the minimum wage to the median wage. That will create a real wage floor and limit wage inequality because the minimum wage will automatically increase as median wages rise with productivity.

5. Do it all

It is important these measures are enacted as a comprehensive package.

Implemented alone they will be far less successful.

Without tackling the trade deficit, fiscal stimulus and the benefits from cauterizing the housing market will leak out of the economy. Similarly, increasing union membership and wages will result in an acceleration of job and investment off-shoring.

Fixing the trade deficit without fixing the income generation process and lightening households' debt burden will leave the economy permanently short of demand.

Escaping the Great Recession requires jumpstarting the economy by increasing demand. Preventing the economy falling back into stagnation requires rebuilding the income and demand generating process. That is why success needs the full policy package.

Posted on the FT Economists' Forum on September 6, 2010. Also posted at thomaspalley.com on September 8, 2010.

INCOME DISTRIBUTION: A QUESTION OF POWER

September 20, 2006

Recently, there has been growing recognition of the enormous increase in U.S. income inequality that has occurred over the last twenty-five years, bringing back inequality levels not seen since 1929. Paul Krugman has written of the danger of a new oligarchy, whose wealth is such that it may be able to control an economy and society even as large as the United States.

So real is growing inequality that even libertarian-minded Alan Greenspan has mused on its dangers to "democratic society" – though his fear is not the undemocratic character of oligarchy, but rather that too much inequality may promote economically disruptive political rebellion from below.

This expanding recognition of the income distribution problem by the prominent and powerful is extremely welcome. However, it raises the question "what is the cause?" One short answer is changed economic power between workers and corporations. This change has affected wage bargaining and whose interests get taken into account in business and economic policy decision-making. The power explanation stands in sharp contrast to economists' stories about increased income inequality being due to rising returns to skill and education. What is so important about the power story is that it torpedoes the standard explanation of income distribution. And with it sinks much other economics about the adverse effects of trade unions, the idea of a natural rate of unemployment, and many claims about the benefits of globalization.

The power story has been around for a long time, but now the economic data have become so clear that it is forcing itself upon the business friendly economics profession. A recent research paper by Becker and Gordon of Northwestern University, "Where Did the Productivity Growth go?" reports that productivity growth has been largely captured by those in the top one percent of the income distribution, especially those in the top one-tenth of one percent. This challenges full on the conventional wisdom that rising income inequality is due to increased economic premiums to skill and education. Wage and salary income of individuals at the 90th percentile grew just 34 percent between 1972 and 2001. That's about the rate of productivity growth, so being a college graduate earned normal returns and was not a ticket to the income stratosphere.

This finding should come as no surprise. For the past two decades the Economic Policy Institute has documented rising income inequality in its bi-annual publication, *The State of Working America*. The 2004 edition reported that hourly wages of those with less than a college degree fell between 1979 and 2003; wages of college degree holders rose by less than one percent a year over that period; and those of advanced degree holders grew by less than 1.1 percent per year. Consequently, the notion of enormous returns to education is a myth.

Despite these facts, the economics profession has continued touting its education story, which confuses correlation and causation. Wages of college-educated persons grew fairly normally over the last thirty years, but wages of those with less than a college degree fell. *Ergo*, the increase in income inequality was positively correlated with educational attainment, but returns to education were normal and not the cause of increased inequality.

The education story has been popular because it serves the social and political purposes of the powerful and favored. First, it implicitly blames the victims for their plight. Workers are responsible for their condition, having been too stupid or lazy to finish high school and go to college. With glib ease, Washington "suits" can then dismiss amazingly skilled welders, mechanics, and blast furnace operators as unskilled. Second, the education story allays fears about globalization and rising corporate power because these supposedly have little to do with rising inequality, which is instead attributed to skill-rewarding technological change. Third, investing in education provides a convenient solution for elite policymakers. Fourth, the education story is consistent with the dominant economic theory of income distribution, and therefore saves that theory.

That dominant theory (known as marginal productivity theory) claims that free markets ensure that workers are not exploited and are paid their contribution to production. The logic is that markets prevent exploitation since a firm that won't pay a worker her contribution will find that worker poached away by another firm that is willing pay slightly more.

The education hypothesis fits neatly with this theory. The claim is that technology has increased the productivity of more educated workers, and firms operating in competitive markets have therefore increased wages of these workers. The only problem is the facts don't fit the theory. Returns to education have not been stellar and cannot explain the pattern of wage and income change that has occurred.

The marginal product theory of economists has always appealed to the elite, being a combination of explanation and justification of income distribution. Free markets pay workers what they are worth, justifying wages and explaining them. Furthermore, free markets prevent exploitation, making unions and minimum wages unnecessary. Indeed, the theory allows the rich and powerful to claim that these essential worker protections are bad and increase unemployment by pricing workers out of jobs.

The conventional economic theory of income distribution has always been a stretch. Like beauty, a worker's contribution is in the eye of the beholder, which raises the question of whose eye. It has now become clear that the theory does not explain the worsening of income distribution. That means another theory is needed – one that admits the role of power, institutions, and socially created perceptions of who adds value. Rather than skilled welders and machinists needing retraining, it is economists that need re-training and re-education.

Posted as "A question of power" on September 20, 2006 on The Guardian, Comment Is Free. Also posted at www.thomaspalley.com on September 28, 2006.

A GLOBAL MINIMUM WAGE SYSTEM

July 18, 2011

The global economy is suffering from severe shortage of demand. In developed economies that shortfall is explicit in high unemployment rates and large output gaps. In emerging market economies it is implicit in their reliance on export-led growth. In part this shortfall reflects the lingering disruptive effects of the financial crisis and Great Recession, but it also reflects globalization's undermining of the income generation process. One mechanism that can help rebuild this process is a global minimum wage system. That does not mean imposing U.S. or European minimum wages in developing countries. It does mean establishing a global set of rules for setting country minimum wages.

The minimum wage is a vital policy tool that provides a floor to wages. This floor reduces downward pressure on wages, and it also creates a rebound ripple effect that raises all wages in the bottom two deciles of the wage spectrum. Furthermore, it compresses wages at the bottom of the wage spectrum, thereby helping reduce inequality. Most importantly, an appropriately designed minimum wage can help connect wages and productivity growth, which is critical for building a sustainable demand generation process.

Traditionally, minimum wage systems have operated by setting a fixed wage that is periodically adjusted to take account of inflation and other changing circumstances. Such an approach is fundamentally flawed and inappropriate for the global economy. It is flawed because the minimum wage is always playing catch-up, and it is inappropriate because the system is difficult to generalize across countries.

Instead, countries should set a minimum wage that is a fixed percent (say fifty percent) of their median wage - which is the wage at which half of workers are paid more and half are paid less. This design has several advantages. First, the minimum wage will automatically rise with the median wage, creating a true floor that moves with the economy. If the median wage rises with productivity growth, the minimum wage will also rise with productivity growth.

Second, since the minimum wage is set by reference to the local median wage, it is set by reference to local economic conditions and reflects what a country can bear. Moreover, since all countries are bound by the same rule, all are treated equally.

Third, if countries want a higher minimum wage they are free to set one. The global minimum wage system would only set a floor: it would not set a ceiling.

Fourth, countries would also be free to set regional minimum wages within each country. Thus, a country like Germany that has higher unemployment in the

219

former East Germany and lower unemployment in the former West Germany could set two minimum wages: one for former East Germany, and one for former West Germany. The only requirement would be that the regional minimum wage be greater than or equal to fifty percent of the regional median wage. Such a system of regional minimum wages would introduce additional flexibility that recognizes wages and living costs vary within countries as well as across countries. This enables the minimum wage system to avoid the danger of over-pricing labor, while still retaining the demand side benefits a minimum wage confers by improving income distribution and helping tie wages to productivity growth.

Finally, a global minimum wage system would also confer significant political benefits by cementing understanding of the need for global labor market rules and showing they are feasible. Just as globalization demands global trade rules for goods and services and global financial rules for financial markets, so too labor markets need global rules.

In sum, globalization has increased international labor competition, which has contributed to rupturing the link between wages and productivity growth. That rupture has undermined the old wage based system of demand growth, forcing a turn to reliance on debt and asset price inflation to drive growth. It has also increased income inequality. Restoring the wage – productivity growth link is therefore vital for both economic and political stability. A global minimum wage system can help accomplish this.

Posted on the FT Economists' Forum on July 18, 2011 and on thomaspalley.com.

THE IMMIGRATION DEBATE:
WORKER RIGHTS ARE MISSING

May 3, 2006

A lot of newspaper ink has been spilled over immigration. So why write another op-ed? The reason is that the economics behind the debate remains badly out of focus and understanding that economics is key to carving a passage through this nastiest of political wedge issues.

As of now, Congress is deadlocked over how to deal with undocumented workers. House Republicans favor a get-tough on immigrant workers approach. The Senate supports a more business friendly approach that establishes a guest worker program while also offering existing illegal immigrants a path to citizenship. Both approaches are deeply flawed because they lack a "worker rights" dimension, and failure to address worker rights means that policy is failing to help those who have been harmed by illegal immigration.

First, some basic economics. In my view, economists (such as George Borjas and Lawrence Katz of Harvard University) have got it right when they say that illegal immigration has negatively impacted wages, especially for low skilled native-born Americans. That is simple supply and demand analysis. The flood of undocumented immigrants has increased low skilled labor supply, driving down wages relative to what they would have been absent any immigration.

However, mainstream economists are mistaken in their claim that the economic contribution of undocumented immigrants is very low. Their logic is that low skilled immigrants are paid little because their productive contribution (what economists term marginal product) is very low. *Ergo*, even though immigrants may be far better off than they were in their native countries, the U.S. economy benefits little. However, this logic ignores the fact that illegal immigrants are vulnerable to massive exploitation, so that their contribution may significantly exceed what they are paid with the surplus being captured by the exploiters.

That spotlights a crucial point. Having a huge pool of illegal immigrants who are stripped of legal rights and driven underground creates the perfect environment for exploitation. That environment hurts all workers because the fears of immigrants can be used to lower wages below what a fair market would pay. Those fears can also be leveraged to undermine the bargaining position of native-born workers, especially when it comes to union organizing efforts.

This reality was starkly illustrated in a case from 1999 that came before the National Labor Relations Board. In that case, management for a Holiday Inn Express in Minnesota terminated workers' employment and reported them to the Immigration and Naturalization Service shortly after they had voted to join Hotel Employees and Restaurant Employees Local 17. The management knew all along that the workers were undocumented, but only reported them to bust a union organizing drive.

The lesson from the Holiday Inn case is that lack of worker rights for immigrants has adverse wage impacts on all workers. There are estimated to be eleven million undocumented workers in the U.S., and these workers are here to stay because awful conditions here are still better than conditions in their home countries. Given that fact, the law and policy must change in two ways. First, undocumented workers must be given full worker rights. Second, business must be discouraged from trying to take advantage of the vulnerability of undocumented workers.

With regard to worker rights, undocumented workers must be given the full protection of labor law – such as back pay for firings without cause. Additionally, undocumented workers should be given "safe harbor" status that protects them from deportation when employers report them as part of a strategy of busting unions and frustrating union organizing efforts. Labor law must apply uniformly to all workers regardless of immigration status because when it comes to the workplace, an injury to one is an injury to all.

With regard to business, the law must impose stiff penalties on businesses that hire workers without making reasonable efforts to verify their legal status. Additionally, the direction of enforcement efforts must be changed. Instead of going after illegal immigrants, prosecuting them, and deporting them, enforcement efforts should be directed against business. Business has played an important role in fostering illegal immigration by offering the prospect of employment. Cutting off the supply of jobs to undocumented workers will reduce the pull of illegal immigration. Pairing this with robust border enforcement can then make a real dent in the problem.

Congress is also wrestling with the issue of amnesty or pathways to citizenship for undocumented workers. This is the most difficult of issue because it can appear to condone breaking of the law. Congress must be honest and recognize that it has tacitly encouraged illegal immigration by its past unwillingness to deter business from hiring undocumented workers. At this stage having a large exploitable population of workers is morally repugnant, and it also undermines the economic well-being of least well-off workers. That speaks to giving undocumented workers a speedy path to legal status. Allowing them to emerge from the shadows of exploitation will raise their wages, and in doing so it will boost the wages of low skill native-born workers.

Taking undocumented workers out of the underground economy can also yield another benefit for society. The underground economy pays no taxes, and it has a tendency to spread like a contagion. That is bad for tax revenues and shifts tax burdens on to the above ground economy. Once touched by the underground economy, it is easy for business to get further involved so that a culture of tolerance for illegal transactions can rapidly expand. Reducing the number of undocumented workers can shrink the underground economy as these workers do not want to be there.

In sum, a comprehensive "worker rights" approach can tackle the painful problem of illegal immigration. It includes giving undocumented workers the full protection of labor law, creating pathways to legal status for such workers, legal and policy measures deterring firms from hiring undocumented workers, and robust border enforcement. The minimum wage should also be raised to compensate for the depressing wage effect of illegal immigration.

This comprehensive approach is currently missing. The House bill makes progress on penalizing employers who hire undocumented workers, but its categorization of these workers as felons is cruel and will increase exploitation by driving them further underground. The Senate bill makes progress with its pathways to citizenship proposal, but this comes at the cost of a guest worker program. This placates business by promising a continued guaranteed supply of cheap labor, but it will continue placing downward pressure on wages. Neither addresses the issue of worker rights of undocumented workers.

What is needed is to keep the employer penalties, expand the pathways to citizenship program, improve border security, address worker rights, and raise the minimum wage, while jettisoning the felon provisions and guest worker program.

Originally posted as "Immigration anxiety" on May 3, 2006 in TomPaine.com. Also posted as "Immigration anxieties: Worker rights is the solution" at thomaspalley.com on May 12, 2006.

EXPAND SARBOX, NOT SHRINK IT

February 16, 2007

There is a growing business chorus calling for shrinking the Sarbanes – Oxley Act (Sarbox) regulating U.S. capital markets. Recently, a self-appointed "blue ribbon" committee financed by Wall Street interests called for making shareholder class action suits more difficult to bring, lowering the legal liability of auditors and directors, and easing accounting certification requirements. In response, the Securities and Exchange Commission (SEC) appears to be moving to implement some of this wish list.

However, corporate behavior over the last few years speaks for expanding Sarbox, not shrinking it. Thus, the CEO pay problem has continued – exemplified by recent massive termination payments to Messrs. Bob Nardelli of Home Depot and Henry Mckinnell of Pfizer. Major accounting restatements continue at large corporations. And most importantly, there is the CEO stock option backdating scandal, which may extend to one thousand companies and appears to implicate boards of directors, including outside directors.

This backdating scandal scotches the notion that America's corporate governance problem concerns a "few bad apples" and makes plain that the problem is the "barrel". That speaks to expanding Sarbox rather than shrinking it.

Here is a set of reforms entirely different from those in the Wall Street blue ribbon Committee's report. These reforms address the rotten barrel problem, thereby truly improving corporate governance and making America a better place for savers and investors.

Reform # 1. Require that the CEO and Chairman of the Board be different persons. Under current arrangements CEOs frequently also act as Board Chairman. That creates an absolute monarch who is almost completely free of accountability. Power tends to corrupt, and absolute power corrupts absolutely. Current U.S. corporate governance arrangements have proven the truth of this aphorism, which speaks for having an independent chairman to whom the CEO is accountable.

Reform # 2. Stop share buy-backs. If companies want to increase pro-form earnings per share they can cancel existing shares (with stock options being cancelled proportionately). If companies want to return excess capital to shareholders they can pay special dividends. Stock buy-backs have terrible incentive properties. On the surface, they increase the share price, which benefits shareholders. Unfortunately, share buy-backs may be engineered to increase the share price in order to enhance the value of mangers' stock options. Consequently, firms may waste capital by overpaying for shares, and shareholders actually lose though managers benefit.

224

Reform # 3. Allow shareholders with large long-held investments to nominate directors for election on the corporate proxy ballot. Under current rules, shareholders seeking to oust incompetent management must wage a costly proxy fight to get the question put. That advantages incumbent management that has the right, under the corporate proxy, to nominate whomever and propose whatever resolutions it wishes. Giving large committed shareholders access to the corporate proxy will make challenging incumbent management easier, thereby improving accountability and responsiveness to shareholders - which is what shareholder democracy is all about.

Reform # 4. Impose rules on management participation in buy-outs. A hard line would prohibit senior managers from participating for two years after leaving a company. A softer line would say that management must make available to shareholders the buy-out business plan. Currently, shareholders are being fleeced by management buyouts. Participating in buy-outs creates conflicts of interest, including locking firms into paying deal-breaker fees that discourage other buyers from making offers. Managers are the agents of shareholders and have access to proprietary information, yet they are allowed to use this privileged position to benefit themselves at the expense of shareholders.

Reform # 5. Make it obligatory for management to hold vested options for a period of three years. Some portion might even be required to be held longer. Under current arrangements managers often sell options as soon as they vest. That creates an undesirable incentive for short-term management that drives up today's stock price, perhaps at the expense of long-term profits and long-term shareholder value. Requiring managers to hold on to vested options can realign incentives in a beneficial way.

Reform # 6. Managers should be required to refund performance bonuses paid on the basis of results that are subsequently revised down.

Reform # 7. Make CEO pay accountable and transparent. This can be done by requiring CEO pay packages be submitted to shareholders for approval. All options should be fully expensed. Pay packages should be presented with a comparison of the average pay-package of similarly positioned CEOs, along with metrics of relative performance such as return on equity. Such measures can guard against over-payment and also encourage pay-for-performance, which is the justification of these generous pay incentives.

Reform # 8. Strictly limit the number of directorships of publicly listed companies an individual can hold. The current system has created a "club" network in which CEOs and Directors are cozy with each other. This coziness weakens oversight and promotes CEO excess. Increasing the size of the director pool can help restore a more professional arms-length relationship in boardrooms between directors, board chairs, and CEOs. It also speaks to having worker directors on the board.

Rather than supporting a rollback of Sarbanes – Oxley, the facts of current U.S. corporate behavior speak to expanding it. Business conservatives have invited a debate over Sarbox. Progressive investor activists should accept that invitation and make the case for expanding Sarbox and deepening corporate accountability.

Posted on February 16, 2007 at thomaspalley.com.

A BETTER WAY TO REGULATE FINANCIAL MARKETS: ASSET BASED RESERVE REQUIREMENTS

November 10, 2009

There is widespread recognition that the financial crisis which triggered the Great Recession was significantly due to financial excess, particularly regarding real estate lending. Now, policymakers are looking to reform the financial system in hope of avoiding future crises. But like the drunk who looks for his lost keys under the lamp post because that is where the light is, policymakers remain fixated on capital standards because that is what is already in place.

There is a better way to regulate financial markets through asset based reserve requirements (ABRR) which would extend margin requirements to a wide array of assets held by financial institutions. ABRR are easy to implement, use the tried and tested approach of reserve requirements, are compatible with existing regulation (including capital standards), and would fill a hole regarding adequacy of financial policy instruments.

The toleration of periodic bouts of financial excess over the past two decades reflects profound intellectual failure among central bankers and economists who believed inflation targeting was a complete and sufficient policy framework. It also reflects lack of policy instruments for directly targeting financial market excess. With central banks relying on the single instrument of short term interest rates, this supported the argument using interest rates to target asset prices would inflict massive collateral damage on the rest of the economy. ABRR offer a simple solution to this problem by providing a new set of policy instruments that can target financial market excess, leaving interest rate policy free to manage the overall macroeconomic situation.

ABRR require financial firms to hold reserves against different classes of assets, with the regulatory authority setting adjustable reserve requirements on the basis of its concerns with each asset class. One concern may be an asset class is too risky; another may be an asset class is expanding too fast and producing inflated asset prices.

By obliging financial firms to hold reserves, the system requires they retain some of their funds as non-interest-bearing deposits with the central bank. The implicit cost of forgone interest must be charged against investing in a particular asset category, reducing its return. Financial firms will therefore reduce holdings of assets with higher reserve requirements, and shift funds into other relatively more profitable asset categories.

The effectiveness of this approach requires system-wide application. If applied only to banks, ABRR would simply encourage lending to shift outside the banking sector. To succeed, reserve requirements must be set by asset type, not by who holds the asset.

A system of ABRR that covers all financial firms can increase the efficacy of monetary policy. Most importantly, it enables central banks to target sector imbalances without recourse to the blunderbuss of interest rate increases. For example, if a monetary authority was concerned about a house price bubble generating excessive risk exposure, it could impose reserve requirements on new mortgages. This would force mortgage lenders to hold some cash to support their new loans, raising the cost of such loans and cooling the market.

A similar logic holds for stock market bubbles. If a monetary authority wanted to prevent stock market inflation from generating excessive consumption, it could impose reserve requirements on equity holdings. This would force financial firms to hold some cash to back their equity holdings, lowering the return on equities and discouraging such investments.

ABRR also act as automatic stabilizers. When asset values rise or when the financial sector creates new assets, ABRR generate an automatic monetary restraint by requiring the financial sector come up with additional reserves. Conversely, when asset values fall or financial assets are extinguished, ABRR generate an automatic monetary easing by releasing reserves previously held against assets. In all of this, ABRR remain fully consistent with the existing system of monetary control as exercised through central bank provision of liquidity at a given interest rate.

At the microeconomic level, ABRR can be used to allocate funds to public purposes such as inner city revitalization or environmental protection. By setting low (or no) reserve requirements on such investments, monetary authorities could channel funds into priority areas, much as government subsidized credit and guarantee programs and government-sponsored secondary markets have expanded education and home ownership opportunities and promoted regional development. Conversely, ABRR can be used to discourage asset allocations that are deemed socially counterproductive.

Finally, ABRR have other significant policy benefits that are especially valuable now. First, ABRR increase the demand for reserves which will prove helpful as central banks seek to exit the current period of quantitative easing to avoid future inflation. By gradually raising asset reserve ratios, central banks can implement a form of reverse quantitative easing that smoothly transitions the system to a new more stable regime.

Second, by increasing the demand for reserves ABRR will increase seigniorage revenue for governments at a time of fiscal squeeze. To the extent required reserves constitute a tax on financial institutions, that tax is economically efficient given the costs of financial crises. It will also shrink a system that many believe is bloated.

Posted on the FT Economists' Forum on November 10, 2009 and at thomaspalley.com on November 16, 2009.

A NEW TRADE AGENDA: TROPICAL TRADE LIBERALIZATION PLUS LABOR STANDARDS

May 11, 2006

The Doha round of trade liberalization negotiations is in deep trouble, and with good reason. Though positioned as a "development" round intended to benefit the world's poorest countries, it in fact does little in that regard. On close examination Doha turns out to be a Trojan horse that pushes the type of trade liberalization that has made globalization so deeply unpopular and unfair.

At this stage, the Doha architecture should be discarded. The agricultural access negotiations should be transformed into a tropical products access agreement, and the manufacturing and services access negotiations abandoned entirely. Such a proposal can yield immediate development benefits, and rejection of the manufacturing and services agenda can send a signal that new thinking is needed in these areas. This can set the stage for a 21st century trade agenda that rectifies the structural failings of today's trading system.

Much attention has been focused on agriculture, and agricultural products access has been used deceptively to try and enlist civil society support for trade liberalization. Yet, it is now clear that Doha's agricultural access provisions would do little to alleviate global poverty, and might well increase it. A recent Carnegie Endowment Report estimates that these agricultural provisions would raise global GDP by just two one-hundredths of one percent. Moreover, all of those gains would accrue to consumers in northern (developed) economies, and developing countries as a group would actually lose.

The reasons for this pattern are clear and simple. Northern countries would commit to reduce agricultural subsidies, but since they produce foodstuffs – cereals, meat, and dairy – the elimination of subsidies would tend to raise global food prices and harm food-importing developing countries. Second, northern countries would also reduce their agricultural product quotas, driving down prices in northern markets. Though quotas restrict imports, they provide higher prices to those developing countries with quota access and they would lose this benefit.

Finally, developing countries would have reciprocal obligations to improve agricultural product access in their own economies. In many countries, agriculture is dominated by small-scale farming that may be unable to compete with large northern agro-businesses. Prices would fall in these countries benefiting urban consumers, but there is also the potential for massive rural dislocation, the costs of which are not even caught in conventional economic models that are calibrated in terms of prices and quantities.

Instead of generalized agricultural trade liberalization, the world should enact tropical products liberalization. Global poverty is heavily concentrated in the tropics – a region lying roughly within the lines of latitude demarcating Mexico and Bolivia. A tropical products round could give freer access to agricultural products and processed derivative products from this region. That means commodities such as sugar, cotton, rice, orange juice, and coffee.

Such a tropical products round has clear win – win potential, and is consistent with the true logic of comparative advantage. By taking northern produced foodstuffs off the negotiating table, food-importing developing countries will be saved from higher food prices. Most northern agriculture interests would also be unaffected. The exceptions are those with no economic justification – sugar cane growing in Florida, rice farming in Japan, and excessive sugar beet production in Northern Europe.

Meanwhile, increasing market access for tropical products can significantly lower prices for northern consumers. Additionally, they will be saved from paying expensive subsidies to farmers who have no comparative advantage in these products and should not be producing them. Finally, northern countries will be saved from the environmental damage wrought by such farming, as evidenced by sugar cane growing in Florida's everglades.

Doha's manufacturing and services access negotiations represent a traditional trade liberalization of the type that has made globalization so contentious. Whereas the logic of comparative advantage is crystal clear in agriculture and primary products, it is much less clear in manufacturing. From the standpoint of northern workers, in a world where capital and technology are fully mobile, manufacturing and services trade are increasingly driven by labor arbitrage rather than by advantages in comparative productivity. From the standpoint of developing countries, elimination of tariffs eliminates a policy instrument that has proven useful historically in helping countries (including the U.S.) catch up and industrialize. It also takes away a vital means of raising tax revenues to finance public infrastructure investment since developing countries usually lack cost-effective and non-distorting alternative ways of raising revenue.

The spread of technology, the lowering of transportation costs and the improvements in electronic communication and long-distance management mean that the classical era of free trade is over. The world is increasingly one market rather than many markets linked by international trade. That speaks to the need for a new agenda.

The new agenda must tackle the question of labor and environmental standards. This is a problem that industrialized countries tackled in the last century when they put in place rules determining what constitutes legitimate competition. Competition based on slavery, discrimination, child labor, and the suppression of workers' right to organize was disallowed. Now similar rules need to be established for the single global economy that is subsuming national economies. This is obviously good for workers, but it can also help developing countries capture more of the economic value they produce by preventing destructive competition between them. Today, value is increasingly captured by corporations situated at the retail and distribution end of the value chain (think Gap and Nike) that can put developing countries in competition with each other. Standards can limit that power.

The agenda must also tackle the system of global intellectual property rights (IPR) that was set up with the establishment of the WTO. Insistence on a single global system is an infringement of developing country sovereignty, and is nothing short of economic imperialism. Sovereign countries have the right to establish their own internal laws regarding copyright and patents. In addition to the sovereignty argument, it makes no sense for countries that differ so widely in terms of economic endowments and stage of development to have the same IPR laws. This is sub-optimal policy that generates economic inefficiency.

Finally, the post-Doha trade agenda must confront the question of exchange rates. International competition must be based on product quality and productive efficiency, not on under-valued exchange rates. Today's disorganized system of exchange rates risks recreating the beggar-thy-neighbor economics of the 1930s when countries sought to gain international competitive advantage by devaluing their exchange rates. Competitive devaluation is a negative sum game that makes the world economy worse off. One countries competitive gain is another's loss, while all lose because of the financial and monetary uncertainty that competitive devaluation produces.

Responsible world leaders must resist scare tactics of those who claim failure of the Doha round will bring down the global trading system. That is nonsense. There is no evidence supporting the metaphor that the global economic system is like a bicycle that requires more liberalization to keep rolling. Indeed, the opposite is true. Liberalization tends to result in economic lock-in, and we should avoid locking-in bad liberalizations. Optimal economic decision theory recommends "when you don't know, go slow."

Originally posted as "Workers of the world, unite" on May 11, 2006 in The Guardian, Comment is Free. Also posted as "Time for a new trade agenda" on May 26, 2006 at thomaspalley.com.

EXCHANGE RATES: THERE IS A BETTER WAY

October 30, 2007

The world economy is poorly served by the current system of exchange rates. That system has contributed to today's global financial imbalances, which are widely viewed as posing significant economic risk. These imbalances have also created political tensions between countries over how to adjust them, and within countries over job losses. Exchange rates matter more than ever under globalization, which means the world needs a better system.

Today's global imbalances concern the U.S. trade deficit, which has spiraled out of control after years of dollar over-valuation. This problem is particularly acute with China. A few years back the problem of over-valued exchange rates afflicted Latin America, and to a lesser degree East Asia. Now, with the dollar weakening, the burden of over-valuation is shifting on to the euro.

This pattern of rolling exchange rate misalignment is bad for the global economy. Such misalignments often end in costly economic crises, and they also cause inefficiency by distorting trade. That is because rather than competing on productivity, too often countries compete through under-valued currencies that confer an exchange rate subsidy.

These costs have been obscured by the debt-financed boom of the last few years. In the U.S., the costs of manufacturing job loss have been camouflaged by a house price bubble. Other countries have dismissed the U.S. trade deficit problem because it has created matching trade surpluses that have spurred export-led growth. But this picture is vulnerable to credit retrenchment and reversal of the dollar's over-valuation. History repeatedly shows that conditions look artificially rosy when wracking up debt, and the hangover only sets in when the financial punch bowl is removed.

The current global exchange rate system is a sub-optimal arrangement. There are many theoretical reasons explaining why foreign exchange markets are prone to mis-pricing, and the empirical evidence shows exchange rates persistently depart from their warranted fundamental levels. Moreover, the system permits strategic manipulation so that some countries (particularly in East Asia) actively intervene to under-value their currencies. That has made for a lop-sided world in which half play by free market rules and half are neo-mercantilist, creating threatening tensions.

It is possible to do better than the current system. The immediate need is for a coordinated global re-alignment of exchange rates that begins to smoothly unwind existing imbalances. The 1985 Plaza currency accord provides a model of how this can be done. China's participation is key as it has large trade surpluses with both the U.S. and Europe. Moreover, other East Asian countries with trade surpluses will resist revaluing unless China revalues for fear they will become uncompetitive. Finally, markets must believe this realignment it will hold. Absent that, business will not make the changes to production and investment patterns needed to restore equilibrium.

Beyond such realignment, there is need for systemic reform to avoid recurring misalignments. That suggests a system of managed exchange rates for major currencies in which countries cooperatively set exchange rates.

Such a system needs rules of intervention. Historically, the onus of defense has fallen on the country whose exchange rate is weakening, which requires it to sell foreign exchange reserves. That is a fundamentally flawed arrangement because countries have limited reserves and the market knows it. Speculators therefore have an incentive to try and "break the bank" by shorting the weak currency, and they have a good shot at success given the scale of low cost leverage financial markets can muster.

Instead, the onus of intervention must be placed on the strong currency country. Its central bank has unlimited amounts of its own currency for sale so it can never be beaten by the market. Consequently, if this intervention rule is credibly adopted, speculators will back off, making the target exchange rate viable.

Intervening in this way will also give an expansionary tilt to the global economy. When weak countries defend exchange rates they often use high interest rates to make their currency attractive, which imparts a deflationary global bias. If strong surplus countries do the intervening, they may lower their interest rates and impart an expansionary bias.

A sensible managed exchange rate system can increase the benefits from trade, diminish exchange rate induced distortions, and reduce country conflict over trade deficits. The means are at hand, but so far the politics have lagged.

In the U.S., discussion of exchange rate policy is still blocked by simplistic free market nostrums. It is also blocked by mistaken fears that a managed system would surrender sovereignty and control. Yet, that is implicitly what has been happening. By absenting itself from the market, the U.S. has *de facto* allowed other countries to set the exchange rate, and that means the U.S. has been letting itself be strategically out-gamed.

Impetus for change has also been reduced because other countries have been beneficiaries of the over-valued dollar. However, many are now starting to suffer from the dollar's weakness.

Putting the pieces together, increasing awareness of the dangers of global imbalances and uncertainty about the dollar has created space for change. The still missing ingredient is political leadership that recognizes there is a better way.

Originally posted as "There is a better way" on The Guardian, Comment Is Free on October 20, 2007. Also posted at thomaspalley.com on October 31, 2007.

EXCHANGE RATES, LABOR STANDARDS, AND DEMOCRACY: WHY CHINA MUST CHANGE

November 28, 2005

For the past five years the global economy has been flying on one engine. That engine is the U.S. consumer who has been on a consumption binge financed by borrowing, in turn backed by a housing price bubble. This situation poses the threat of a serious hard landing when that engine eventually stalls, as it must. Ever inflating house prices and rising debt-to-income levels are not sustainable. And as the late Herbert Stein, Chairman of President Nixon's Council of Economic Advisers, wryly observed: "If something cannot go on forever, it will stop."

This view, regarding the global economy's excessive dependence on the U.S. and the financial fragility of the U.S. economy, is not just held by progressive economists. It is also shared by Wall Street. Thus, Stephen Roach, Chief Economist for Morgan Stanley, recently wrote in the *Financial Times* (November 4, 2005): "there is now about a forty percent probability of a hard landing in the next twelve months." And in a research brief, Roach singles out China as being particularly dependent on the U.S.: "China's export prowess is balanced on the head of a pin – a pin made in America. Fully thirty-five percent of Chinese exports go to the United States."

Roach's Wall Street warnings are sobering. But they miss a more profound point, which is that the global economy has been heading in the wrong direction, hollowing out the middle class in America while failing to create a big enough middle class in the developing world. That hollowing-out process has long been visible in U.S. statistics on wages and family income distribution, and it has been rendered keenly concrete by Delphi Corp.'s recent bankruptcy filing. It is only because of successive stock market and housing price bubbles, combined with a massive increase in consumer access to credit, that the hollowing-out has not been worse.

A major cause of these dangerous trends is the flawed structure of the global economy. Spurred by our own policy makers, the International Monetary Fund, and the World Bank, developing countries have adopted an export-led approach to manufacturing growth and development. This approach has two critical features. First, countries rely on selling in foreign markets rather than their own domestic markets. Second, countries use under-valued exchange rates to subsidize their products, thereby making them hyper-competitive. China exemplifies this model, exporting over half of its manufacturing output and having an exchange rate that is up to forty percent undervalued.

The focus on export-led growth has distorted the global economy. First, it has created the global financial imbalances that Wall Street is so apprehensive about, as manifested in the record U.S. trade deficit. Second, U.S. manufacturing has been undermined by unfair competition subsidized by under-valued currencies. This in turn has accelerated the hollowing of America's middle. Third, export-led growth promotes the global race-to-the-bottom since countries look for international competitive advantage however possible. Consequently, workplace standards, wages, and the environment are all subject to persistent retrograde pressures, impeding the development of a middle class in developing countries.

The implication is that the global economy must shift from export-led development to domestic market-led development. In an export-led world, higher wages undermine employment. In a domestic market-led world, higher wages can promote employment. This is where labor standards and unions enter. The challenge is to establish a system that has wages rising with productivity so that workers can buy what they produce, rather than dumping it on world markets. Setting wages by government edict does not work, as evidenced by the former socialist economies. Instead, labor standards and unions are the way forward, since they provide a decentralized mechanism that links wages and productivity through bargaining. History supports this. Every country that has ever made the transition to developed industrialized status has traveled this route.

China is the poster-child for export-led manufacturing growth. It has the most under-valued exchange rate, the worst labor repression, and is by far the largest developing country exporter. As such, China is the gravitational attractor for the race to the bottom. Other countries must change too, but they can only do so if China changes so that none lose relative competitive advantage. If China revalues its exchange rate, other East Asian countries can also do so. Likewise, if China raises wages, so too can others.

One area where China is showing leadership is its stated commitment to increase social spending. This will be good for China's citizenry, and it will also contribute to incomes and domestic demand in China which will be good for the global economy. However, there is also a problem that is unique to China. Labor standards and trade unions are key to domestic market-led development, but China's political system prevents them. That creates an additional political roadblock that must be solved. Democratic reform in China is not a nicety. It is a necessity for the global economy to work.

Originally posted as "Why China must change" on TomPaine.com. Also posted on December 10, 2005 at thomaspalley.com.

MARKETS AND THE COMMON GOOD

June 8, 2006

Like a modern-day Rip Van Winkle, there are indications that the Democratic Party may finally be awakening from its long slumber and realizing it lacks a compelling identity. That lack of identity is especially clear regarding the economy, and it contrasts with Republicans who have long emphasized free markets. The current moment of Republican unraveling offers Democrats an historic opportunity to close this identity gap and change the direction of American politics.

The Republican free market message resonates with deep-seated cultural attachments to individualism and freedom, and their message tacitly treats free markets as identical to society. Democrats should challenge this message with one about "markets *and* society," meaning that markets should serve both individuals and society. Whereas free markets are especially good at promoting the interests of individuals, there are important societal interests (such as democracy and community) that they fail to address and may actively harm. That calls for institutions other than markets to represent those interests, and also for thoughtfully balancing markets with society's other interests.

For most of the past 30 years voters have regarded Republicans as the party they feel most comfortable with managing of the economy. This standing has enormously benefited Republicans in both elections and their ability to determine the daily economic policy agenda. The public is not made up of policy experts and people have neither the time nor the willingness to become informed on technical economic policy issues. Thus, the party that gains the public's confidence and frames the economic debate has a huge advantage. It is consistently given first mover advantage and the benefit of the doubt, while the party on the outside must always defend before it can propose.

Now, due to a combination of failed policies and policy excess, the continuation of Republican economic policy dominance is an open question. The economic recovery following the last recession has been the weakest since World War II. And most importantly, there may be increasing support for the belief that the Republican Party is less a party of small government and efficient markets and more a party of profits for big business and tax relief for the super-wealthy.

These developments create a momentous opportunity for Democrats, but at this stage they face a choice between a Phoenix and cuckoo response. One would imitate the Phoenix, a mythical bird that periodically incinerates itself to emerge revived and regenerated from the ashes. The other would imitate the cuckoo, which lays its eggs in the nests of smaller birds and has them raise its offspring in place of the original eggs.

The cuckoo strategy is being pressed by new Democrats who aim for a softer version of the current policy program, inaugurated by Ronald Reagan in 1980. According to this strategy, Democrats should use the current moment to occupy the economic policy nest created by Republicans and redecorate it. This would involve continuing with the themes of budget austerity, free trade, and deregulated markets that Republicans pioneered. However, these themes would be softened by "compassionate" initiatives like greater income supports for the poor and tax incentives to help low paid workers save.

Significant steps in line with such a strategy have already been taken by former Treasury Secretary Robert Rubin, who has established his Hamilton Project at the Brookings Institution. The goal is to build an intellectual infrastructure that can be paired with the political expertise of the former Clinton administration, thereby establishing policy hegemony within the Democratic Party.

In sharp contrast, a Phoenix strategy would build on the progressive legacy of Franklin Roosevelt's New Deal and Harry Truman's Fair Deal, bringing back to life the economic logic and vision that inspired them. This is a far more difficult enterprise that not only aims to wrest control of the policy debate, but also to redirect it. Instead of merely making minor adjustments to the Republican framework, a Phoenix strategy would dramatically alter understandings of the nature of markets and their relation to society.

Changing the understanding of markets is key. Economic conservatives have hoodwinked Americans into accepting a view of the economy that saddles them with economic fatalism. Compare this to the Roosevelt-Truman era, when people believed the economy could be shaped by policy. The conservative lie is that "natural" market forces mean little can be done about low wages, disappearing pension and health benefits and degenerate competition predicated on international outsourcing. This is Margaret Thatcher's infamous TINA--there is no alternative. It is untrue. Changing tax laws, the method of providing health insurance, the conduct of monetary policy and the rules governing corporations, labor markets and international trade can transform the market into a force for race to the top progress rather the race to the bottom exploitation.

Labor Democrats, African-Americans and immigrants constitute the natural core constituency of a Phoenix strategy since these groups are dealt the worst hand and face the most blighted future under the current policy regime. However, that constituency must be broadened to include middle class America if it is to sustain lasting political victory. This can be accomplished because questions about the nature of markets and their relation to society are central to all Americans. Not only is individual economic well-being at stake, so too are values regarding family and community.

A successful Phoenix strategy cannot rest on taking from the top draw a list of policy proposals cobbled together over the past 20 years. Instead, it will require a clear articulation of the purpose of society and the relation of markets to society. In short, the development of a philosophy in which markets serve society, rather than society serving markets, is necessary. Out of this statement and vision can then flow a new progressive policy agenda in which all elements are mutually reinforcing.

This is exactly what radical conservatives accomplished 40 years ago with their capstone notion of free markets, which, in turn, drove policies of free trade, deregulation, attacking unions and small government. The conservative philosophical trick was to assert the existence of natural free markets and then claim an identity between markets and the interests of society. That trick worked well, but the fallacy of its assumptions is now showing up in the corruption in political markets and the gross inequities evident in markets more generally.

A markets and society agenda resonates strongly with themes that run deep in America's identity. Americans are committed to individualism and freedom, but they are also committed to democracy and country. Markets speak to individualism and freedom. Society speaks to democracy and the common-good embodied in country. That is an agenda that can trump the conservative position that deregulated free markets are all that is needed.

Originally posted on June 8, 2006 on ourfuture.org. Also posted at thomaspalley.com on June 12, 2006.

Thomas I. Palley is an economist living in Washington D.C. He is currently an associate of the Economic Growth Program of the New America Foundation in Washington D.C. He was formerly chief economist with the U.S. – China Economic and Security Review Commission. Prior to joining the Commission he served as director of the Open Society Institute's Globalization Reform Project and as assistant director of Public Policy at the AFL-CIO.

Dr. Palley holds a B.A. degree from Oxford University and a M.A. degree in International Relations and Ph.D. in Economics, both from Yale University.

Thomas Palley is the author of:

Plenty of Nothing: The Downsizing of the American Dream and the Case for Structural Keynesianism (1998).

Post Keynesian Economics: Debt, Distribution and the Macro Economy (1996).

From Financial Crisis to Stagnation: The Destruction of Shared Prosperity and the Role of Economics (2012).

He has published in numerous academic journals, and written for *The Atlantic Monthly, American Prospect* and *Nation* magazines. His numerous op-eds are posted on his website.

www.thomaspalley.com